POLITICAL CONSPIRACIES IN AMERICA

POLITICAL CONSPIRACIES IN AMERICA

A Reader

Edited by
Donald T. Critchlow, John Korasick,
and Matthew C. Sherman

Indiana University Press
BLOOMINGTON | INDIANAPOLIS

This book is a publication of

Indiana University Press
601 North Morton Street
Bloomington, Indiana 47404-3797 USA

http://iupress.indiana.edu

Telephone orders 800-842-6796
Fax orders 812-855-7931
Orders by email iuporder@indiana.edu

The paper used in this publication meets the minimum requirements of American National Standard for Information Sciences—Permanence of Paper for Printed Library Materials, ANSI Z39.48-1984.

Manufactured in the United States of America

Library of Congress Cataloging-in-Publication Data

Political conspiracies in America : a reader / edited by Donald T. Critchlow, John Korasick, and Matthew C. Sherman.
p. cm.
Includes bibliographical references and index.
ISBN-13: 978-0-253-35079-4 (cloth : alk. paper)
ISBN-13: 978-0-253-21964-0 (paper : alk. paper) 1. Conspiracies—United States—History—Sources. 2. United States—Politics and government—Sources. I. Critchlow, Donald T., date II. Korasick, John. III. Sherman, Matthew C.
E183.P65 2008
364.1'300973—dc22

2007038024

1 2 3 4 5 13 12 11 10 09 08

Contents

Introduction

Democratic governance in the United States is premised on the belief that the political universe is rational and that an open society is essential to the preservation of democracy. Free speech and a free press help to protect democracy from subversive agents who would seek to usurp power and destroy the system. Democracies strike a careful balance in protecting rights essential to political dissent while instituting anti-subversive measures necessary to preserve democratic society itself. Although this balance has not always been maintained, ultimately democratic government rests on the trust of the people in their public officials. Fear of conspiracy manifests mistrust in political leadership and in its ability to maintain order because it has been corrupted by subversive forces. Given the continued persistence of alleged conspiracies in American history, from the colonies' first settlement until today, the American democratic regime has shown remarkable endurance.

Political conspiracy is a secret and illegal agreement to undertake unlawful or wrongful acts to affect the political system. The Plot of Brutus and his brother-in-law Cassius to assassinate Julius Caesar on March 15, 44 BCE, was a conspiracy. In American history, the Aaron Burr conspiracy (1805–07) involved a plot to remove the western territories and the Louisiana Purchase from the United States. The plot by financiers Jay Gould and James Fisk to corner the gold market, based on inside information provided by President Ulysses Grant's brother-in-law Abel Corbin and Assistant Secretary of the Treasury General Daniel Butterfield in 1869, was a financial conspiracy involving people high in government. In the twentieth century, the infiltration of Soviet spies into the U.S. government during the Franklin Roosevelt administration was a political conspiracy conducted behind closed doors within the Kremlin to illegally obtain American secrets.

While these and other examples can be found throughout history, most political conspiracies have been imagined. Those who promulgate such conspiracies present a fantastic view of the world in which a small group of men and women, operating secretly, can dictate world events with improbable exactitude. Conspiracy theorists believe that the "hidden history" behind such conspiracies is revealed only through close study and deciphering of apparently random events. Having attained this knowledge, conspiracy theorists believe they have an obligation to warn their fellow citizens of the dark, subversive forces operating in secret. They employ a conspiracy language that allows ideological groups to convey shared worldviews. When an American conspiracist speaks disparagingly of "Rome" or "the New World Order" or "the Bilderbergers," for example, those who share the speaker's political outlook understand the full implications of the reference. As such, the language of conspiracy encapsulates larger presumptions about the world and how it operates, and code words become a tool to rally followers and to gain new recruits to specific political positions on both ends of the political spectrum.

In this way there is at times but a thin line between irrational and rational fears. Indeed, the extent of conspiratorial fears within the history of western democracies, especially the United States, seems to belie political rationality. Conspiratorial fears were evident among the first settlers in New England, the Puritans and the Pilgrims, in their conviction that high officials in the Church of England were intent on betraying the Protestant Reformation and returning to the practices and theology of Roman Catholicism, with its promotion of idolatry, superstition, ignorance, and hierarchical corruption. Fears of conspiracy abounded throughout colonial America, as seen in relations with Native Americans, the Salem witch trials, repression of religious dissent, and relations with the mother country. Historian Bernard Bailyn, in *The Ideological Origins of the American Revolution,* argued that the fear of a conspiracy—one that reached into the highest circles of the king's court—to subvert the liberties of a free people was central to the ideology of the American revolutionaries. As such, rational Enlightenment thought combined with an irrational fear of conspiracy to produce American republican ideology.

Conspiracy plays other roles in politics as well. Conspiratorial worldviews, for those who subscribe to them, have extrinsic value by rationalizing the world, even though these worldviews might be intrinsically irrational. Furthermore, to have value, conspiracy beliefs must appear to be substantiated. Thus conspiracists spend an inordinate amount of time discovering and mastering "evidence" to substantiate their views. This allows conspiracy believers to present themselves as scholars of a different sort, autodidacts who know better than the experts. In this way, conspiracy offers a mechanism for citizens to acquire and sort confusing and complex political, economic, and social information into a carefully filtered construction of the world. Conspiracy provides a narrative for understanding how the world is ordered. At the same time, conspiracy enhances the self-esteem of the believer by imparting "secret" and "hidden" knowledge that the rest of the polity does not know. As a result, believers in conspiracy find power, but of a certain type: subversive power. It expresses, quite often, the desire of the weak or those seeking further power to exert power through their unique knowledge and understanding of the world. Further, conspiracy provides a bonding experience for believers, a sense of community of shared intimate and personal information.

This community experience is especially important in times of social change, when conspiracy theories seem to become most prominent. And, finally, among its myriad of roles, conspiracy theories allow people to isolate "others," those groups or people who are categorized as unhealthy or corrupting influences on the general population.

Because a conspiracy theory voices discontent with the established political order and helps bond true believers through their shared subversive knowledge, it can appear more intense—and operationally useful—when a dominant political regime is experiencing change. During periods when the established political order comes under attack, conspiracy theories can obtain greater acceptability among some political leaders and elements of the electorate. In such situations, both those defending the established regime and those challenging the established order may subscribe to such theories. American political history is replete with examples of the relationship between regime change and the projection of conspiracy. As the Federalist Party entered into a decline that led to the triumph of the Jeffersonian Democratic-Republicans, archconservatives within the party, led by New England ministers such as Timothy Dwight and Jedidiah Morse, drew upon an anti-Enlightenment literature found in revolutionary France and England revealing a Masonic conspiracy of the Bavarian Illuminati. In the 1820s, anti-Anglo financial conspiracies emerged as the political order again underwent change, giving rise to Jacksonian democracy. Anti-Masonic tendencies found expression in the Whig Party that rose to challenge the Democratic Party. And in the volatile politics of the 1850s, political conspiracies abounded, focusing on nativist, anti-Catholic, and anti-Mormon sentiments.

This pattern finds sharper relief when examined in those states and regions experiencing intense political competition in the absence of a dominant political party able to gain hegemony among the electorate. In antebellum America, these theories found their most violent expression in frontier states and territories that were up for grabs politically, creating a hothouse for conspiracies. The decline of the Whig Party in the 1850s also fueled this phenomenon. Anti-Mormonism led to explosive outbreaks of violence in Missouri and Illinois in the 1820s and 1830s; the slave conspiracy, which mirrored the abolitionist conspiracy, exploded in Missouri and Kansas in the 1850s. Similarly, conspiracies of the monied interests found political expression in the Greenback Parties in states such as Indiana, Illinois, and Missouri in the 1870s. The Republican ascendancy of the 1890s coincided with the outbreak of anti-Catholic, anti-immigrant, anti-Semitic, and anti-monied conspiracies. Such views could be found in every social class and region, though these prejudices were not unique to any one political party: they reflected the rhetoric of conspiracy used to rally supporters and to express base prejudices found among followers of various parties.

The political realignment brought about by the Great Depression and the ascendancy of the New Deal order provided fertile ground for conspiracists on the right to attack the Roosevelt administration on a variety of charges, including manipulation of money for the benefit of internationalists, infiltration of the government by communists, and engineering America's entry into the Second World War. Fears of conspiracy, however, were found also on the left, as rumors spread of a military takeover of the government. In the postwar era, the right raised conspiratorial fears of the subversion of national sovereignty through communist infiltration and internationalism operating under a variety of guises, including the United Nations and groups such as the Bilderbergers. As liberalism came under challenge by an ascendant conservative political order, conspiracists both revived older theories and devised new ones that represented racial and ethnic fears in a global age. And in the modern era, conspiracy theory often incorporates a multitude of conspiracies. Money conspiracies might include anti-Jewish, anti-corporate, and anti-internationalist perspectives, which are not unique to the left or right. Other such perspectives that may be found regardless of ideology include anti-elitism, anti-corporatism, and anti-internationalism.

Modern technology has helped disseminate conspiracy theories to the larger public. Books, pamphlets, movies, television, and the internet have inundated American culture with conspiracy theories. Popular novelist John Grisham has incorporated conspiratorial themes into many of his books, including *The Firm* (1991), *The Pelican Brief* (1992), and *The Runaway Jury* (1996). Filmmaker Oliver Stone has promulgated conspiracy at the box office with two movies based on U.S. presidents, *JFK* (1993) and, more implicitly, *Nixon* (1995). Arguably the leading source of conspiratorial visions in contemporary America has been the popular television series *The X-Files,* which focuses on two F.B.I. agents—the unconvinced Dana Scully (Gillian Anderson) and the conspiracist Fox Mulder (David Duchovny)—who are constantly trying to uncover government conspiracies, ranging from alien colonization of the Earth to the government's testing of biological weapons on American citizens. The popularity of the show was remarkable. It consistently ranked among the top programs during its run from 1993 to 2002, and in 2006 *TV Guide* placed *The X-Files* in its list of the top fifty shows of all time. Clearly, popular culture has greatly influenced interest in conspiratorial thinking in modern America.

The internet has provided an important technological component in the distribution and accessibility of conspiracy theories. Conspiracists can maintain their own web sites, create a blog discussing conspiracies, and transcribe texts from older conspiracy books to post on their website. The internet has proved especially powerful in promoting conspiracies about the terrorist attacks that occurred on September 11, 2001. Conspiracy theorists undertook extensive evaluation of video relating to the attacks. Some conspiracists claim that frozen frames of video reveal splinters of information proving that the attacks were planned by the military, that explosives caused the collapse of the World Trade Center, or that the Pentagon was attacked by a missile rather than a hijacked airliner. These contemporary conspiracists, like those before them in American history, are autodidacts who constantly seek new methods of inquiry and analysis to disseminate their conspiracy theories.

This collection of edited documents, many of which have not appeared in print since they were first published, captures the poignant role conspiracy has played in American political life. These selections are intended to provide students and the general reader with an understanding of the rhetoric of conspiracy, as well as the rich variety of conspiracy theories from the founding of the republic until the present day. The documents show that, whether progressives or reactionaries, elite factions or popular interests, representatives of established political parties or challengers to party control, Americans have often used conspiracy to promote their political agendas. No single factor explains the intensity of conspiracy theory at any one moment in American political history.

These readings will enable readers to develop a deeper appreciation of the detrimental effects that conspiracy theory has for democratic governance. If large numbers of people within a democracy distrust their leaders and fear that the system is being manipulated by secret groups or organizations, democracy itself becomes threatened. To facilitate an understanding of the important role conspiracy has played in the American political order, each section begins with a brief introduction that summarizes the period and the role conspiracy played at the time. In addition, each reading is prefaced by a short description of the original author and the historical context in which the article appeared. In order to allow readers a full measure of the tone and construction of conspiracist argument, the editors of this volume have been careful not to reduce the documents to a simple excerpt. Instead, readers are invited to engage with the conspiracist authors in order to understand the attraction (and repulsion) of the arguments made at the time and repeated later by others.

The editors of this volume are not conspiracy theorists, and we abhor the conspiracies expressed in this book. We selected materials based on their originality, political influence, representational themes, and their importance for understanding political events at the time and in American political history in general. This volume includes a wide sampling of various conspiracies but is limited to political conspiracies, which tend to include social, economic, and cultural perspectives. A similar sampling of purely economic, cultural, or social conspiracies, to say nothing of an exhaustive record of political conspiracies, could fill multiple volumes. We believe that the present book should encourage further study of conspiracy theory in American history, even though readers will find selections abhorrent in their paranoia and bigotry. We believe that the dark views expressed in these selections take root when hidden from the light of serious inquiry. Thus, those conspiracies that embody prejudice toward ethnic, racial, and religious groups should be exposed and revealed for what they are in fact: deep and willful ignorance parading as insider knowledge.

The editors would like to thank Professor Jeffrey Pasley at the University of Missouri, Columbia, and Professor Gregory Schneider at Emporia State University for their good advice. In addition, we acknowledge the assistance of archivists and librarians at the University of Missouri, Columbia, the Missouri State Archives, Saint Louis University, Moorland-Springarn Research Center at Howard University, and the Eagle Forum Archives in Clayton, Missouri. The Social Philosophy and Politics Center at Bowling Green State University provided a fellowship to Donald T. Critchlow that allowed him time to work on this volume following completion of a larger project, *The Conservative Ascendancy: How the GOP Right Made Political History.* In addition, the editors wish to thank Robert Sloan at Indiana University Press for his support of this volume, and the excellent editorial staff at the press.

The editors undertook this project as a collaborative effort. We discussed at great length which selections to include and which documents to exclude. We were overwhelmed by the wealth of materials available, many of which have not appeared in print since their first publication.

POLITICAL CONSPIRACIES IN AMERICA

SECTION ONE

Conspiracy in a New Nation

During the late eighteenth and early nineteenth centuries, the fledgling American political experiment was still far from being a success. As the new nation struggled with establishing a government and its institutions, threats remained. The ocean that provided the nation's main defense had been routinely traversed for centuries. The nations that were, or could potentially be, hostile—Britain, France, and Spain—all maintained colonial possessions on the North American continent. In addition to military threats, the new republic faced a host of domestic challenges. Among these were conflicts over the form of the new government and over just how much democracy was desirable. These factors gave rise to fears of conspiracies threatening the independence, and even existence, of the new nation and its ideals.

The United States was born of conspiracy, real and imagined. Fears of a ministerial conspiracy to deprive the American colonists of their liberty drove the Americans to war and, ultimately, to independence. During the early years, fears that liberty and democracy would degenerate into licentiousness and mob rule were given credence by social unrest in Pennsylvania and Massachusetts. In addition, fears of domestic conspiracies, designed to undermine or overthrow the government, took root.

Conspiracy fears among American colonists stretch back to the earliest settlements but gained strength by the mid-eighteenth century. Following the French and Indian War (1754–63) and England's reexertion of control, American colonists became increasing fearful of dark forces at work in Parliament and behind the crown. The Stamp Act (1765) brought the colonists and the British into open conflict. The controversy stemmed from whether or not Parliament had the right or the power to impose taxes on the colonies. Viewing the Parliamentary acts as a conspiracy to deny traditional liberty, and therefore impose slavery on the colonies, the rhetoric grew increasingly hostile. The American belief in a ministerial conspiracy and increasing frustration with the inaction of their supposed defender, King George III, resulted in a protest being transformed into a rebellion. The records of the Continental Congress are replete with references to a ministerial conspiracy prior to the spring of 1776. As the conflict continued, it became clear that the king would not intercede on behalf of the colonists, and the Americans responded with one of the greatest indictments against tyranny in history, the Declaration of Independence.

After the Revolution, new conspiracies against liberty and democracy arose. The war left the nation economically devastated. One reaction to the economic hardships came from Massachusetts, in the form of Shays' Rebellion (1786), in which farmers led by Daniel Shays sought to prevent foreclosures by closing the courts. The weak central government, under the Articles of Confederation, had been powerless to impact the social and economic conditions that gave rise to Shays' Rebellion. In response, Federalists called for a strong federal government and a new constitution, while conspiracy theories took root and prospered among their opponents.

In the first years of the nation, the rhetoric of Federalist Party political leaders such as Alexander Hamilton, George Cabot, and Timothy Dwight, among others, led to suspicions of encroaching monarchism. Disputes with France, anti-egalitarianism, and the adoption of the Alien and Sedition Acts during the Adams administration all gave rise to Republican belief in a conspiracy to establish an American monarchy.

The Federalists, for their part, developed conspiracy theories involving Republicans. Unable to come to grips with just how radicalized the nation became during the Revolution, the Federalists, already in decline and no longer in step with contemporary public opinion, adopted reactionary and repressive policies. Many Federalists viewed Jeffersonian Republicans as treasonous. The Whiskey Rebellion (1794), in which Pennsylvania farmers revolted over a tax, as well as domestic disturbances stemming from the ratification of Jay's Treaty (1795), were viewed as Republican conspiracies aimed at overthrowing the government. Even more serious was the connection between Republicans and the revolutionaries in France.

When the Terror during the French Revolution began, Federalists concluded that the French revolutionaries had little in common with the Americans. The French were completely destroying the social order, denying religion and morality, and spiraling into licentiousness and unrestrained freedom, with no checks to enforce the public good. Thomas Jefferson, the leader of the Republicans, was identified as the greatest proponent of the French revolutionaries. Drawing upon anti-Enlightenment literature, notably Edmund Burke's "Reflections on the Revolution in France," Federalist orators took the Republicans to task. In his 1798 sermon "The Duty of Americans at the Present Crisis," Timothy Dwight maintained that the driving force behind the French chaos was Freemasonry, specifically the Bavarian Illuminati and their anti-Christian licentiousness. He drew heavily from continental literature, including John Robison's *Proofs of a Conspiracy* (1797) and Abbé Barruel's *Memoirs Illustrating the History of Jacobinism* (1797–98), and charged that Illuminati influence had spread across Europe and reached the United States. Thus in Dwight's mind there was an international conspiracy to undermine the basic tenets underlying the creation of the United States, and it had domestic support.

After the Republicans gained supremacy in 1801, they too faced political difficulties. The nation was growing rapidly. The Louisiana Purchase effectively doubled the size of the nation. But there remained a divide between the people and the central government, which was only exacerbated by the increase in territory. Once the boundaries of the nation pushed west of the Mississippi River, there arose the possibility of national disintegration, heightened by the conspiracy of Aaron Burr, a rogue general, and others to establish a second republic on the continent. The final details of this conspiracy are lost to history, however; we only know that Burr escaped punishment though clearly something was afoot.

Finally, as the nation became more assured of its viability, some Americans perceived a new threat of immense power and diabolical design: the Freemasons. From the 1820s through mid-century, anti-Masons worked to expose the alleged secrets of Freemasonry, its oaths and practices that they saw as antithetical to American republican ideology. The Masons were viewed as a shadow government, usurping the law and local authority and turning the power of these institutions to their own purposes. Some even spread the notion that the Masons had materially contributed to the election of President Andrew Jackson, himself a Mason of high rank.

Conspiracies, real and imagined, had a real and tangible impact on the early development of the United States, and some of these early conspiracies persisted well into the nineteenth century. They were embraced by those searching for answers to events that could not be easily explained. The Federalists saw the Jeffersonians as disloyal and so attributed their successes to conspiracy. The far-flung reaches of the nation were too far from the centers of power, making them ripe for Burr's conspiracy to separate them from the rest of the United States. Secret societies, like those Timothy Dwight had warned about, arose on American shores, and anecdotal evidence indicated that they would sanction horrible crimes against those outside their own society. This threat was considered the most insidious of all by conspiracists, because in this case the enemy was in their midst.

To the People of Great-Britain

John Jay

The belief in a ministerial conspiracy to enslave the colonists was a major factor in the outbreak of the American Revolution. Following the Seven

Years or French and Indian War, Parliament found the British treasury nearly depleted and thus decided that the colonies should bear some of the cost of the war. The Americans disagreed, seeing the Sugar Act (1764), Currency Act (1764), Quartering Act (1764), Stamp Act (1765), Townsend Acts (1767), Tea Act (1773), and the Coercive Acts (1774)—the latter directed specifically at Massachusetts—as attempts by Parliament to usurp their rights. The controversy stemmed from the traditional method of governing the colonies. At one point Parliament participated only in the governance of Britain itself, leaving the colonies to the crown and its representatives in North America. The colonies developed their own legislatures and worked with the royal governors to govern themselves. But this was tradition rather than rule. When Parliament, which sat no representatives from the colonies, began to take an interest in their operation for the purpose of raising revenue, many perceived a conspiracy, as expressed in the motto "No taxation without representation."

On October 11, 1774, the Continental Congress unanimously approved the appointment of a committee to draft a message to the people of Great Britain and Ireland. The committee members outlined a conspiracy against the colonists' "British" liberty; they disavowed any intention of seeking independence and did not mention the king as one of their tormentors—in stark contrast with the Declaration of Independence. (From John Jay, William Livingston, and Richard Henry Lee, "To the People of Great Britain," *Journal of the Continental Congress,* October 21, 1774, pp. 82–90.)

Friends and fellow subjects,

When a nation, led to greatness by the hand of liberty, and possessed of all the glory that heroism, munificence, and humanity can bestow, descends to the ungrateful task of forging chains for her friends and children, and instead of giving support to freedom, turns advocate for slavery and oppression, there is reason to suspect she has either ceased to be virtuous, or been extremely negligent in the appointment of her rulers.

In almost every age, in repeated conflicts . . . against many and powerful nations, against the open assaults of enemies, and the more dangerous treachery of friends, have the inhabitants of your island, your great and glorious ancestors, maintained their independence and transmitted the rights of men, and the blessings of liberty to . . . their posterity.

Be not surprised . . . that we, who are descended from the same common ancestors; that we, whose forefathers participated in all the rights, the liberties, and . . . who have carefully conveyed the same fair inheritance to us . . . should refuse to surrender them to men who found their claims on no principles of reason, and who prosecute them with a design, that by having our lives and property in their power, they may with greater facility enslave you.

The cause of America is now the object of universal attention. . . . This unhappy country has not only been oppressed, but abused and misrepresented; and the duty we owe to ourselves and posterity to your interest, and the general welfare of the British Empire, leads us to address you on this very important subject.

Know then, that we consider ourselves, and do insist, that we are and ought to be as free as our fellow-subjects in Britain, and that no power on earth has a right to take our property . . . without our consent. That we claim all the benefits secured . . . by the English constitution, and particularly . . . trial by jury. That we hold it essential to English liberty, that no man be condemned unheard, or punished for supposed offences, without having an opportunity of making his defense. That we think the Legislature of Great Britain is not authorized . . . to establish a religion, fraught with sanguinary and impious tenets, or, to erect an arbitrary form of government, in any quarter of the globe. These rights we . . . deem sacred. And yet sacred as they are, they have, with many others, been repeatedly and flagrantly violated.

Are not the proprietors of the soil of Great Britain lords of their own property? Can it be taken from them without consent? Will they yield it to the arbitrary disposal of any man, or number of men . . . ?

Why then are the proprietors of the soil of America less lords of their property . . . why should they submit it to the disposal of your Parliament, or any other Parliament . . . not of their election? Can . . . the sea that divides us, cause disparity in rights, or can any reason be given, why English subjects, who live three thousand miles from the royal palace, should enjoy less liberty than those who are three hundred miles distant from it?

Reason looks with indignation on such distinctions, and freemen can never perceive their propriety. And yet, however chimerical and unjust . . . the Parliament assert, that they have a right to bind us in all cases . . . that they may take and use our property when and in what manner they please. . . . Such declarations we consider as heresies in English polities. . . .

At the conclusion of the late war—a war rendered glorious by the abilities and integrity of a Minister, to whose efforts the British Empire owes its safety and its fame. At the conclusion of this war, which was succeeded by an inglorious peace, formed under the auspices of a Minister of principles, and of a family unfriendly to the protestant cause, and inimical to liberty—we say at this period, and under the influence of that man, a plan for enslaving your fellow subjects in America was concerted, and has ever since been pertinaciously carrying into execution.

Prior to this era you were content to drawing from us the wealth produced by our commerce. You restrained our trade in every way that could conduce to your emolument. . . . You named the ports and nations to which . . . our merchandise should be carried, and with whom we should trade; and though some of the restrictions were grievous, we . . . did not complain. . . .

We call upon you yourselves, to witness our loyalty and attachment to the common interest of the . . . empire. Did we not, in the last war; add all the strength of this vast continent to the force which repelled our common enemy? Did we not leave our native shores . . . to promote the success of British arms in foreign climates? Did you not thank us for our zeal, and even reimburse us large sums of money, which, you confessed, we had advanced beyond our proportion and far beyond our abilities? You did.

To what causes . . . are we to attribute the sudden change of treatment, and that system of slavery which was prepared for us at the restoration of peace?

Before we had recovered from the distresses which ever attend war, an attempt was made to drain this country of all its money by the oppressive Stamp Act. Paint, glass, and other commodities, which you would not permit us to purchase of other nations, were taxed. . . . These and many other impositions were laid upon us most unjustly and unconstitutionally, for the express purpose of raising a revenue. In order to silence complaint, it was . . . provided that this revenue should be expended in America for its protection and defense. These exactions, however, can receive no justification from a pretended necessity of protecting and defending us. They are lavishly squandered on court favorites and ministerial dependents, generally avowed enemies to America and employing themselves, by partial representations, to traduce and embroil the Colonies. For the necessary support of government here, we ever were and ever shall be ready to provide. And whenever the exigencies of the state may require it, we shall . . . cheerfully contribute our full proportion of men and money. To enforce this . . . unjust scheme of taxation, every fence that . . . our . . . ancestors erected against arbitrary power, has been violently thrown down in America, and the . . . right to trial by jury taken away. . . . It was ordained, that whenever offences should be committed in the colonies against particular acts imposing various duties and restrictions upon trade, the prosecutor might bring his action . . . in the Courts of the Admiralty. . . .

When the design of raising a revenue from the duties imposed on the importation of tea into America had . . . been rendered abortive by our ceasing to import that commodity, a scheme was concerted by the Ministry with the East India Company, and an Act passed enabling and encouraging them to transport and vend it in the colonies. Aware of the danger of giving success to this insidious maneuver . . . various methods were adopted to elude the stroke. The people of Boston, then rule by a Governor, whom . . . all America considers as her enemy, were exceedingly embarrassed. The ships which has arrived with the tea were by his management prevented from returning. The duties would have been paid; the cargoes landed and exposed to sale; a Governor's influence would have procured many purchasers. While the town was suspended by deliberations . . .

the tea was destroyed. Even supposing a trespass was thereby committed, and the proprietors . . . entitled to damages . . . the East India Company . . . did not think proper to commence any suits, nor did they even demand satisfaction. . . . The Ministry . . . officiously made the case their own. . . . Diverse papers, letters, and other unauthenticated ex parte evidence were laid before them; neither the persons who destroyed the tea, or the people of Boston, were called upon to answer the complaint. The Ministry, incensed by being disappointed in a favorite scheme, were determined to recur from the little arts of finesse, to open force and unmanly violence. The port of Boston was blocked . . . and an army placed in the town. Their trade was . . . suspended, and thousands reduced to . . . gaining subsistence from charity, till they should submit to pass under the yoke, and consent to become slaves, by confessing the omnipotence of Parliament, and acquiescing in whatever disposition they might think proper to make of their lives and property.

Let justice and humanity cease to be the boast . . . examine your records . . . and show us a single instance of men being condemned to suffer for imputed crimes, unheard, unquestioned, and without even the specious formality of a trial; and . . . by laws made expressly for the purpose, and which had no existence at the time of the fact committed. If it be difficult to reconcile these proceedings to the genius and temper of your laws and constitution, the task will become more arduous when we call upon our ministerial enemies to justify, not only condemning men untried and by hearsay, but involving the innocent in one common punishment with the guilty, and for the act of thirty or forty, to bring poverty, distress and calamity on thirty thousand souls, and those not your enemies, but your friends, brethren, and fellow subjects.

It would be some consolation to us, if the catalog of American oppressions ended here. It gives us pain to be reduced to the necessity of reminding you that under the confidence reposed the faith of government, pledged in a royal charter . . . the forefathers of . . . Massachusetts Bay left their former habitations, and established that great, flourishing, and loyal Colony. Without incurring or being charged with the forfeiture of their rights, without being heard, without being tried, without law, and without justice, by an act of Parliament, their charter is destroyed, their liberties violated, their constitution and form of government changed; and all this upon no better pretence, than because in one of their towns a trespass was committed . . . and because the Ministry were of opinion, that such high political regulations were necessary to compel due subordination and obedience to their mandates.

Nor are these the only capital grievances under which we labor. We might tell of dissolute, weak and wicked Governors having been set over us; of Legislatures being suspended for asserting the rights of British subjects; of needy and ignorant dependents on great men, advanced to the seats of justice and to other places of trust and importance; of hard restrictions on commerce, and a great variety of lesser evils, the recollection of which is almost lost under the weight and pressure of greater and more poignant calamities.

Now mark the progression of the ministerial plan for enslaving us.

Well aware that such hardy attempts to take our property from us; to deprive us of that valuable right of trial by jury; to seize our persons, and carry us for trial to Great Britain; to blockade our ports; to destroy our charters, and change our forms of government, would occasion, and had already occasioned, great discontent in all the colonies, which might produce opposition to these measures; an act was passed to protect, indemnify, and screen from punishment such as might be guilty even of murder, in endeavoring to carry their oppressive edicts into execution; and by another act the dominion of Canada is to be so extended, modeled, and governed, as that by being disunited from us, detached from our interests, by civil as well as religious prejudices, that by their numbers daily swelling with Catholic emigrants from Europe, and by their devotion to administration, so friendly to their religion, they might become formidable to us, and on occasion, be fit instruments in the hands of power, to reduce the ancient free Protestant Colonies to the same state of slavery with themselves.

This was evidently the object of the Act;—and in this view, being extremely dangerous to our liberty and quiet, we cannot forebear complaining of it, as hostile to British America. Suppurated to these considerations, we cannot help deploring the . . . condition to which it has reduced . . . many English settlers, who, encouraged by the Royal Proclamation, promising the enjoyment of all their rights, have purchased estates in that country. They are now the subjects of an arbitrary government. . . . Nor can we suppress our astonishment, that a British Parliament should ever consent to establish in that country a religion that has deluged your island in blood, and dispersed impiety, bigotry, persecution, murder and rebellion through every part of the world.

This being the true state of facts let us beseech you to consider to what end they lead. Admit that the Ministry, by the powers of Britain, and the aid of our Roman Catholic neighbors, should be able to carry the point of taxation, and reduce us to a state of perfect humiliation and slavery. Such an enterprise would doubtless make some addition to your national debt, which already presses down your liberties. . . . We presume, also, that your commerce will somewhat be diminished. However, suppose you should prove victorious; in what condition will you then be? What advantages or what laurels will you reap from such conquest?

May not a Ministry with the same armies enslave you? It may be said, you will cease to pay them; but remember the taxes from America, the wealth, and we may add, the men, and particularly the Roman Catholics of this vast continent will then be in the power of your enemies, nor will you have any reason to expect, that after making slaves of us, many among us should refuse to assist in reducing you to the same abject state. . . .

We believe there is yet much virtue, much justice, and much public spirit in the English nation. To that justice we now appeal. You have been told that we are seditious . . . and desirous of independence. Be assured that these are not facts, but calumnies. Permit us to be as free as yourselves, and we shall over esteem a union with you to be our greatest glory . . . we shall ever be ready to contribute . . . to the welfare of the Empire. . . .

But if you are determined that your Ministers shall wantonly sport with the rights of mankind; if neither the voice of justice, the dictates of law, the principles of the constitution, or the suggestions of humanity can restrain your hands from shedding . . . blood in such an impious cause, we must tell you, that we will never submit to be hewers of wood or drawers of water for any ministry or nation in the world.

Place us in the same situation that we were at the close of the last war, and our former harmony will be restored. But lest the same supineness and the same inattention to our common interest . . . should continue, we think it prudent to anticipate the consequences.

By the destruction of the trade of Boston, the Ministry have endeavored to induce submission to their measures. The like fate may befall us all, we will endeavor therefore to live without trade, and recur for subsistence to the fertility and bounty of our native soil, which will afford us all the necessaries . . . of life. . . .

It is with the utmost regret, however, that we find ourselves compelled by the overruling principles of self-preservation, to adopt measures detrimental in their consequences to numbers of our fellow subjects in Great Britain and Ireland. But we hope, that the magnanimity and justice of the British nation will furnish a Parliament of such wisdom, independence and public spirit, as may save the violated rights of the whole empire from the devices of wicked Ministers and evil Counselors whether in or out of office, and . . . restore that harmony, friendship and fraternal affection between all the inhabitants of his Majesty's kingdoms and territories so ardently wished for by every true and honest American.

The Duty of Americans at the Present Crisis

Timothy Dwight

During the early years of the American Republic, fears of foreign and domestic conspiracies aimed at overthrowing the fledgling government were rife. The Federalists, the ascendant faction in American politics, had backed the creation of a strong national government under the Constitution. They were suspicious of the Republicans, a faction that emerged during the early 1790s that espoused the opposite position. From the Federalist point of view, the Republicans were subversives. Republican leaders, such as Thomas Jefferson, embraced and cheered the French Revolutionaries and their radical Enlightenment ideals; they were slow to distance themselves from the French after the Revolution devolved into madness and carnage in the name of reason. In examining the origins of the French Revolution, Timothy Dwight (1752–1817), a Congregational minister, President of Yale, and arch-Federalist, cites the French Enlightenment thinkers and a new conspiratorial threat, the Illuminati, as the prime movers in an international movement dedicated to eradicate religion and promote licentiousness and vice, all in the name of reason and the spread of Masonry. (From Timothy Dwight, "The Duty of Americans at the Present Crisis," a sermon delivered July 4, 1798, New Haven.)

. . . About the year 1728, Voltaire, so celebrated for his wit and brilliancy, and not less distinguished for his hatred of Christianity and his abandonment of principle, formed a systematical design to destroy Christianity, and to introduce in its stead a general diffusion of irreligion and atheism. For this purpose he associated with himself Frederic the II, King of Prussia, and Mess. D'Alembert and Diderot, the principle compilers of the Encyclopedie; all men of talents, atheists, and in the like manner abandoned. The principal parts of this system were 1st, the compilation of the *Encyclopédie;* in which with great art and insidiousness the doctrines of Natural as well as Christian Theology were rendered absurd and ridiculous; and the mind of the reader was insensibly steeled against conviction and duty. 2. The overthrow of the religious orders in Catholic countries; a step essentially necessary to the destruction of the religion professed in those countries. 3. The establishment of a sect of philosophists to serve, it is presumed, as a conclave, a rallying point, for all their followers. 4. The appropriation to themselves, and their disciples, of the places and honors of members of the French Academy, the most respectable literary society in France, and always considered as containing none but men of prime learning and talents. In this way they designed to hold out themselves, and their friends, as the only persons of great literary and intellectual distinction in that country, and to dictate all literary opinions to the nation. 5. The fabrication of Books of all kinds against Christianity, especially such as excite[s] doubt, and generate contempt and derision. Of these they issued . . . an immense number; so printed as to be purchased for little or nothing, and so written, as to catch the feelings, and steal upon the approbation, of every class of men. 6. The formation of a Secret Academy, of which Voltaire was the standing president, and in which books were formed; altered, forged, imputed as posthumous to deceased writers of reputation, and sent abroad with the weight of their names. These were printed and circulated, at the lowest price, through all classes of men, in an uninterrupted succession, and through every part of the kingdom.

Nor were the labors of this Academy confined to religion. They attacked also morality and government, unhinged gradually the minds of men, and destroyed their reverence for every thing heretofore esteemed sacred.

In the mean time, the Masonic Societies . . . were, especially in France and Germany, made the professed scenes of debate concerning religion, morality, and government, by these philosophists, who had in great numbers become Masons. For such debate the legalized existence of Masonry, its profound secrecy, its solemn and mystic rites and symbols, its mutual correspondence, and its extension through most civilized countries, furnished the greatest advantages. All here was free, safe, and calculated to encourage the boldest excursions of restless opinion and impatient ardor, and to make and fix the deepest impressions. Here, and in no other place, under such arbitrary governments, could every innovator in these important subjects utter every sentiment, however daring, and attack every doctrine and institution, however guarded by law and sanctity. In the secure and unrestrained debates of the dodge, every novel, licentious, and alarming opinion was resolutely advanced. Minds, already tinged with philosophism, were here speedily blackened with a deep and deadly die; and those, which came fresh and innocent to the scene of contamination, became early and irremediably corrupted. A stubborn incapacity of conviction, and a flinty insensibility to every moral and natural tie, grew of course out of this combination of causes; and men were surely prepared . . . for every plot and perpetration. In these hot beds were sown the seeds of that astonishing Revolution, and all its dreadful appendages, which now spreads dismay and horror throughout half the globe.

While these measures were advancing the great design with a regular and rapid progress, Doctor Adam Weishaupt, professor of the Canon law in the University of Ingolstadt, a city of Bavaria . . . formed, about the year 1777, the order of Illuminati. This order is professedly a higher order of Masons . . . and grafted on ancient Masonic Institutions. There secrecy, solemnity, mysticism, and correspondence of Masonry, were in this new order preserved and enhanced; while the ardor of innovation, the impatience of civil and moral restraints, and the aims against government, morals, and religion were elevated, expanded, and rendered more systematical, malignant and daring.

In the societies of Illuminati doctrines were taught, which strike at the root of all human happiness and virtue; and every such doctrine was either expressly or implicitly involved in their system.

The being of God was denied and ridiculed.

Government was asserted to be a curse, and authority a mere usurpation.

Civil Society was declared to be the only apostasy of man.

The possession of property was pronounced to be robbery.

Chastity and natural affection were declared to be nothing more than groundless prejudices.

Adultery, Assassination, poisoning, and other crimes of the like infernal nature, were taught as lawful, and even virtuous actions.

To crown such a system of falsehood and horror all means were declared to be lawful, provided the end was good.

In this last doctrine men are not only loosed from every bond, and from every duty; but from every inducement to perform any thing which is good, and, abstain from any thing which is evil; and are set upon each other, like a company of hellhounds to worry, rend, and destroy. Of the goodness of the end every man is to judge for himself; and most men, and all men who resemble the Illuminati, will pronounce every end to be good, which will gratify their inclinations. The great and good ends proposed by the Illuminati, as the ultimate objects of their union, are the overthrow of religion, government, and human society civil and domestic. These they pronounce to be so good, that murder, butchery, and war, however extended and dreadful are declared by them to be completely justifiable, if necessary for these great purposes. With such an example in view, it will be in vain to hunt for ends, which can be evil. . . .

The names by which this society was enlarged, and its doctrines spread, were of every promising kind. With unremitted ardor and diligence the members insinuated themselves into every place of power and trust, and into every literary, political and friendly society; engrossed as much as possible the education of youth, especially of distinction; became licensers of the press, and directors of every literary journal; waylaid every foolish prince, every unprincipled civil officer, and every abandoned clergyman; entered boldly into the desk, and with unhallowed hands, and satanic lips, polluted the pages of God; enlisted in their service almost all the booksellers, and of course the printers, of Germany; inundated the country with books, replete with infidelity, irreligion, immorality, and obscenity; prohibited the printing, and prevented the sale, of books of the contrary character; decried and ridiculed them when published in spite of their efforts; panegyrized and trumpeted those of themselves and their coadjutors; and in a word made more numerous, more diversified, and more strenuous exertions, than an active imagination would have preconceived.

To these exertions their success has been proportioned. Multitudes of the Germans, notwithstanding the gravity, steadiness, and sobriety of their national character, have become either partial or entire converts to these wretched doctrines; numerous societies have been established among them; the public faith and morals have been unhinged; and the political and religious affairs of that empire have assumed an aspect, which forebodes its total ruin. In France, also, Illuminatism has been eagerly and extensively adopted; and those men, who have had, successively, the chief direction of the public affairs of that country, have been members of this society. . . .

Nor have England and Scotland escaped the contagion. Several societies have been erected in both of those countries. Nay in the private papers, seized in the custody of the leading members in Germany, several such societies are recorded as having been erected in America, before the year 1786.

It is a remarkable fact, that a large proportion of the sentiments, here stated, have been publicly avowed and applauded in the French legislature. . . .

I presume I have sufficiently . . . shown, that doctrines and teachers . . . have arisen in the very countries specified, and that they are rapidly spreading through the world, to engage mankind in an open and professed war against God. . . .

. . . It may be necessary to remind you, that personal obedience and reformation is the foundation, and the sum of all national worth and prosperity. If each man conducts himself aright, the community cannot be conducted wrong. . . .

Individuals are often apt to consider their own private conduct as of small importance to the public welfare. This opinion is wholly erroneous and highly mischievous. . . . On the contrary, the advantages to the public of private virtue, faithful prayer and edifying example, cannot be calculated. . . .

Among the particular duties required by this precept, and at the present time, none holds a higher place than the observation of the Sabbath.

. . . Religion and Liberty are the two great objects of defensive war. Conjoined, they unite all the feelings, and call forth all the energies, of man. . . . Religion and liberty are the meat and the drink of the body politic. . . . Without religion we may possibly retain the freedom of savages . . . but not the freedom of New-England. . . .

Another duty . . . is an entire separation from our enemies. Among the moral duties of man none hold a higher rank than political ones, and among our own political duties none is more plain, or more absolute. . . .

Another duty, to which we are . . . called, is union among ourselves. . . .

The great bond of union to every people is its government. This destroyed, or distrusted, there is no center left of intelligence, counsel, or action; no system of purposes, or measures; no point of rallying, or confidence. . . .

Another duty . . . is unshaken firmness in our opposition.

A steady and invincible firmness is the chief instrument of great achievements. It is the prime mean of great wealth, learning, wisdom, power and virtue; and without it nothing noble or useful is usually accomplished. Without it our separation from our enemies, and the union among ourselves, will avail to no end. . . . Great sacrifices of property, of peace; and of life, we may be called to make, but they will fall short of complete ruin. If they should not, it will be more desirable, beyond computation, to fall in the honorable and faithful defense of our families, our country, and our religion, than to survive, the melancholy, debased and guilty spectators of the ruin of all. . . .

From two forces only are we in danger of irresolution; Avarice, and a reliance on those fair professions, which our enemies have begun to make, and which they will doubtless continue to make, in degrees, and with insidiousness still greater.

. . . Will you rely on men whose principles justify falsehood, injustice, and cruelty? Will you trust philosophists; men who set truth at naught, who make justice a butt of mockery, who deny the being . . . of God, and laugh at the interests and sufferings of men? Think not that such men can change. They can scarcely be worse. There is not a hope that they will become better.

But perhaps you may be alarmed by the power, and the successes of your enemies. I am warranted to declare, that the ablest judge of this subject in America has said, that, if we are untied firm, and faithful to ourselves, neither France, nor all Europe, can subdue these States. . . . Three thousand miles of ocean spread between us and our enemies, to enfeeble and disappoint their efforts. They will not here contend with silken Italians, with divided Swissers, nor with self-surrendered Belgians and Batavians. They will find a hardy race of freemen, uncorrupted by luxury, unbroken by despotism; enlightened to understand their privileges, glowing with independence, and determined to be free, or to die: men who love and who will defend, their families, their country, and their religion: men fresh from triumph, and strong in a recent and victorious Revolution.

Aaron Burr's Conspiracy

Thomas Jefferson

Though young democratic nations are susceptible to coups d'etat and fragmentation, the United States successfully transferred power between competing political factions following the election of Thomas Jefferson to the presidency in 1800. As the nation expanded to the Mississippi River valley and acquired the Louisiana Territory from France, however, its sheer size and low population density made it vulnerable to uprising, especially in the West. It was there that Aaron Burr, Jefferson's onetime rival and vice president during his first term in office, had plotted in 1795 to seize territory with the apparent intention to establish a new government, although the details of the plot remain unknown. What is known is that Burr, the grandson of theologian Jonathan Edwards and a cousin of Timothy Dwight, attempted to create a new nation forged from Mexican territory and territory west of the Appalachian Mountains. Burr's detractors charged that the conspiracy involved overthrowing the United States. Involved in this plan was General James Wilkinson, commander of the U.S. Army at New Orleans and governor of the Louisiana Territory.

Wilkinson, however, betrayed Burr and reported to President Jefferson that Burr was planning a revolution. Jefferson ordered Burr's arrest on grounds of treason. Burr was subsequently released, but Jefferson ordered him to be rearrested. In a trial presided over by Supreme Court chief justice John Marshall in 1807, Burr was acquitted, largely because the Constitution requires a strict definition and proof of treason. Burr's intentions were never clear, and the government failed to prove its charge of treason that Burr and Wilkinson planned to form an independent nation in North America. In this 1807 report to Congress, Jefferson outlines the charges of conspiracy and treason against Burr before he was brought to trial. (From Thomas Jefferson, "Burr's Conspiracy," American State Papers 037, Miscellaneous Volume 1, 9th Congress, 2nd Session, Publication No. 217, pp. 468–69.)

To the Senate and House of Representatives of the United States:

Agreeably to the request of the House of Representatives, communicated in their resolution of the 16th instant, I proceed to state, under the reserve therein expressed, information received touching an illegal combination of private individuals against the peace and safety of the Union, and a military expedition planned by them against the territories of a Power in amity with the United States, with the measures I have pursued for appeasing the same.

I had . . . been in the constant expectation of receiving such further information as would enable me to lay before the Legislature the termination, as well as the beginning and progress of this scene of depravity, so far as it has been acted on the Ohio and its waters. From this, the state of safety of the lower country might have been estimated on probable grounds, and the delay was indulged the rather because no circumstance had yet made it necessary to call in the aid of the legislative functions. Information, now recently communicated, has brought us nearly to the period contemplated. The mass of what I have received, in the course of these transactions, is voluminous, but little has been given under the sanction of an oath, so as to constitute formal and legal evidence. It is chiefly in the form of letters, often containing such a mixture of rumors, conjectures, and suspicions, as renders it difficult to sift out the real facts, and unadvisable to hazard more than general outlines, strengthened by concurrent information, or the particular credibility of the relator. In this state of the evidence, delivered sometimes, too, under the restriction of private confidence, neither safety nor justice will permit the exposing names, except that of the principal actor, whose guilt is placed beyond question.

Some time in the latter part of September I received intimations that designs were in agitation in the western country, unlawful, and unfriendly to the peace of the Union, and that the prime mover in these was Aaron Burr, heretofore distinguished by the favor of his country. The grounds of these intimations being inconclusive, the objects uncertain, and the fidelity of that country known to be firm, the only measure taken was to urge the informants to use their best endeavors to get further insight into the designs and proceedings of the suspected persons, and to communicate them to me.

It was not until the latter part of October, that the objects of the conspiracy began to be perceived; but still so blended and involved in mystery, that nothing distinct could be singled out for pursuit. In this state of uncertainty . . . I thought it best to send to the scene . . . as person in whose integrity, understanding, and discretion, entire confidence could be reposed, with instructions to investigate the plots going on, to enter into conference . . . with the Governors, and all other officers, civil and military, and, with their aid, to do . . . whatever should be necessary to discover the designs of the conspirators . . . and to call out the force of the country to suppress any unlawful enterprise in which it should be found they were engaged. By this time it was known that many boats were under preparation, stores of provisions collecting, and an unusual number of suspicious characters in motion on the Ohio and its waters. Besides dispatching the confidential agent . . . orders were . . . sent to the Governors of the Orleans and Mississippi Territories, and to the commanders of the land and naval forces there, to be on their guard against surprise, and in constant readiness resist any enterprise . . . and on the 8th of November instructions were forwarded to General Wilkinson to hasten an accommodation with the Spanish commandant on the Sabine, and . . . to fall back with his principal force to the hither bank of the Mississippi, for the defense of the interesting points on that river. By a letter received from that officer of the 25th of November . . . we learned that a confidential agent of Aaron Burr had been deputed to him, with communications . . . explaining his designs, exaggerating his resources, and making such offers of emolument and command, to engage him and the army in his unlawful enterprise, as he had flattered himself would be successful. The general, with the honor of a soldier, and the fidelity of a good citizen, immediately dispatched a trusty officer to me . . . proceeded to establish . . . an understanding with the Spanish commandant . . . and to enter on measures for opposing the projected enterprise.

The general's letter . . . and some other information received a few days earlier . . . developed Burr's general designs, different parts of which only had been revealed to different informants. It appeared that he contemplated two distinct objects, which might be carried on either jointly or separately, and either the one or the other first, as circumstances should direct. One of these was the severance of the union of these States by the Allegany [*sic*] mountains; the other an attack on Mexico; a third object was provided, merely ostensible, to wit, the settlement of a pretended purchase of a tract of country on the Washita [River], claimed by a Baron Bastrop. This was to serve as the pretext for all his preparations, an allurement for such followers as really wished to acquire settlements in that country, and a cover under which to retreat in the event of a final discomfiture of both branches of his real design.

He found at once that the attachment of the western county . . . was not to be shaken; that its dissolution could not be effected with the consent of its inhabitants; and that his resources were inadequate . . . to effect it by force. He took his course then at once; determined to seize on New Orleans, plunder the bank there, possess himself of the military and naval stores, and proceed on his expedition to Mexico; and to this object all his means and preparations were now directed. . . .

This was the state of my information of his proceedings about the last of November; at which time, therefore, it was first possible to take specific measures to meet them. The proclamation of November 27 . . . was now issued. Orders were dispatched to every interesting point on the Ohio and Mississippi [Rivers], from Pittsburgh to New Orleans, for the employment of such force, either of the regulars or of the militia, and of such proceedings also of the civil authorities, as might enable them to seize on all boats and stores provided of the enterprise, to arrest the persons concerned, and to suppress effectually the further progress of the enterprise. A little before the receipt of these orders . . . our confidential agent, who had been diligently employed in investigating the conspiracy, had acquired sufficient information to open himself to the Governor of that State [Ohio], and to apply for the immediate exertion . . . of the State to crush the combination. Governor [Edward] Tiffin and the Legislature . . . effected the seizure of all the boats, provisions, and other preparations within their reach; and thus gave a first blow, materially disabling the enterprise in its outset.

In Kentucky a premature attempt to bring Burr to justice . . . had produced a popular impression in his favor, and a general disbelief of his guilt. This gave him an unfortunate opportunity of hastening his equipments. The arrival of the proclamation and orders . . . at length awakened the authorities of that State to the truth, and then produced the same promptitude and energy of which the neighboring State had set the example. Under an act of their Legislature . . . militia was instantly ordered to different important points, and measures taken for doing whatever could yet be done. Some boats . . . and persons . . . had, in the meantime, passed the falls of Ohio to rendezvous at the mouth of Cumberland [River], with others expected down that river.

Not apprised . . . that any boats were building on the Cumberland, the effect of the proclamation had been trusted for some time in the State of Tennessee; but on the 19th of December similar communications . . . were dispatched by express to the Governor, and a general officer of the western division of the State; and on the 23rd of December our confidential agent left Frankfort for Nashville. . . . But by information received yesterday, I learned that on the 22nd of December Mr. Burr descended the Cumberland, with two boats merely of accommodation, carrying with him from that State no quota towards his unlawful enterprise. Where after the arrival of the proclamation, of the orders, or of our agent, any exertion which could be made by that State, or the orders of the Governor of Kentucky, for calling out the militia at the mouth of Cumberland, would be in time to arrest these boats, and those form the falls of Ohio, is still doubtful.

On the whole, the fugitives from the Ohio, with their associates from Cumberland, or any other place in that quarter, cannot threaten serious danger to the city of New Orleans. . . .

Surmises have been hazarded that this enterprise is to receive aid from certain foreign Powers, but these surmises are without proof or probability. The wisdom of the measures sanctioned by Congress . . . has placed us in the paths of peace and justice with the only Powers with whom we had any differences, and nothing has happened since which makes it either their interest or ours to pursue another course. No change of measures has taken place on our part; none ought to take place at this time. With the one, friendly arrangement was proposed; and the law, deemed necessary on the failure of that, was suspended, to give time for a fair trial of the issue. With the same Power friendly arrangement is now proceeding, under good expectations, and the same law, deemed necessary on failure of that, is still suspended. . . . With the other, negotiation was in like manner preferred, and provisional measures only taken to meet the event of rupture. With the same Power negotiation is still preferred, and provisional measures only are necessary to meet the event of rupture. While, therefore, we do not deflect in the slightest degree from the course we then assumed, and are still pursuing with mutual consent to restore a good understanding, we are not to impute to them practices as irreconcilable to interest as to good faith, and changing necessarily the relations of peace and justice between us to those of war. These surmises are, therefore, to be imputed to the vauntings of the author of this enterprise, to multiply his partisans by magnifying the belief of his prospects and support.

By letters from General Wilkinson of the 14th and 18th of December . . . I received the important affidavit, a copy of which I now communicate, with extracts of so much of the letters as comes within the scope of the resolution. By these it will be seen that of three of the principal emissaries of Mr. Burr, whom the General had caused to be apprehended, one had been liberated by habeas corpus, and two others . . . have been embarked . . . to ports in the Atlantic States. . . . As soon as these persons shall arrive, they will be delivered to the custody of the law, and left to such course of trial . . . as its functionaries may direct. The presence of the highest judicial authorities to be assembled at this place within a few days, the means of pursuing a sounder course of proceedings here than elsewhere, and the aid of the Executive means, should the judges have occasion to use them, render it equally desirable for the criminal as for the public, that, being already removed from the place where they were first apprehended, the first regular arrest should take place here, and the course of proceedings receive here their proper direction.

January 22, 1807
Thomas Jefferson

Address to the People of Massachusetts

John Quincy Adams

The fear of a Masonic conspiracy infiltrating all levels of government and establishing a shadow government had a powerful impact in the early nineteenth century. Rumors of Masons serving as jurors refusing to convict fellow Masons, of sheriffs packing juries with Masons, of elected officials ignoring the will of the people in favor of the will of the Masons, and of unchristian acts and beliefs alarmed many who saw a secret society placing itself above the people, the law, and God. John Quincy Adams (1767–1848), sixth president of the United States, diplomat, and statesman, was a prominent opponent of the Masonic movement. Adams believed that Masons had actively worked against him politically and cost him reelection as president in favor of Andrew Jackson, a Mason. In 1834 Adams ran for governor of Massachusetts as an Anti-Mason in a four-way race, but no candidate received the requisite vote and Adams subsequently withdrew from the race to support Whig candidate John Davis. The following selection is from a letter in which Adams announced that he was withdrawing from contention, outlining the reasons for his candidacy and exposing what he saw as the crimes and immorality of Freemasons. (From John Quincy Adams, "Address to the People of Massachusetts," in *Letters and Opinions of the Masonic Institution*, 1851.)

Fellow-Citizens: For the first time within nearly half a century, you have been . . . unable to agree upon the person to whom the office of . . . Chief Magistrate should be committed for the ensuing year. . . .

Of the four candidates, having the highest number of votes, my name stands the second . . . I have deemed it my duty to withdraw . . . and to request the members of the House of Representatives to withhold their votes from me, with the assurance of my determination . . . not to accept the appointment. . . .

I have not thought it necessary . . . to assign to the Legislature the reasons which have brought me to this determination. . . . This exposition . . . is, however . . . due to . . . my fellow-citizens, who honored me by their nomination. . . .

In accepting the nomination of the Antimasonic Convention . . . I was aware of the dissentions which agitated the Commonwealth. . . . I knew that the Antimasons . . . constituted a minority of the people of the Commonwealth. That they were for the most part a detachment from . . . the . . . National Republicans, and who . . . had embraced at least three-fourths of the people of the State. That their views . . . both with regard to the administration of the General Government, and to that of the Commonwealth, still coincided with those of that party, and I believed . . . that this breach should be repaired. . . . The Masonic controversy was the only point upon which the two divisions of the party were separated, but that separation I feared was irreconcilable. The party in opposition to the State government, and friendly to the present federal administration, was necessarily Masonic, by adherence to their chief; himself illustrious with Masonic acquirements and dignities. . . . It was with extreme reluctance that I consented to be placed within the wind of this commotion, for I saw that it would bring me in collision with the party . . . wielding the power of the State, and with whose principles and policy my own were in full accord.

I had recently been re-elected . . . in the congressional district where I resided, to . . . the House of Representatives of the United States. I had previously been nominated by a convention of the members of that party, as well as by an Antimasonic, and also a Republican convention, to represent the District of Plymouth in the last Congress. . . .

I had freely avowed my opinions of Masonry and Antimasonry, when the people of the District selected me to represent them in Congress. They were not the opinions of a majority of the people whom I was to represent. . . . They were unpopular opinions, and therefore not the ground to be occupied by persons aspiring to popularity, or to its rewards. . . . In forming his political opinions every citizen must be governed by his own honest judgment. . . . To obtain the information necessary for forming a correct opinion upon political questions is a duty specially incumbent upon those who possess . . . the public confidence; and having been . . . honored with the confidence . . . of my fellow-citizens, I have thought it my indispensable duty to make myself acquainted with the facts . . . involved in the controversy relating to the Masonic Institution.

The authentication of the facts . . . was necessarily slow and gradual. The struggle between the common rights of the people, and the exclusive privileges of an oath-bound association, organized for extensive secretly concerted action, has been long protracted, and there is no present prospect of its termination. The kidnapping and murder of William Morgan, for merely avowing the intention to reveal the secrets of Freemasonry, was the first act which roused the attention of the people to the nature and character of this Institution. . . .

At the time of the murder . . . I was . . . President of the United States. Neither the penalties of Freemasonry, nor the practical execution of them, by the Masons who murdered him, were known to the public in general, nor to me. Freemasonry exercised an absolute control over all the public journals edited by members of the Institution, and over many others by terror and intimidation. . . .

But the trials of the Masonic outrages in the State of New York have exhibited other expositions of Masonic law. Masonic juries have been packed by Masonic sheriffs, for the express purpose not only of screening the guilty . . . but of falsifying the facts by presentiments and verdicts known to themselves to be untrue. Masonic witnesses have refused to testify, and suffered imprisonment. . . . When conscience . . . has constrained Masonic witnesses to testify to crimes in which they themselves shared, and to the secrets of the craft, solitary Masonic jurors have refused to assent to verdicts . . . on the avowed resolution that they would not believe any testimony of a seceding Mason.

The extent to which the public justice of the country had been baffled, and the morals of the people vitiated by Freemasonry, was therefore disclosed to me gradually. . . . Absorbed by other cares . . . I was for years very imperfectly informed either of the laws of Masonry, or of the ascendancy they were maintaining over the laws of the land, or of the deep depravity with which they were cankering the morals of the people. . . . It was not until the 4th of July, 1828, that the Convention of seceding Masons, held at Le Roy, made public the secrets, oaths, obligations and penalties of the higher degrees—nor were the proceedings of that Convention made known to me till I found them in David Bernard's *Light on Masonry* [1829]. . . . To David Bernard . . . the world is indebted for the revelation of the most execrable mysteries of Masonry. . . .

From the time of that publication, the whole system of the Masonic laws, and their practical operation, having relation to the disclosure of their secrets, have been gradually unfolding themselves and the law and its execution have been continual commentaries upon each other. . . .

I saw a code of Masonic legislation, adapted to prostrate every principle of equal justice, and to corrupt every sentiment of virtuous feeling in the soul of him who bound his allegiance to it. I saw the practice of common honesty, the kindness of Christian benevolence, even the abstinence from atrocious crimes, limited exclusively, by the lawless oaths, and barbarous penalties, to the social relations between the brotherhood of the Craft. I saw slander organized into a secret, wide-spread and affiliated agency, fixing its invisible fangs into the hearts of its victims, sheltered by the darkness of the lodge room, and armed with the never-ceasing penalties of death. I saw self-invoked imprecations of throats cut from ear to ear, of heart and vitals torn out and cast forth to the wolves and vultures, of skulls smitten off, and hung on spires. I saw wine drunk from a human skull with solemn invocation of all the sins of its owner upon the head of him who drinks from it. And I saw a wretched mortal man dooming himself to eternal punishment . . . as a guarantee for idle and ridiculous promises. Such are the laws of Masonry, such their indelible character, and with that character perfectly corresponded the history of the abduction and murder of Morgan, and the history of the Masonic Lodges, Chapters and Encampments, from that day to the present. . . .

All this . . . have I seen, through a succession of time. . . . To inform myself of the facts I deemed a duty of paramount obligation upon me, as a man, a citizen, and a Christian; especially after my release from the arduous duties of public office. . . .

Yet I did not intrude myself as a volunteer in the controversy. It had been erroneously stated in a newspaper, edited by a high Masonic dignitary in Boston, that I was a Mason. In answer to an inquiry . . . I had declared that I was not, and never should be. This letter . . . crept into the public prints; and from that day the revenge of Masonic charity, from Maine to Louisiana marked me for its own. At the critical moment of the Presidential election, in the counties of New York where Antimasonry was most prevailing, a hand-bill was profusely circulated, with a deposition . . . of an individual . . . swearing that he had been present at two different times . . . with me at meetings of a Masonic Lodge at Pittsfield, a town, in which I had never entered a house in my life.

This was the first punishment inflicted upon me by Masonic law, for declaring that I never should be a Mason. The influence of Masonry upon that Presidential election was otherwise exerted with considerable effect; and of the more recent election it decided, perhaps, the fate. . . .

I have stated . . . the reasons and motives which have actuated me in the part that I have taken in the Masonic and Antimasonic controversy. To obtain an accurate knowledge of the facts, and of the real laws of Freemasonry, and to bring them to the test of pure moral principles, I believed to be my indispensable duty, and having done that, it was no less my duty to bear my testimony on every suitable occasion both to facts and principles. . . .

In concluding this exposition of my own motives for assenting to the nomination of the Antimasonic Convention, and now for withdrawing from the contest, let me give the parting advice of a friend to the remnant of the party styling themselves National Republicans, with whom I have generally concurred in opinion upon most of the great interests of the nation. . . .

The opinions of their addressing committee are no doubt of great weight upon subjects which they understand—but in the utter ignorance of the nature, character and condition of the Masonic Institution which their address displays, it is not from them that you will receive a dictation how you shall look upon it. They speak of Freemasonry as "an inefficient and almost superannuated institution." An institution which . . . was convulsing all the free States of this Union; an institution in the support of which, under the transparent mask of neutrality, they were addressing you with pages of invective and slander upon its adversaries. . . .

And since when is it inefficient and almost superannuated? Had the committee which penned that address heard the eloquent orator of the craft at New London, in July, 1825? He spoke of the then present time, and said, "It is powerful—it comprises men of rank, wealth, office and talent—power and out of power, and that in almost every place where power is of any importance. And it comprises among other classes of the community, to the lowest, in large numbers, active men united together, and capable of being directed by the efforts of others so as to have the force of concert throughout the civilized world. They are distributed too with the means of knowing one another, and the means of co-operating in the desk, in the legislative hall, on the bench, in every gathering of business, in every party of pleasure, in every domestic circle, in peace and in war, among enemies and friends, in one place as well as in another."

Is this the inefficient and almost superannuated institution of the committee? And upon this faithful Masonic representation of Masonic power, did you mark this concerted secret faculty of mutual recognition for the purposes of co-operation, in the legislative hall? Did you mark its ascent upon the very bench of justice? . . . What must be the result of a mutual secret recognition for the purposes of co-operation between a judge on the bench, and a suitor or a culprit at the bar? Inquire of the records of the judicial tribunals of New York, and they will furnish the answer.

Has the institution . . . been suddenly struck with inefficiency and superannuation? If the committee had consulted Masonic authority, they would have found that the interval of fifteen months between the delivery of this discourse and the murder of William Morgan, was one of unparalleled prosperity to the Order and unexampled multiplication of its members. Since the execution of the law of Masonry upon Morgan . . . the Institution has been, and continues to be, a church militant; and if in the prosecution of that warfare it has lost some of its efficiency, to whom and to what is this diminution of its power attributable? To Antimasonry—to political Antimasonry alone. All the measures taken to bring the murderers of Morgan . . . to justice, were taken by political Antimasons. . . . The disclosure of the Masonic oaths, obligations and penalties, was made by political Antimasonry, and that alone, has prostrated the power of Masonry throughout the whole of that region of . . . New York, where the most atrocious of her crimes had been committed. . . .

Political Antimasonry sprang from the bosom of the people themselves, and it was the cry of horror from the unlearned, unsophisticated voice of the people at the murder of Morgan—at the prostration of law and justice in the impunity of his murderers, and at the disclosure of the Masonic obligations. That cry arose, not from the mansions of the wealthy, nor from the cabinets of the learned or of the great . . . it came from the broad basis of the population; from the less educated and most numerous class of the community. So it is with all great moral reforms.

SECTION TWO

Conspiracy in an Age of Democracy

Conspiracy fears continued unabated through the early years of the American Republic. By the 1830s it was apparent that the American experiment was a success. Control of the government had been successfully and peacefully transferred between political factions on numerous occasions, proof of the system's resilience. The western territories witnessed explosive population and economic growth and the Market Revolution ushered in the beginnings of the Industrial Age. Still, Americans perceived conspiracies threatening their way of life.

King Cotton became the engine that drove the American economy. Cotton, whether sold to mills in the North or in England, was the commodity that forced industrialization. The large-scale cultivation of cotton in the South drove an agricultural boom in the Midwest, itself necessary to feed the people of the South, and it promoted the development of transportation, including canals, steamboats, and railroads. Great Britain was the dominant economic power in the world and possessed the capital to invest in American industry and transportation. This foreign capital was a double-edged sword, however: the cash influx was good, but some Americans perceived the potential for foreign manipulation of the national economy as a threat. Bankers and industrialists were accused by some radicals of selling out the nation to a foreign power, and Great Britain in particular became the centerpiece of a conspiracy theory that reemerges throughout American history.

Industrialization was fueled in part by cheap immigrant labor. Driven from Europe by economic hardship and famine, many new immigrants saw the United States as a beacon of hope and a fresh beginning. Nativist forces, however, opposed immigration, especially when unemployment dramatically increased in the Depression of 1837. Many of the new immigrants were Roman Catholics from Ireland and Central Europe, which aroused intense anti-Catholic fears on the part of nativists. Anti-Catholic conspiracies had been around since the colonial period, but the large migration of Catholics at this time lent credence to the idea that Rome sought to undermine the American government by sending to North America hordes of people who looked to the pope for leadership. Nativists argued that the great tyrants of Europe were Catholics who feared democracy, in contrast to the freedom-loving Protestants who founded the United States. Thus the nativists promulgated the notion that the influx of Catholic immigrants was a plot by European tyrants to destroy American liberty.

The emergence of Mormonism, a Protestant sect founded in 1830, gave rise to other conspiracies. The Mormon religion, officially called the Church of Jesus Christ of Latter-day Saints, was a part of the Second Great Awakening, a period of intense religious revivalism in the United States. The Mormons lived communally and established an elaborate Church hierarchy. Mormons professed to be the possessors of the original church, the Church of Jesus Christ. In the early 1830s they moved to Ohio, Missouri, and Illinois, where their communal ways, belief in polygamy, and lack of slaves alienated many Americans. This resulted in armed conflict in Missouri and the murder of church founder Joseph Smith in Illinois. In the mid-1840s the Mormons moved to what later became the state of Utah. The rhetoric of the church led many to believe that the Mormons sought to separate part of the nation and create a new religious empire. Furthermore, the Mormon belief in polygamous marriage, based on the tenets of the Old Testament, aroused deep anti-Mormon prejudice, which contributed to several unsuccessful attempts at gaining statehood for Utah. It was not until after the Mormon Church officially repudiated polygamy that Congress voted to admit Utah as a state in 1896. Nonetheless, even today conspiracies concerning Mormon attempts to attain domination over the country resurface. These are fueled, in part, by the insularity of the church.

The following selections illustrate the fear of foreign or nonwhite, non-Anglo-Saxon, non-Protestant influence on the nation. Senator Hugh Lawson White, supporting President Andrew Jackson's veto of the Second Bank of the United States, warned against the influence of Anglo bankers. Elijah Lovejoy, minister and editor, decried the efforts of Jesuits to silence his abolitionist press. Samuel Morse further stressed the dangers of Catholic immigration. In 1838, the State of Missouri went to war against the Mormon Church. Sampson Avard, a Mormon testifying for the state against Joseph Smith, related plans for the creation of "the millennial kingdom" in Jackson County, Missouri. Efforts by residents of Utah to be admitted to the Union were thwarted several times by people such as John Cradlebaugh, a federal judge and delegate from the Nevada Territory who related his experiences with the Mormons and their alleged attempts to overthrow civil authority.

These conspiracy theories were presented in print, in the courtroom, and on the floor of Congress. All have survived into the twenty-first century, although as distinctly minority views. These views reflect a fear of societal and cultural change at a time of rapid industrial growth, coupled with changing demographic patterns in urban areas. The nation was growing quickly, and many in the land of individual liberty sought to preserve a cultural homogeneity that may have existed only in their memories.

Bank Veto

Hugh Lawson White

By the 1830s, there was no serious threat of foreign military domination in the United States. However, one major threat remained in the minds of many Americans: a conspiracy of British financiers working with American bankers. The Second Bank of the United States was chartered in 1816 as a private/public institution. The bank was especially unpopular in the South and West. With the bank's charter set to expire in 1836, supporters pushed through recharter legislation in 1832. President Andrew Jackson, a staunch opponent of the bank, vetoed the bill. In the following selection, Tennessee senator Hugh Lawson White (1773–1840) defends the veto and cites one of the concerns of the bank opponents, foreign influence on the bank and the potential for that influence to be brought to bear upon the nation in times of crisis. He alludes to talk of a previous conspiracy in chartering the Second U.S. Bank but dismisses it. He suggests that English bankers took advantage of a dire financial situation following the War of 1812. (From Hugh Lawson White, "The Bank Veto Speech of Mr. White of Tennessee. Delivered in the Senate of the United States, Wednesday, July 11, 1832." *Nile's Weekly Register,* August 18, 1832, p. 446.)

Mr. President: . . . I must crave the indulgence of the Senate, while I attempt some answer to the matters urged by the senator from Massachusetts to the message accompanying the bill, now ordered to be re-considered.

I rejoice that for once we have a document from the present chief magistrate, acknowledged by the opposition to be frank, plain and susceptible of only one interpretation. . . . Here it is admitted we have a document so worded, as to be understood ever where alike. The honorable senator thinks this frankness . . . ought to be met in a corresponding spirit, by those who differ from him in opinion. Approving of this course, I shall endeavor to be equally as explicit . . . in answer to his argument.

The Senator thinks if the charter of this bank is not renewed, ruin to the country is to be the consequence, because the bank must wind up all its concerns. This is nothing but the old argument used in 1811, when the then existing bank applied for a renewal of its charter. Distress to the community, and ruin to the country were predicted by the advocates of the bank. The predictions were not verified. The capital employed by the bank was not annihilated. It still existed, and in loans to individuals, or in some other shape, it was applied to the uses of the community. . . .

Let us look at this matter as it is. Immediately before the election, the directors apply for a charter, which they think the president at any other time will not sign, for the express purpose of compelling him to sign contrary to his judgment, or of encountering all their hostility in the canvass, and at the polls. . . .

Sir, if under these circumstances the charter is renewed, the elective franchise is destroyed, and the liberties and prosperities of the people are delivered over to this moneyed institution, to be disposed of at their discretion. Against this I enter my solemn protest. . . .

The honorable senator has wearied himself a good deal with a criticism upon the word "monopoly." He says it is used, at least, twenty times in this message, and never correctly. That the act only confers exclusive privileges, and the word monopoly means the sole power of trading.

Mr. President, I do think upon this great subject the minds of statesmen may be more profitably employed than in close criticisms upon the definition of particular words; but I am content to take the senator's definition and insist it is appropriately used. The charter does grant the sole power of banking for fifteen years to this company. They, therefore, have the sole power of trading in the manner pointed out in that charter for the period of its duration. To make it a monopoly, the company need not have the exclusive right of trading in every thing; the sole right to carry on a particular branch of business, is sufficient, and as this company is to have this sole, or exclusive right, it appears to me the word is properly used. The honorable senator fears much mischief may follow from the objections urged against foreigners owning stock in the bank, unless something shall be done to remove their erroneous impressions. He says we are interested in encouraging them to make loans for public purposes to the general and state governments, and that heretofore it has been our policy to encourage them to hold property among us.

Mr. President, this never has been our policy as to lands; the respective states have, and ought ever to have, the exclusive right to determine who shall hold lands within their limits. It has generally been . . . their policy to prevent aliens from acquiring freeholds within their limits. . . . As to our public stocks, I think with the senator, foreigners may well make loans to the government, or purchase stock owned by our citizens. Much benefit may result from this, and we have no injury to fear. As to our public stocks; foreigners owning them, can have no agency whatever in creating them, or managing them. At the end of each quarter, the government pays the stipulated interest, and at the time agreed on, discharges the principal. The holder of the stock, by no act of his, can make his profits more or less. But the case is not so as to bank stock. Although the foreigner can neither vote, nor be a director, yet he can . . . have an indirect influence on the operations of the bank, and by regulating exchanges favorably for the bank and injuriously for the citizens can increase the profits . . . and thus benefit himself. Will any gentleman say he is of the opinion of the Barings, who own a million of stock, can have no influence on the profits to be made by this institution? I think not. . . .

Mr. President, we must remember that in case of a war, this bank . . . must be your main dependence for raising money, and yet there is no provision by which it is bound to loan us one cent. Now suppose it to have existed during the last war, and the stock to have been owned by British subjects and a few of our own citizens, and those citizens to have belonged to that sect in politics who were seeking to change our federal rulers—who had sent an embassy to this city to request the then president to resign. Does any man believe the administration could have procured a loan for one cent? Those politicians, I am willing to suppose, were acting honestly—that they believed the war impolitic, unjust and wicked, so much so that they would not aid it with their good wishes. Does any one suppose that they would not have held it treason against good morals, to have loaned pecuniary aid? Surely, they would. We must then have been without money, and without the means of obtaining any. Peace must have been made, and upon any terms, dictated by the bank or by the enemy. . . .

The honorable member has alluded to that part of the message which speaks of the investigation of the bank being unwillingly yielded—and at the same time, he says, as it does not allude to this branch of the legislature, we cannot notice it.

Sir, is not this statement true? Was not the creation of a committee opposed? The bank had its agents here, no doubt. Gentlemen of the house, confiding in the statements of the agent, thought the investigation useless, therefore they opposed it. It was unwillingly yielded. Who is blamed for this in the message? Not the House—not the members of the House—let any candid mind examine the whole paragraph, and he must see it is those who applied for a renewal of the charter, and persisted in the application after this limited and unsatisfactory examination. The honorable senator thinks the message is unfortunate, in ascribing to the patriots of the revolution the spirit of compromise, which ought not to be imitated. Mr. President, if the message did read as the senator has read it, it would have been substantially correct. The leading patriots . . . were the leading men in framing and adopting the constitution, and it is the spirit of compromise which these men manifested in adopting the constitution. . . . It has been argued, that it is strange the message should intimate the executive ought to have been called upon for a draft of the project of a bank.

I submit, Mr. President, that it is not at all strange. In every instance heretofore the bank projects have proceeded for the treasury, and so they ought. Although the bank established in general Washington's day may have been the best that could be devised as things then were; yet the increase of population—numerous changes in almost every thing, might make it a very unsuitable plan at this time. The secretary of the treasury, whose duty it is to watch the finances of the country and the operations of the bank, could better judge of the details proper for a bill than any other officer, and now, as in time past, ought to have been consulted.

Mr. President: In submitting this message, one of the highest duties of the chief magistrate has been performed. Under peculiar and trying circumstances, he has given his sentiments plainly and frankly, as he believed his duty required.

When the excitement of the time in which we act shall have passed way, and the historian and biographer shall be employed in giving his account of the acts of our most distinguished public men, and comes to the name of Andrew Jackson;—when he shall have recounted all the great and good deeds done by this man, in the course of a long and eventful life, and the circumstances under which this message was communicated shall have been stated, the conclusion will be, that in doing this, he has shown a willingness to risk more to promote the happiness of his fellow men, and to secure their liberties, than by the doing of any other act whatever.

"To My Fellow Citizens"

Elijah Lovejoy

The following selection deals with two conspiracies: the slave power and Catholicism. In 1835, St. Louis enacted ordinances that prohibited antislavery speech and provided for the establishment of "vigilance committees" for enforcement. The primary targets of the ordinance were Elijah Lovejoy and the *St. Louis Observer.* Lovejoy (1802–37), a native of Maine, was a schoolteacher, Protestant minister, newspaper editor, and also one of the most outspoken abolitionists of the era. On numerous occasions, his printing presses were destroyed by pro-slavery mobs. In the following selection, Lovejoy addresses the citizens of St. Louis and decries the usurpation of civil liberties by the pro-slavery majority. At the same time, Lovejoy goes one step further and blames the Catholic Church and the Jesuits for the ordinances. St. Louis was strongly Catholic, dating to French and Spanish rule. Unlike many other American cities of the era, immigrants to St. Louis were largely Protestant. In 1836 Lovejoy fled St. Louis and began publishing a newspaper in Alton, Illinois, a port city across from St. Louis on the Mississippi River. It was there in 1837 that he was killed by a pro-slavery mob while protecting a new printing press. (From Elijah Lovejoy, "To My Fellow Citizens," *St. Louis Observer*, November 5, 1835, p. 2.)

Recent well known occurrences in this city, and elsewhere, have, in the opinion of some of my friends, as well as my own, made it my duty to address myself to you personally. And in so doing, I hope to be pardoned for the apparent egotism which, in such an address, is more or less unavoidable. I hope also to write in that spirit of meekness and humility that becomes a follower of the Lamb, and at the same time with all that boldness and sincerity of speech, which should mark the language of a freeman and a Christian minister. It is not my design or wish to offend any one, but simply to maintain my rights as a republican citizen, free-born, of these United States, and to defend, fearlessly, the cause of TRUTH and RIGHTEOUSNESS.

It is confidently reported through the State, and the charge is distinctly made in a paper of this city that I am an abolitionist. And this is made use of to excite against me the public mind, and threats of personal violence are coming to my ears daily. Under almost any circumstances I should consider it a matter altogether too unimportant to trouble the public with. . . . But inasmuch as the public have thought otherwise, I feel myself bound to give them every explanation possible.

In the first place, therefore, I declare that I am not an Abolitionist. By abolitionist I understand one who wishes to have the slaves amongst us immediately set free. Not only do I not desire such an event, but I should deplore it as one of the greatest evils that could afflict our community—injurious greatly to masters and slaves. . . .

But, with equal frankness, I declare to you . . . that I am an emancipationist. I am, and while I exist, whether on earth or in heaven, I expect to be opposed to the system of slavery. . . .

I come now to the specific charge made in one of the city papers, that I circulated abolition pamphlets, such as "Human Rights," &c.; by sending them in a box of Bibles to Jefferson City. . . .

The facts are simply these. In the discharge of my official duty, I sent to the order of the Cole County Bible Society, a quantity of Bibles. In putting them into the box obtained for the purpose, I found that the box was not filled. I therefore gathered together the loose papers in the office . . . put them promiscuously into the box, nailed it up and sent it off. Not long afterward, I received from my friend . . . a letter informing me that amongst the newspapers sent in the box was a copy of the "Emancipator," and . . . moreover . . . some persons were disposed to believe that I had sent it purposely.

Let this statement, fellow-citizens, show you the impropriety and the danger of putting the administration of justice into the hands of a mob. I am assured that had I been in the city, at the time . . . I should surely have suffered the penalty of the whipping-post or the tar-barrel, if not both . . . !

And now, fellow-citizens, having made the above explanation, for the purpose of undeceiving such of you as have honestly supposed me in error; truth and candor require me to add that had I desired to send a copy of the "Emancipator" or any other newspaper to Jefferson City, I should not have taken the pains to box it up. I am not aware that any law of my country forbids my sending what document I please to a friend or citizen. . . .

I come now to the proceedings had at the late meeting of our citizens. . . .

I freely acknowledge the respectability of the citizens who composed the meetings referred to. And were the question under consideration to be decided as mere matters of opinion, it would become me . . . to bow in humble silence to the decisions of . . . my fellow-citizens. But I cannot surrender my principles, though the whole world besides should vote them down—I can make no compromised between truth and error, even though my life be the alternative.

Of the first resolution . . . I have nothing to say. . . .

The second resolution, strictly speaking, neither affirms nor denies any thing, in reference to the matter in hand. No man has a moral right to do anything improper. Whether, therefore, he has the moral right to discuss the question of slavery, is a point with which human legislation or resolutions have nothing to do. The true issue . . . is, whether he has the civil, the political right, to discuss it, or not. In Russia, in Turkey, in Austria, nay, even in France, this right most certainly does not exist. But does it exist in Missouri? We decide this question by turning to the Constitution of State. The 16th section, Article 13b, of the Constitution of Missouri, reads as follows:

"That the free communication of thoughts and opinions is one of the invaluable rights of man, and that every person may free speak, write, and print on any subject, being responsible for the abuse of that liberty."

Here then, I find my warrant for using . . . all freedom of speech. If I abuse that right I freely acknowledge myself amenable to the laws. But it is said that the right to hold slaves is a constitutional one, and therefore not to be called in question. I admit the premise, but deny the conclusion. . . . The Constitution declares that this shall be a perpetual republic, but has not any citizen the right to discuss . . . the comparative merits of despotism and liberty? And if he has eloquence and force of argument sufficient, may he not persuade us all to crown him our king . . . ?

See the danger, and the natural and inevitable result to which the first step here will lead. Today a public meeting declares that you shall not discuss the subject of slavery, in any of its bearings, civil or religious. Right or wrong, the press must be silent. Tomorrow, another meeting decides that it is against the peace of society, that the principles of popery shall be discussed, and the edict goes forth to muzzle the press. . . . The truth is . . . if you give ground a single inch, there is no stopping place. I deem it, therefore, my duty to take my stand upon the Constitution. . . . We have slaves, it is true, but I am not one. I am a citizen of these United States, a citizen of Missouri, free-born; and having never forfeited the . . . privileges attached to such a condition. . . .

What shall I, what can I, say of the 4th resolution? It was adopted . . . with but a few dissenting voices. Many of our most respectable citizens voted for it—Presbyterians, Methodists, Baptists, Episcopalians, Roman Catholics; those who believe the Bible is the Word of God and those who do not, all united in voting for the resolution that the Bible sanctions slavery as it now exists in the United States. . . .

The fifth resolution appoints a Committee of Vigilance consisting of seven for each ward, twenty for the suburbs and seven for each township in the county . . . whose duty is shall be to report to the Mayor or the other civil authorities, all persons suspected of preaching abolition doctrines, . . . and should the civil authorities fail to deal with them, on suspicion, why then the Committee are to call a meeting of the citizens and execute their decrees—in other words, to lynch the suspected persons. . . .

I turn, for a moment, to my fellow Christians, of all Protestant denominations.

Respected and beloved fathers and brethren. As I address myself to you, my heart is full, well nigh to bursting, and my eyes overflow. It is indeed a time of trial and rebuke. The enemies of the cross are numerous and bold and malignant, in the extreme. From the situation in which the Providence of God has placed me, a large portion of their hatred, in this quarter, has concentrated itself on me. You know that, now for nearly two years, a constant stream of calumnies and personal abuse of the most viperous kind has been poured upon me. . . . You know also, that I have never, in a single instance, replied to or otherwise noticed these attacks. And now not only is a fresh attack, of ten-fold virulence, made upon my character, but violence is threatened to my person. Think not that it is because I am an abolitionist that I am so persecuted. . . . In the progress of events slavery has doubtless contributed its share . . . to the bitterness of hatred with which the *Observer,* and I as connected with it are regarded. But the true cause is the open and decided stand which the paper has taken against the encroachment of Popery. . . .

I repeat it, the real origin of the cry, "Down with the *Observer,*" is to be looked for in its opposition to Popery. The fire that is now blazing and crackling through this city, was kindled on Popish altars, and has been assiduously blown up by Jesuit breath. And now . . . shall we flee before it, or stay and abide its fury, even though we perish in the flames? For one, I cannot hesitate. The path of duty lies plain before me, and I must walk therein, even tho' it lead to the whipping-post, the tar-barrel, or even the stake. . . .

But, O my brethren, what shall I say to those of you who recorded your votes in favor of the resolution that the Bible sanctions slavery? . . .

O, were the Church united at such a crisis as this, what a triumph we might achieve! But it never can be united, until you come over to us. Did you ever hear of a Christian, once holding a contrary doctrine, giving it up for yours? Never . . .

unless at the same time he gave up his Christianity with it. But there are instances, daily, of conversions from your side to ours. . . . Let us unitedly take our stand upon the principles of truth and righteousness. . . .

Fellow-citizens of St. Louis; above you have my sentiments . . . on the great subjects now agitating the public mind. Are they such as render me unworthy of that protection which regulated Society accords to the humblest of its members? Let me ask you, why is it that this storm of persecution directed at me? What have I done? Have I libeled any man's person or character? No. Have I been found in gambling-houses, billiard rooms or tippling shops? Never. Have I ever disturbed the peace and quiet of your city by midnight revelings, or riots in the streets? It is not pretended. . . .

I do, therefore, as an American citizen, and Christian patriot, and in the name of Liberty, and Law, and Religion, solemnly protest against all these attempts, howsoever or by whomsoever made, to frown down the liberty of the press and forbid the free expression of opinion. . . .

Fellow citizens; they told me that if I returned to the city . . . you would surely lay violent hands upon me. . . . I have appeared openly amongst you, in your streets and market places, and now I openly and publicly throw myself into your hands. I can die at my post, but I cannot desert it.

Imminent Dangers to the Free Institutions of the United States through Foreign Immigration

Samuel F. B. Morse

Nativist conspiracies stressed the threat to the nation of unchecked subversives seeking to undermine American political institutions. Anti-Catholic nativists pointed to massive immigration from Eastern and Central Europe and Ireland as a threat to American liberty. Not only did these immigrants lack a common cultural heritage with the natives (i.e., Anglo-Saxon), they were beholden to a foreign potentate, the pope. Fear and suspicion of Catholics continued throughout the nineteenth century and into the twenty-first. Samuel F. B. Morse (1791–1872), artist and inventor and son of a well-known anti-Masonic conspiracist, was an active nativist author. Raised in a Congregational Church, Morse distrusted Catholics from childhood. As an aspiring artist, he traveled to Italy, where he was berated by a soldier for failing to remove his cap as the pope's procession passed. It was this image of Catholicism as a religion of force that stayed with him. In the following selection, Morse contends that an association of Catholics, led by the Austro-Hungarians and in partnership with the Jesuits, orchestrated the mass migrations to the United States in order to overthrow American democracy, based on a study that found Protestantism more favorable to democracy and Catholicism favorable to monarchy. Writing in 1835, Morse cites the Protestant Reformation and the American Revolution as examples of Protestant-led drives toward individual liberty. (From Samuel F. B. Morse, *Imminent Dangers to the Free Institutions of the United States Through Foreign Immigration* [New York: E. B. Clayton, 1835; reprint, New York: Arno Press and the New York Times, 1969].)

The great question regarding Foreigners, and a change in our Naturalization laws, is a National question, and . . . a very serious one. It is . . . with deep regret that I perceive an attempt made by both parties . . . to turn the just National excitement on this subject each to the account of their own party. The question, whether Foreigners shall be subjected to a new law of naturalization . . . is one entirely separate at present from party politics . . . and is capable of being decided solely on its own merits. The organs of the two parties, however, are noticing the subject, and both engaged in their usual style of recrimination. . . . I cannot but advert to this crying evil at a moment when a great and pressing danger to the country demands the attention of Americans of all parties, and their cool and dispassionate examination of the evidence. . . .

The danger to which I would call attention is not imaginary. It is a danger arising from a new position of the social elements in the onward march of the world to liberty. The great struggle for some years has till now been principally confined to Europe. But we cannot exclude . . . the influence of foreign movements upon our own political institutions, in the great contest between liberty and despotism. . . . To deny the danger, is to shut one's eyes. . . . And to seek to allay the salutary alarm arising from a demonstration of its actual presence among us, by attributing this alarm to any but the right cause, is worse than folly . . . it is flinging away our liberties . . . without a struggle . . . at the fist appearance of the enemy. . . .

Our country, in the position it has given foreigners who have made it their home, has pursued a course in relation to them, totally different from that of any other country in the world. This course, while it is liberal without example, subjects our institutions to peculiar dangers. . . .

In the other countries of Europe, the right of naturalization in each particular case, belongs to the Executive branch of government. It is so in France, in

Bavaria, and all the German States. In France . . . a residence of 10 years gives to the alien all the rights of a citizen, even that of becoming a member of the Chamber of Deputies, but the limited suffrage in that country operates as a check on any abuse of this privilege.

This country on the contrary opens to the foreigner, without other check than an oath, that he has resided five years in the country, a direct influence on its political affairs. . . .

Europe has been generally at rest from war for some 20 years past. The activity of mind which has so long been engaged in war, in military schemes of offence and defense in the field, was, at the general pacification of the world, to be transferred to the Cabinet, and turned to the cultivation of the arts of peace. It was at this period . . . that a Holy Alliance of the Monarchs of Europe was formed. . . . The "General Peace" was, and still is, the ever ready plea in excuse for every new act of oppression at home, or of interference abroad. The mental elements, however, set in motion remotely by the Protestant Reformation, but more strongly agitated by the American Revolution, are yet working among the people of these governments to give the Tyrants of the earth uneasiness. . . .

There is danger of reaction from Europe; and it is the part of common prudence to look for it, and to provide against it. The great political truth has recently been promulgated at . . . Vienna, and by one of the profoundest scholars of Germany (Frederick Schlegel, a devoted Roman Catholic, and one of the Austrian Cabinet), the great truth clearly and unanswerably proved, that the political revolutions to which European governments have been so long subjected, from the popular desires for liberty, are the natural effects of the Protestant Reformation. That Protestantism favors Republicanism, while Popery as naturally supports Monarchical power. In these lectures, deliverer by Schlegel for the purpose of strengthening the cause of absolute power, at the time that he was Counselor of Legation in the Austrian Cabinet, and the confidential friend of Prince Metternich, there is a most important allusion to this country; and as it demonstrates one of the principal connecting points between European and American politics, and is the key to many of the mysterious doings that are in operation against American institutions under our own eyes. . . . Is it not the most natural and obvious act for Austria to do, with her views on the influence of Popery upon the forms of government, its influence to pull down Republicanism, and build up monarchy; I say, is it not her most obvious act to send Popery to this country if it is not here, or give it a fresh and vigorous impulse if it is already here? At any rate she is doing it. She has set herself to work with all her activity to disseminate throughout the country the Popish religion. Immediately after the delivery of Schlegel's lectures . . . in the year 1828, a great society was formed in the Austrian capital. . . . The late Emperor, and Prince Metternich, and the Crown Prince . . . and all the civil and ecclesiastical officers of the empire, with the princes of Savoy and Piedmont, uniting in it, and calling it after the name of a canonized King, St. Leopold. This society is formed for a great and express purpose . . . of promoting the greater activity of Catholic mission is America. . . . Yes; these foreign despots are suddenly stirred up to combine and promote the greater activity of Popery in this county; and this, too, just after they had been convinced of the truth . . . that Popery is utterly opposed to Republican liberty. . . .

I have shown that a Society (the "St. Leopold Foundation") is organized in a Foreign Absolute government . . . for the purpose of spreading Popery in this country. . . . It is not a small private association, but a great and extensive combination. It embraces . . . not merely the wide Austrian Empire, Hungary, and Italy, but it includes Piedmont, Savoy, and Catholic France; it embodies the civil and ecclesiastical authorities of all these countries. . . . With its head-quarters at Vienna, under the . . . direction . . . of Metternich . . . it makes itself already felt through the republic. Its emissaries are here. And who are these emissaries? They are JESUITS. This society of men, after exerting their tyranny for upwards of 200 years, at length became so formidable to the world, threatening the entire subversion of all social order, that even the Pope, whose devoted subjects they are, . . . was compelled to dissolve them. They had not been suppressed . . . for 50 years, before the waning influence of Popery and Despotism required their useful labors, to resist the spreading light of Democratic liberty. . . . And do Americans need to be told what Jesuits are? If any are ignorant let them inform themselves of their history without delay. . . . Their workings are before you in every day's events: they are a secret society, a sort of Masonic order, with superadded features of most revolting odiousness, and a thousand times more dangerous. . . .

To return to the subject; it is in the Roman Catholic ranks that we are principally to look for the materials to be employed by the Jesuits, and in what condition do we find this sect at present in our country? We find it spreading itself into every nook and corner of the land; churches, chapels, colleges, nunneries and convents, are springing up as if by magic every where;. . . . And who are the members of the Roman Catholic communion? What proportion are natives of this land, nurtured under our own institutions, and well versed in the nature of American liberty? Is it not notorious that the greater part are Foreigners from the various Catholic countries of Europe? Emigration has . . . been specially promoted among this class of Foreigners, and they have been in the proportion of three to one of all other emigrants arriving on our shores; they are from Ireland, Germany, Poland, and Belgium. . . .

It will doubtless appear to most intelligent Americans . . . that I might have spared myself . . . some time in seriously combating the claim of strangers, of foreigners . . . to any rights or privileges in it, except such as are granted by the gracious permission . . . of the Sovereign of the United States . . . the People. . . . Emigrants have been induced to prefer such arrogant claims, they have nurtured their foreign feelings and their foreign nationality to such a degree, and manifested such a determination to create and strengthen a separate and a foreign interest, that the American people can endure it no longer, and a direct hostile interest is now in array against them. . . . The naturalized citizen who conducts consistently, who has become an American in reality, and not merely by profession, is not touched by any censure of mine. Neither is the foreigner who is temporarily or officially here; he is professedly an alien, and meddles not . . . with our politics. It is that anomalous, nondescript, hermaphrodite, Jesuit thing, neither foreigner nor native, yet a moiety of each, now one, now the other, both or neither, as circumstances suit . . . a man who from Ireland, or France, or Germany, or other foreign lands, renounces his native country and adopts America . . . and still, being received and sworn to be a citizen, talks . . . of Ireland as "his home," as "his beloved country." . . .

We have now to resist the momentous evil that threatens us from Foreign Conspiracy. The Conspirators are in the foreign importations. Innocent and guilty are brought over together. We must of necessity suspect them all. . . . A subtle attack is making upon us by foreign powers. The proofs are as strong as the nature of the case allows. . . . The arbitrary governments of Europe,—those governments who keep the people in the most abject obedience at the point of the bayonet . . . have combined to attack us in every vulnerable point. . . . They are impelled by self-preservation to attempt our destruction,—they must destroy democracy. It is with them a case of life and death,—they must succeed or perish. . . . Americans, you are marked for their prey, not by foreign bayonets, but by weapons surer of effecting the conquest of liberty than all the munitions of . . . Europe. . . . Fly to protect the vulnerable places of your Constitution and Laws. Place your guards; you will need them, and quickly too. And first, shut your gates. Shut the open gates. . . . Your enemies, in the guise of friends, by the thousands, are at this moment rushing in to your ruin through the open portals of naturalization. Stop them, or you are lost, irrevocably lost. . . .

Have you no reward? Oh, yes; your country is filling with a noble foreign population, all friends of liberty, all undoubted Democrats, taught in the school of Democratic Europe, accustomed to huzza with one voice for liberty, and under the guidance of Jesuit leaders well trained; far famed, long tried friends of Democracy; and to make assurance doubly sure, selected with the greatest care by Austria's Democratic Emperor, and Rome's Democratic Pope, who watch them with jealous eyes, and if not faithful in upholding Democracy, will deprive them of their stipulated wages, and recall them home, to receive their merited punishment—an Arch-bishop's see, or a Cardinal's hat. Democracy is safe with such keepers. The country is in no danger. Sleep on.

Missouri Mormon War

Sampson Avard

In 1838 open conflict broke out between Mormons and non-Mormons in northwestern Missouri. Since the early 1830s, Mormons had migrated to the western portion of the state based on their belief that God had revealed to Joseph Smith that Christ would return in Jackson County, Missouri. The influx of Mormons, along with their social structures, alienated many Missourians. Attempts by the state legislature to keep the peace by creating new counties for Mormon settlement, Caldwell and Daviess Counties, failed when the Mormons refused to be contained. Soon violence erupted between individuals and eventually involved armed bands. The state militia was called out and Governor Lilburn Boggs issued the "Extermination Order" that stated Mormons had to leave the state or die. Shortly thereafter John P. Greene published a book, *Facts Relative to the Expulsion of the Mormons, or Latter Day Saints, From the State of Missouri, Under the "Extermination Order,"* (1839), decrying the treatment of the Mormons in Missouri. Angered by the one-sided nature of the book, the Missouri General Assembly authorized the Missouri secretary of state to publish a record of the conflict. The following selection comes from the Missouri state publication in a case of treason, *State of Missouri v. Joseph Smith, Jr. et al.* (1838). In the trial, Sampson Avard testified that he had been appointed head of a secret paramilitary army, the Danites, organized to seize control of Illinois. He revealed the nature of the group and their plans for the establishment of "the millennial kingdom." His testimony against Mormons was used as further evidence of a Mormon conspiracy against the United States. (From James Lawrence Minor, Missouri Secretary of State, *Documents Containing the Correspondence, Orders, &c.: In relation to the Disturbances with the Mormons* [Fayette: Boonslick Democrat, 1841], 97–107.)

Sampson Avard, a witness produced, sworn, and examined on behalf of the State, deposeth and saith: That about four months ago, a band, called the Daughters of Zion, (since called the Danite band,) was formed of the members of the Mormon church, the original object of which was to drive from the county of Caldwell all those who dissented from the Mormon church; in which they succeeded admirably and to the satisfaction of those concerned. I consider Joseph Smith, Jr., as

Head Quarters of the Militia
City of Jefferson
Octr 27 1838

Sir

Since the order of this morning to you directing you to cause 400 mounted men to be raised within your division I have received by Amos Rees Esqr of Ray & Wiley C. Williams Esq one of my Aids information of the most appalling Character which entirely changes the face of things and places the Mormons in the attitude of an open and avowed defiance of the laws and of having made war upon the people of this State Your orders are therefore to hasten your operations with all possible speed The Mormons must be treated as enemies and must be exterminated or driven from the State if necessary for the public peace their outrages are beyond all description If you can increase your force you are authorized to do so to any extent you may consider necessary I have just issued orders to Major Genl Willock of Marion Co to raise 500 men and to march them to the Northern part of Daviess and there unite with Genl Doniphan of Clay who has been ordered with 500 men to proceed to the same point for the purpose of intercepting the retreat of the Mormons to the North. they have been directed to communicate with you by express, you can also communicate with them if you find it necessary. Instead therefore of proceeding as at first directed to reinstate the citizens of Daviess in their homes you will proceed immediately to Richmond and there operate against the Mormons Brig Genl Parks of Ray has been ordered to have four hundred of his Brigade

53

Mormon Extermination Order, October 27, 1838. Missouri governor Lilburn Boggs issued Executive Order 44, known as the “Extermination Order,” which authorized mobilization of the state militia to remove a perceived Mormon threat. *Mormon Extermination Order, Special Collections, Mormon War Papers, Missouri State Archives.*

the prime mover and organizer of this Danite band. The officers of the band . . . were brought before him . . . together with Hiram Smith and Sidney Rigdon: The three composing the first presidency of the whole church. Joseph Smith, Jr., blessed them, and prophesied over them; declaring that they should be the means . . . of bringing forth the millennial kingdom. It was stated . . . that it was necessary this band should be bound together by a covenant, that those who revealed the secrets of the society should be put to death. The covenant taken by all the Danite band was as follows, to whit: They declared, holding up their right hands, "In the name of Jesus Christ, the Son of God, I do solemnly obligate myself ever to conceal, and never to reveal, the secret purposes of this society called the Daughters of Zion. Should I ever do the same, I hold my life as the forfeiture." The prophet . . . together with his two counselors . . . were considered as the supreme head of the church; and the Danite band felt themselves as much bound to obey them, as to obey the Supreme God. Instruction was given . . . that if any of them should get into a difficulty, the rest should help him out; and that they should stand by each other right or wrong. . . .

At the election last August, a report came to Far West [the Mormon settlement in Caldwell County] that some of the brethren in Daviess County were killed. I called for twenty volunteers to accompany me to Daviess to see into this matter. I went; and about one hundred and twenty Mormons accompanied me. . . . When I arrived . . . I found the report exaggerated. None were killed. We visited Mr. Adam Black—about 150 or 200 men of us armed. Joseph Smith was commander; and if Black had not signed the paper he did, it was the common understanding and belief that he would have shared the fate of the dissenters. . . .

As regards the affair at DeWitt, I know little personally; but I heard Mr. S. Rigdon say they had gone down to DeWitt [Missouri], where it was said a mob had collected to wage war upon the Mormons residing in Carroll County; and that Joseph Smith, Jr., with his friends went down to DeWitt to give aid and help to his brethren. . . . I heard . . . say they were in Hinkle's camp (at DeWitt) several days. When the Mormons returned from DeWitt, it was rumored that a mob was collecting in Daviess County. Joseph Smith, Jr. . . . gave notice that he wished the whole county collected on the next day (Monday) at Far West. He declared . . . that all who did not take up arms in defense of the Mormons of Daviess should be considered as Tories, and should take their exit from the county.

At the meeting on Monday . . . Joseph Smith, Jr., took the pulpit, and delivered an address, in which he said that we had been an injured people, driven violently from Jackson County; that we had appealed to the Governor, magistrates, judges, and even to the President . . . and there had been no redress for us; and that now a mob was about to destroy the rights of our brethren of Daviess County, and that it was high time that we should take measures to defend our own rights. A vote was taken whether the brethren should embody and go down to Daviess to attack the mob. This question was put by the prophet . . . and passed unanimously. . . . Captains Patten and Brunson were appointed commanders of the Mormons. . . . After we arrived at 'Diahmon, in Daviess, a council was held. . . . In the above referred to council, Mr. Smith spoke of the grievances we had suffered in Jackson, Clay, Kirtland, and other places; declaring that we must in future stand up for our rights as citizens of the United States, and as saints of the most high God; and that it was the will of God we should do so; that we should be free and independent, and that as the State of Missouri and the United States, would not protect us, it was high time we should be up, as saints of the most high God, and protect ourselves, and take the kingdom. Lyman Wight observed, that, before the winter was over, he thought we would be in St. Louis, and take it. . . . The council was called on to vote the measures of Smith, which they did unanimously. On the next day Captain Patten . . . took command of about one hundred armed men, and told them that he had a job for them to do, and that the work of the Lord was rolling on, and they must be united. He then led the troops to Gallatin, saying he was going to attack the mob there. He made a rush into Gallatin, dispersing the few men there, and took the goods out of Stolling's store, and carried them to 'Diahmon, and I afterwards saw the storehouse on fire. When we returned to 'Diahmon, the goods were deposited in the Lord's storehouse. . . . When Patten returned from Gallatin . . . the goods were divided . . . among those engaged; and these affairs were conducted under the superintendence of the first presidency. A part of the goods were brought to Far West. . . . I saw a great many cattle, furniture, etc., brought into our camp by the Mormons. . . . The troops were kept together until the [Missouri] militia came. . . . There were from 500 to 800 men . . . under arms. After the militia had been near Far West awhile, in an address, Smith said that those troops were militia, and that we were militia too . . . and he advised them to know nothing of what had happened; to say nothing; and to keep dark. . . . The troops were constantly kept prepared, and in a situation to repel attack. . . . Some months ago I received orders to destroy the paper concerning the Danite Society; which order was issued by the first presidency, and which paper, being the constitution for the government of the Danite Society, was in my custody, but which I did not destroy. . . . This paper was taken into President Rigdon's house, and read to the prophet and his councilors, and was unanimously adopted by them as their rule and guide in future. After it was thus adopted, I was instructed by the council to destroy it, as, if it should be discovered, it would be considered treasonable. . . . This paper was drawn up about the time the Danite band was formed. Since the drawing up of the paper against the dissenters it was that this constitution of the Danite band was drafted . . . which constitution, above referred to, is as follows:

"Whereas, in all bodies laws are necessary for the permanency, safety, and well-being of society, we, the members of the Society of the Daughters of Zion, do agree to regulate ourselves under such laws as . . . shall be deemed necessary for the preservation of our holy religion, and of our most sacred rights. . . . And now, to prove ourselves worthy of the liberty conferred on us . . . we do agree to be governed by such laws as shall perpetuate these high privileges . . . and of which privileges wicked and designing men have tried to deprive us, by all manner of evil, and that purely in consequence of the tenacity we have manifested in the discharge of our duty towards our God, who had given us those rights and privileges, and a right, in common with others, to dwell on this land. But we, not having the privileges allowed unto us, have determined . . . to resist tyranny. . . . Our rights we must have, and our rights we shall have, in the name of Israel's God.

"Art. 1st. All power belongs . . . to the people, and they have a right to dispose of it as they shall deem fit; but, as it is inconvenient . . . to convene the people in all cases, the legislative powers have been given by them, from time to time, into the hands of a representation composed of delegates from the people themselves. This is and has been the law, both in civil and religious bodies, and is the true principle.

"Art. 2d. The executive power shall be vested in the president of the whole church and his councilors.

"Art. 3d. The legislative powers shall reside in the president and his councilors together, and with the generals and colonels of the society. By them all laws shall be made regulating the society.

"Art. 4th. All offices shall be during life and good behavior, or to be regulated by the law of God.

"Art. 5th. The society reserves the power of electing its own officers. . . . The nominations to go from the presidency to his second, and from the second to the third in rank, and so down through all the various grades. . . .

"Art. 6th. Punishments shall be administered to the guilty in accordance to the offence; and no member shall be punished without law, or by any others than those appointed by law for that purpose. The Legislature shall have power to make laws regulating punishments, as, in their judgments, shall be wisdom and righteousness.

"Art. 7th. There shall be a secretary, whose business it shall be to keep all the legislative records of the society, also to keep a register of the names of every member of the society; also the rank of the officers. He shall also communicate the laws to the generals, as directed by laws made for the regulation of such business by the Legislature.

"Art. 8th. All officers shall be subject to the commands of the Captain General, given through the Secretary of War; and so all officers shall be subjects to their superior rank, according to the laws made for that purpose."

In connection with the grand scheme of the prophet, his preachers and apostles were instructed to preach to and instruct their followers . . . that it was their duty to come up to the State called Far West, and to possess the kingdom; that it was the will of God they should do so; and that the Lord would give them power to possess the kingdom. There was another writing drawn up in June last, which had for its object to get rid of the dissenters, and which had the desired effect.... Since that time ... I have heard the prophet say that it was a fortunate thing that we got rid of the dissenters, as they would have endangered the rolling on of the kingdom of God as introduced, and to be carried into effect, by the Danite band; that they ... were great obstacles in their way; and that, unless they were removed, the aforesaid kingdom could not roll on.

Admission of Utah as a State

John Cradlebaugh

In 1862 Utah submitted its third bid for statehood. By this time Mormonism had been controversial for a quarter century. The issue was seized upon by nativist factions in the United States, along with anti-Catholic and anti-Mason sentiments, as proof of yet another subversive group in the country. Citing the call to create a Mormon Empire, based in Jackson County, Missouri, nativists argued that Mormons sought to overthrow the Constitution. There were also charges that Mormons subverted justice by refusing to testify against or convict other Mormons—basically the same charge made against the Masons four decades earlier. Finally, the issue of polygamy also played on the prurient minds of many Americans. Decrying the immorality of the faith and the damage done to Mormon women, nativists were distracted by the perceived licentiousness and depravity of Mormonism. The following selection is taken from a speech by John Cradlebaugh (1819–1872) in the U.S. House of Representatives, urging the body to reject Utah's 1862 bid for statehood. Cradlebaugh, a federal judge, soldier, mine owner, and delegate from the Territory of Nevada, declared that the power of the church government had made the federal territorial courts powerless, an especially powerful charge given his position as judge. (From John Cradlebaugh, "Admission of Utah as a State," House of Representatives, February 1, 1863.)

Mr. Chairman: Having resided for some time among the Mormons, become acquainted with their ecclesiastical polity, their habits and their crimes, I feel that, I would not be discharging my duty, if I failed to impart such information as I have acquired, in regard to this people in our midst who are building up, consolidating and daringly carrying out a system, subversive of the Constitution and laws, and fatal to morals and true religion.

The remoteness of Utah from the settled regions of our country, and the absence of any general intercourse between the Mormons and the masses of our people have served to keep the latter in almost complete ignorance of the character and designs of the former. That ignorance, pardonable at first, becomes criminal when the avenues to a full knowledge are open to us.

Mormonism is one of the monstrosities of the age in which we live. It seems to have been left for the model republic of the world . . . to produce an idle, worthless vagabond of an imposter, who heralds forth a creed repulsive to every refined mind, opposed to every generous impulse of the human heart, and a faith which commands a violation of the rights of hospitality; sanctifies falsehood; enforces the systematic degradation of woman; not only permits, but orders, the commission of the vilest lusts, in the name of the Almighty God himself, and teaches that it is a sacred duty to commit the crimes of theft and murder. It is surprising that such faith taught, too, in the coarsest and most vulgar way, should meet with any success. Yet, in less than a third of a century, it girdles the globe. . . . And, as if to crown its achievements, it establishes itself in the heart of one of the greatest and most powerful governments of the world; establishes therein a theocratic government . . . putting the laws at defiance, and now seeks to consummate and perpetuate itself by acquiring a state sovereignty and by being placed on an equality with the other States of the Union.

Mormonism is in part a conglomeration of ill cemented creeds from other religions and in part founded upon the eccentric production of one Spaulding. . . . He had a smattering of Biblical knowledge, and chose, for his subject, "the history of the lost tribes of Israel." The whole was supposed to be communicated by the Indians, and the last of the series was named, Mormon, representing that he had buried the book. . . . Poor Spaulding at length went to his grave, and the manuscript remained a neglected roll in the possession of his widow.

Then arose Joe Smith, more ready to live by his wits than the labor of his hands. Smith had, early in life, manifested a turn for pious frauds. . . . He announced that he had dug up the book of Mormon which taught the true religion; this was none other than poor Spaulding's manuscript which he had purloined from the widow. In his hands, the manuscript became the basis for Mormonism. Joe became a prophet; the founder of a religious sect; the president of a swindling bank; the builder of the city of Nauvoo; Mayor of the city; General of the armies of Israel; candidate for President of the United States, and, finally, a Martyr, as the saints choose to call him. But the truth is that his villainies, together with the villainies of his followers, brought down upon the just vengeance of the people of Illinois and Missouri, and his career was brought to an end by his being shot while confined in a jail in Carthage. It was unfortunate that such was his end, for his followers raised the old cry of Martyrdom and persecution, and, as has always proved, "the blood of the martyr was the seed of the church."

Mormonism repudiates the celibacy imposed by the Catholic religion upon its priesthood, and takes in its stead the voluptuous impositions of the Mohammedan church. . . . Mormons claim to be favored with marvelous gifts—the power of speaking in tongues, of casting out devils, of curing the sick, and of healing the lame. . . . They recognize the Bible, but interpret it for themselves, and hold that it is subject to be changed by new revelation. . . . They teach the shedding of blood for the remission of sins, or, in other words, that if a Mormon apostatizes, his throat shall be cut, and his blood poured out upon the ground for the remission of his sin. . . . They say that the earth and the fullness thereof is the Lord's; that they are God's chosen people . . . that their mission on earth is to take charge of God's property, and . . . that it is their duty to obtain it, and . . . in obtaining it, they must not get in debt to the Lord's enemies for it: in other words, they teach that it is a duty to rob and steal from Gentiles.

They have christened themselves "The Church of Jesus Christ of Latter Day Saints." They claim that Mormonism is to go on spreading until it overthrows all the nations of the earth, and, if necessary for its accomplishment, its success shall be consummated by the sword; that Jackson County, Missouri, is to be the seat of the empire of the Mormon Church; that hence the Mormons are to be finally gathered, and that from the Zion shall proceed a power that will dethrone kings, subvert dynasties, and subjugate all the nations of the earth. . . .

The Church government established by the Mormons . . . is one of the most complete despotisms on the face of the earth. The mind of one man permeates through the whole mass of the people, and subjects to its unrelenting tyranny the souls and bodies of all. It reigns supreme in church and State, in morals, and even in the minutest domestic and social arrangements. Brigham's [Brigham Young] house is at once tabernacle, capitol, and harem; and Brigham himself is king, priest, lawgiver, and chief polygamist. . . . He taxes his deluded followers to the extent of all surplus property upon their arrival in the Territory. . . . He has through the legislature unrestricted license to tax merchants. . . . By like authority he seizes upon the great highway between our Atlantic and Pacific possessions, grants exclusive rights to erect bridges and ferries across all the streams in the Territory . . . expressly providing in the law that a portion of the receipts shall be paid over to himself, by which means . . . the emigrant to the Pacific coast is forced to build up the Church. . . .

Brigham is both Church and State. True, the atrocities committed in Utah are not committed by him with his own hands, but they are committed by his underlings, and at his bidding. . . . He seeks to avert censure by feigning ignorance of the atrocities of his underlings. Such ignorance can only be supposable on the hypothesis that Mormonism is not a system and Brigham is not its head. That he is a despot without power, or a prophet without the ability to foresee. . . .

It has been said that we have courts in Utah, and the question is frequently asked, why do not the courts act? The uniform testimony of the judges is to the effect that the courts are powerless. More than fifteen Federal judges, who have gone to the Territory, have so stated. They have again and again told you that the entire legislation of the Territory is to prevent the administration of the laws; that the church authorities are determined that the laws shall not be enforced in the Federal courts; that the grand and trial jurors are Mormons, who are taught that the Mormon Church laws are the higher laws, and should prevail, and who refuse, therefore, to discharge their sworn duties, and have invariably refused to punish any Mormon for an offence committed against an anti-Mormon. To such an extent has this been carried, that although the valleys of Salt Lake have been replete with robberies and murders, yet the records of the courts do not show a single instance of the punishment of a Mormon for an offence committed against a Gentile. . . . The Federal courts are powerless to do good, and are used only when they can subserve the purposes of the Mormons.

The weak, timid, temporizing, cowardly policy which has ever been pursued towards Utah by the Federal Government has only led to disorganization and anarchy and to the open violation of the most sacred rights, and has exhibited Utah before the world as the gloomy theater where murder and robbery alternatively shift the scene. . . .

I have endeavored to set before you a fair and impartial abstract of Mormonism and its results as practically exhibited. I am aware that compelled by lack of time, the review has necessarily been meager. I have, however, endeavored to bring out the salient points, and if I know myself have nothing extenuated, nor set down aught in malice. I have given to you nothing but what the truth of history will prove. . . .

The question now presented is, shall this system be permanently fastened upon our body politic. It may be said that under the Constitution of the United States, every man is guaranteed the right to worship God according to the dictates of his own conscience, and that the Government has no right to interfere with this people in the practice of their religious faith. I deny that the Constitution contemplates the protection of every class of persons who may assume to themselves a religious faith at war with the most cherished sentiments of virtue and morality throughout the Christian and civilized world. I contend that we owe it as a duty to manifest our disapprobation of practices and doctrines so odious, and that it is our duty to retain this Mormon people under the general jurisdiction of the Government, so that their institutions may be reached by Federal legislation if necessary, and thus show in a most indubitable manner that we are unwilling that the stain and disgrace shall be fastened upon us. It is a duty enjoined upon us by the common obligations of justice and humanity.

There can be no doubt that the mass of the Mormon community are misled in their errors by a set of heartless, fanatical leaders. Their success may be much attributed to their isolation. That isolation, the fast filling up of the great basin, because of its vast mineral deposits, will soon do away with. Nevada now has a population equal to Utah. Thriving towns and cities are springing up on the Humboldt River, and in near proximity to the Mormons. Brigham sees this, and he knows and feels that he must place himself in a position to prevent the consequences to this system which will grow out of this contiguity of settlement. He feels that he cannot keep his women where they have a chance to get away, unless he can protect himself by legislation, further than he is able to do while his community remains under the general jurisdiction of our Government. It is on that account that he manifests so great a desire to become an independent State. I say he desires to become a State, for under his tyrannical sway, and with the system that is now prevalent, Brigham would be the State, and the State would be Brigham.

I say, again, there does not exist, on the part of this Government, an obligation to withhold from the Mormon people . . . the means of fostering and perpetuating this system. It is involved in the general duty of preserving untarnished the fair fame of our country; it is enjoined by self-respect and the promptings of an enlightened humanity. The civilized world would view with reprobation and disgust, and the American heart would shrink with shame at the admission of Utah in the family of States upon an equality with the other States of the Union.

The people of Utah have nothing but ill will towards our Government. The great masses know nothing of our institutions—they come to Zion, not to America. They are hurried through the settled portions of our country without being allowed to become acquainted with our people or institutions. Upon arriving in Utah they hear nothing but abuse of our people—the whole fountain of patriotism is polluted, and they are taught that they owe neither allegiance or love to our Government. Treason and insubordination are openly taught. God forbid that this people should be admitted into the Union as an independent State. I protest against it in the name of humanity, which would be violated by the admission! I protest against it on behalf of my constituents, who have a deep interest in the institutions that are to prevail in the great American basin! I protest against it in the name and on behalf of the murdered victims of the cruel Mormon faith, whose moldering bones are bleaching in almost every valley in the Territory! I protest against it on behalf of the downtrodden and undone women of Utah, who, with their female posterity, in all time to come, will bless those that would not aid in keeping them in bondage.

SECTION THREE

Conspiracy in a Divided Nation

The more tumultuous the time, the greater the fear of conspiracy. Therefore it should be no surprise that the period from 1850 to 1866 was rife with conspiracy theories. Driven by the sectional crisis, specifically the issue of slavery and then the Civil War, conspiracy fears abounded. Each side had its own conspiracies: abolitionists pointed to "the slave power," while slaveholders accused abolitionists of fomenting slave revolts.

Slavery had been a major political issue since the founding of the nation. How could a nation founded on individual liberty justify slavery? Beginning in the late 1830s among abolitionists, the idea of a cabal of slaveholders wielding excessive political power gained credence amongst northerners until, by the 1850s, non-abolitionists began referring to slave power. The fear that slaveholders were conspiring with northern industrialists, with whom they shared an economic interest, to maintain and expand the nation's reliance on slave labor was common in abolitionist literature. According to the theory, the slave power conspiracy sought to reopen the slave trade, expand the "peculiar institution" throughout the nation, and establish an oligarchy. The idea of a select few ruling the nation was anathema to American political philosophy. Laborers were the most accepting of this conspiracy, as they could envision a disastrous turn of events if the slave power succeeded in its plot. Although American labor was not well organized at the time, the campaign did create a political and social awareness that came to the fore with the establishment of the Republican Party. The campaign also greatly lessened the possibility of sectional reconciliation or even neutrality. By 1850 the phrase slave power had entered the national lexicon.

Conspiracists found further proof of the slave power in the Missouri-Kansas conflict. Beginning in the mid-1850s, armed pro-slavery Missourians, known as the "Blue Lodge," crossed the border into Kansas Territory and voted to make Kansas a slave state. In some cases nearly twice as many pro-slavery ballots were cast as there were registered voters. These were the first skirmishes of the Civil War. The election of Abraham Lincoln in 1860 sparked the secession movement, but blood had already been shed between pro- and anti-slavery forces (to say nothing of slaves themselves) for many years.

Between December 1860 and February 1861 seven states seceded from the Union—South Carolina, Mississippi, Florida, Alabama, Georgia, Louisiana, and Texas—forming the Confederate States of America. The bombardment of Fort Sumter in April 1861 marked the actual beginning of the Civil War. After Lincoln called on the states for troops to quash the rebellion, Virginia, Arkansas, Tennessee, and North Carolina joined the Confederacy. Missouri, Kentucky, Maryland, and Delaware remained in the Union, though Missouri was divided and witnessed a great deal of military action and extreme brutality. West Virginia was formed from Virginia and admitted to the Union in 1863.

War hysteria gripped the Union government. The Republicans were firmly in control, but conservative northern Democrats, known as Copperheads, did constitute an opposition party. War, by its nature, breeds a "for us or against us" mentality. Lincoln authorized a draft, confiscation of slaves, and eventually freed the slaves in the non-Union, non-occupied states. He also authorized measures that would not be condoned in modern times: arbitrary arrests, the suspension of habeas corpus, attacks on the dissident press. Republicans viewed Democratic criticisms of these policies as evidence of disloyalty. The Democrats, who had initially supported the war effort to restore the Union, saw the actions, especially after the Emancipation Proclamation, as an attempt by abolitionists to radically remake the country and stifle dissent.

The brutality of the war was unprecedented. Each side accused the other of conspiracies to assassinate their presidents, Lincoln and Jefferson Davis. Once General Robert E. Lee surrendered to General Ulysses S. Grant at Appomattox Courthouse on April 9, 1865, the war was effectively over. However, on April 14 Lincoln was assassinated in Ford's Theater by John Wilkes Booth. This action set off a storm of conspiracy theorizing. New theories were even presented in the twentieth century, accusing Vice President Andrew Johnson, northern bankers, and the Catholic Church of being behind the assassination. Other conspiracy ideas abounded, including allegations that Jesuits were involved.

This section presents a number of sectional and wartime conspiracies. The first selection, a speech by George W. Julian, a member of Congress from Indiana, outlines the conspiracies that each side saw in the slave power debate. Julian dismisses the southern theories and then details the slave power conspiracy. In the next selection, C. Chauncey Burr takes the Copperhead position, arguing that an abolitionist conspiracy had hijacked the U.S. government. The following two selections discuss Lincoln assassination conspiracy theories, the first detailed by John A. Bingham, the prosecutor in the trial against the conspirators, who makes the case that the assassins were Confederate agents in the employ of Jefferson Davis. In the second, an anonymous author charges that the Knights of the Golden Circle/Order of American Knights/Sons of Liberty, three names for a secret society with a large membership in the western states, were responsible for the assassination.

The Slavery Question

George W. Julian

Slavery became the national issue by the middle of the nineteenth century. Many Americans could not understand why the federal government seemed unwilling to oppose the will of a relative few slaveholders in the southern states and stem the spread of slavery across the continent. This pro-slavery influence was dubbed the "slave power." George Washington Julian (1817–1899), a United States Representative from Indiana, was a staunch opponent of slavery expansion and would be aligned with the Radical Republicans during the Civil War. The following selection is from a speech delivered in the House of Representatives in 1850. At that time Julian was a member of the Free Soil Party, a small third party, and Congress was debating the Compromise of 1850 that brought California into the Union, created the Utah and New Mexico Territories, banned the slave trade in the District of Columbia, and created a new Fugitive Slave law, making it easier for slaveholders to recover runaway slaves. Julian, frustrated with attacks by pro-slavery advocates in the North, argues that southern complaints of northern transgressions were empty and that threats to disband the Union were hollow because of slave power. (From George W. Julian, "The Slavery Question," a speech delivered in the House of Representatives, May 14, 1850.)

Mr. Chairman: Representing, as I do, one of the strongest anti-slavery districts in the Union, I feel called . . . to express . . . the views and feelings of my constituents. . . . I am not vain enough to suppose that anything I may say will influence the action of this committee; yet I should hereafter reproach myself were I to sit here . . . till the close of the session listening to the monstrous heresies . . . of Southern gentlemen, without confronting them on this floor. . . .

Mr. Chairman, we hear much of northern and southern aggression. Nothing is more current in southern speeches and newspapers than the charges that the people of the free States are aggressing upon the rights of the South, and this Union, it seems, is to be dissolved, unless these aggressions shall cease. On the other hand the people of the free States charge the South with being the aggressor. . . . Now, how stands the case? Who is the aggressor? This is the question to be solved, and the one I propose mainly to examine. I wish to do this fairly and dispassionately; for I am fully aware of the differences of opinions which prevail. . . .

The charge of northern aggression I certainly deny. . . . Neither is the charge of southern aggression, perhaps, fully and strictly true. The truth rather seems to be, that under the lead of southern counsels, both sections of the Union have united in enlarging and aggrandizing the slave power. This proposition I shall endeavor to establish.

What are these northern aggressions of which we have heard do much complaint? Of what hostile acts do they consist? Have the people of the free States attempted to interfere, by law, with slavery in the South? This charge, I am aware, is frequently brought against us. You can scarcely open a newspaper from that quarter in which it is not gravely made. It has been . . . denied by northern men on this floor, but southern gentlemen still continue to repeat it. . . . The charge is utterly unfounded in truth. The Whigs and Democrats of the North, as well as the Free Soil men, disclaim all right on the part of Congress as to touch the institution of slavery where it exists. We all agree that the subject is beyond our control. As regards . . . constitutional power, Congress has no more right to abolish slavery in South Carolina than it has to abolish free schools in Massachusetts—no more right to support slavery in one State than in the other. . . . It is true, that some of us in the North claim the right to assault slavery with moral weapons, even in the States. When the slaveholder says to us that on this subject we must keep our thoughts to ourselves, we shall obey him if it suits us. We have a right to employ these moral forces by which reforms of every kind are carried forward. . . .

We are charged with violating the clause in the Federal Constitution relative to fugitives from labor. This is among the gravest accusations preferred against us. Sir, this clause, and the act of Congress made in pursuance of it, have been elaborately argued and solemnly adjudicated upon in the highest court in the nation. Our duty in the free States has been made so plain that a child may understand it. I would not refer to this subject . . . were it not for the unending clamor of the South against us. We are driven to a repetition of the grounds of our defense. We say the slave-hunter may come upon our soil in pursuit of his fugitive, and take him if he is able . . . with or without warrant and we are not allowed to interfere in the race. "Hands off" is our covenant, and the whole of it. If the owner sees fit to sue out a warrant, he must go before a United States officer with his complaint. It is not the duty of our State magistrate to aid him, the execution of the clause in question depending exclusively upon Federal authority. . . . I would like to have Southern gentlemen answer this question; for I insist upon it, that if the Federal Constitution does not require them to assist in the recapture of fugitives, it cannot be an aggression upon southern rights to withhold such assistance, and thus maintain the position of neutrality, or non-action, assigned them by the Constitution. . . . Can it be that the Northern States have any other duties to perform than those which the Constitution itself imposes? Is slavery so endeared to us that we must volunteer in its support? Sir . . . no free State has an yet passed any laws discharging fugitives from the service they owe by the laws of other States, or preventing their recapture; and if this is not done, there can be no reasonable ground of complaint against the North. . . .

As regards the enticement of slaves from their masters, the number of such cases is small. Neither the States, nor the mass of their citizens are accountable, or have any connection whatever with such transactions. . . . Blame not the North for this, but blame your diabolical system. . . .

Another intolerable aggression with which the North is charged is that of scattering incendiary publications in the South, designed to incite insurrections among the slaves. . . . I deny the charge. I deny that the free States "keep up and foster in their bosoms Abolition societies" for any purpose. The Abolition societies . . . belong to what is called the [William Lloyd] Garrison school. They are voluntary associations of men and women, the northern States being no more responsible for their doings than the southern States. . . . I deny that they are guilty of inciting, or of wishing to incite, servile insurrections, or scattering firebrands among the slaves. . . . These Abolitionists are . . . the friends of peace, non-resistants; the enemies of violence and blood; and they would regret as much as any people in the Union to see a servile war. . . .

Mr. Chairman, I have now briefly noticed most of the alleged aggressions of the North. . . . Turning now to the other side of the picture, I propose to glace at that policy and some of those acts by which slavery . . . has been transplanted into new regions, fostered by the Government as a great national interest, and interwoven with the whole fabric of its policy. I shall make no special complaint about "southern aggression," for it will appear . . . that the slave power has built itself up by the cooperation or acquiescence of the non-slaveholding States. . . .

At the time the Federal Constitution was adopted, the States of North Carolina and Georgia claimed certain territory, which they afterwards ceded . . . to the General Government; and out of this territory the three States of Tennessee, Alabama, and Mississippi, were formed and successively admitted into the Union. The compromises by which the northern States had bound themselves in reference to slavery in the old States, were now stretched over these new ones. . . .

In 1803 we gave fifteen millions of dollars for the territory of Louisiana, and the three large slave States of Louisiana, Arkansas, and Missouri, were subsequently carved out of it, and . . . admitted into the Union. . . . Here, again, the obligation of the free States to support slavery was enlarged. . . .

In 1819 we gave five millions of dollars for the territory of Florida. We did not buy it on account of the value of its lands, or of the added wealth it would bring into the Union, but mainly to strengthen the slaveholding interest. . . . Florida was subsequently admitted, by the help of northern votes, into full fellowship with Massachusetts and the other free States, whose relations with slavery were thus again extended. . . .

In 1845 Texas was annexed, containing enough territory for five or six States. That this was a measure "essentially southern in its character," is placed beyond all doubt by the records of the State Department. It is likewise proved by the declarations of southern members of Congress in 1844, and by the avowals of the southern press and of leading men in the South. . . . I do not charge any party in the North with favoring annexation with the design of extending slavery. I speak not as a partisan, but as a seeker of facts, bearing upon the alleged charge of northern aggression; and what I assert is, that while the motive of the South in grasping Texas was unmasked, and was in fact glaringly manifest, the North was induced to come to her rescue, and thus added an empire of slavery to her dominions in the Southwest. . . . Nine slaveholding States have been added to the Union since the date of its formation, and five of them out of soil then the property of foreign nations. All this has been generously done by the free States, for they have had the strength in every instance to prevent these additions and this constantly augmenting southern power. . . .

I pass, in conclusion, to some kindred considerations. . . . The population of the United States in 1840 was seventeen millions. The white population of the South was four millions seven hundred and eighty-two thousand, five hundred and twenty. The number of slaveholders . . . has been estimated from one hundred thousand to three hundred thousand. If we take into the account the actual number of slave owners . . . a fair estimate . . . would probably be at two hundred thousand. . . . The white population of the free States in 1840 was nine millions six hundred and fifty-four thousand eight hundred and sixty-five. By comparing the slaveholders with the non-slaveholders of the South . . . it will appear that the former constitute only about one-twentieth of the white population of the slaveholding States. This is what we call the slave power. This is the force which is to dissolve the Union, and before which northern men bow down. . . . These two hundred thousand slaveholders, composed in part of women and minors, lord it over three millions of slaves; keep in subjection four or five millions of non-slaveholding whites of the South . . . and at the same time control . . . from nine to ten millions of people in the free States, whose Representatives tremble and turn pale at the impotent threats of their southern overseers. Now, bearing in mind that the population of the free States is, and generally has been, about double that of the slave States, let us glance at the monopoly which this slave power has secured to itself of the offices of the Government. . . .

Of the sixty-one years the Government has been in operation, the Presidency, with its immense power and patronage, has been filled by slaveholders about forty-nine years. . . . Seven of our Presidents have been slave owners—four not. . . . The South has secured the important Cabinet offices in the same way. Thus of nineteen Secretaries of State, fourteen have been slaveholders. . . . With the exception of the office of Secretary of the Treasury, the South has had more than her share of all the Cabinet appointments. The slaveholding States have had the important office of Speaker of this House for more than thirty-eight years. . . . The South has had twelve Speakers, the North only eight. . . . Turn to the Judiciary. The Chief Justice has been from the slave states about forty-nine years. . . . And it is a remarkable fact, that at no period since the formation of the Government, has the north had a majority on the Supreme Bench. . . . Why even now, whilst the cry of northern aggression continually meets us, the South has a slaveholding President, elected by northern votes, a slaveholding Cabinet, a slaveholding Supreme Court, a slave holding Speaker of this House, with slaveholding committees in both Houses; whilst slaveholding influences are unceasingly at work in hushing the anti-slavery agitation, and buying up . . . northern men, who are as mercenary in heart as they are bankrupt in moral principle.

Still, southern gentlemen read us daily homilies here on the encroachments of the North; and the threat of disunion is the thunder with which, as usual, we are to be driven from our purpose, and frightened into uncomplaining silence. . . . Had northern politicians resisted the aggressions of the South, as it was their duty to do, in the onset, the unhappy crisis in which the country is now placed would have been averted. . . .

Mr. Chairman, it has become quite fashionable to denounce the anti-slavery agitation of the North. Gentlemen tell us it is disturbing the peace of that country, dividing the nation in "geographical parties," and threatening to destroy the Union. Sir, let me ask, at whose door lies the blame for all this? What are the causes which have given birth to this agitation, and these so-called sectional parties? The South . . . by the help or permission of the North, has controlled the offices of the Government and shaped its policy for the last fifty years. Though her agency slavery has been widening its power, and taking deeper and deeper root in the country every hour of that whole period. Instead of an institution barely to be tolerated in the few States as their own exclusive concern, and that for a time only, it has become nationalized, and demands the protection of this Government "wherever our flag floats." It has grown to be the great interest of the Union, and subordinates all other question to its unholy purposes. . . . And when, after long years of . . . forbearance, a portion of the northern people . . . demand their just rights, refusing to be the absolute slaves of the South, they are denounced as "agitators," enemies of the Union, the builders of geographical parties. Sir, I meet these charges, and I say to southern gentlemen, that they have forced agitation upon us. . . . Agitation is a necessary fruit, an inevitable consequence of southern aggression and northern cowardice; and slavery propagandists and doughfaces must answer for their own political sins. . . . Am I told that we should not wound the pride of the South? Sir, on what occasion has she exhibited any great tenderness for the pride of the North? She has pursued . . . a policy of systematic selfishness from the beginning. . . . When we ask her respectfully to yield us our rights under the Constitution, we are met with browbeating and threats. . . . Sir, their pride is not worth saving at such a sacrifice. It is not the pride of principle, of justice, but the pride of arrogance, pampered into insolence by long indulgence; and, under no circumstances would I yield to it. The history of the world demonstrates, that slavery, regardless of soul or climate, has existed wherever it has not been interdicted by positive legislation. It always establishes itself . . . without law, and then suborns the law into its support.

Harper's Ferry Outbreak—Important Disclosures

Raleigh (N.C.) Register

On October 16, 1859, abolitionist John Brown and twenty-one other men attacked the United States Arsenal in Harper's Ferry, Virginia, in an attempt to capture weapons and lead a slave uprising to destroy slavery in the South. There were antecedents to Brown's attempt to resolve the slavery crisis through violent means. During the bloody conflict in the 1850s over whether Kansas would enter the Union as a slave or free state, Brown and his men had murdered five proslavery men who lived near Pottawattomie Creek, Kansas. Believing his work still uncompleted, Brown sought the support of several New England radical abolitionists—many of whom were members of the Massachusetts Kansas Committee—to fund a war of slave liberation in the South. Over the course of three years, Brown gradually earned the financial support and trust, albeit reluctant at times, of six abolitionists, including Dr. Samuel Gridley Howe, Thomas Wentworth Higginson, Theodore Parker, Franklin Sanborn, George Luther Stearns, and Gerrit Smith. These men gave Brown the means to carry out his conspiracy, and when it was learned that he had their support, northerners and southerners alike began to believe in a larger conspiracy that involved members of the Republican Party. The following selection reflects these fears that grew out of an actual conspiracy. (From the November 2, 1859, edition of the *Raleigh, (N.C.) Register.*)

From our paper of today our readers will see that [John] Brown's foray upon Harper's Ferry is assuming a more important and interesting type than it presented at first, inasmuch as correspondence brought to light, implicates some very prominent men at the North, as accessories to Brown's designs, although, he may have acted prematurely in carrying, or attempting to carry, them into execution. These disclosures are "startling" indeed, and show a settled determination on the part of the abolitionists to leave no means untried to deprive the South of its slave property, and to let no cost of blood stand in the way of the attempt. As long as such men as [abolitionists William Lloyd] Garrison, [Wendell] Phillips, & Co., raved, ranted and blasphemed, and did nothing else, conservative men might afford to look on in anger, sorrow or contempt as the mood prompted them, but when we see Senators of the United States, listening calmly to, and by silence acquiescing in cool and deliberate plans for making actual war upon half of the Union, the subject becomes vastly more grave and important, than any which has been submitted to the consideration of the people of the South and the Union, since the foundation of the government.

We are told that the people of the North by a vast majority hold the late invasion of the South in unmitigated abhorrence. We hope they do. Certainly the tone of the press of the North would warrant us in believing that such is the state of opinion in that section. But, we would ask, why has not the suggestion of the Boston *Courier* been acted upon? Why have not public meetings in the cities and towns of the North, been held to give expression to the conservative feeling of that portion of the Union, and their utter abhorrence of Brown's, and all similar modes, of interfering with the rights and property of the South? They have in their midst rich and powerful men, who are known to have aided and abetted in Brown's outrage, but who perhaps cannot be reached by that law which they have outraged. Should not the conservative neighbors of these men, enforce upon them the law of public opinion at their own homes, and brand them as the incendiary and diabolical miscreants they have proved to be? We know not what others may think about it, but villainously bad as Old Brown is, and dangerous as he has proved to be, we cannot help entertaining for him a *quasi* respect, when we compare him with Gerrit Smith [Massachusetts social reformer], Horace Greeley [editor of the *New York Daily Tribune*] and William H. Seward [Republican senator from New York]. Brown, although in the worst of classes, has displayed pluck and manhood, while Smith, Greeley and Seward, have played the part of sneaking, cowardly miscreants, who would send forward others to do for them deeds of treason, blood and murder, which they have feared to undertake themselves.

As it regards Seward, we do not hesitate to say that it can be proved that he knew of this conspiracy against the lives and property of the citizens of one of the States of this Union—that the plot was unfolded to him, and he, either by his silence, or by the words attributed to him, acquiesced in it—he should be at once expelled from the Senate of the United States, as wholly unworthy of a seat in that body, and to be the associate of honorable men. He will have forfeited his oath to support the Constitution of the United States, and proved himself to be a conspirator against the government of the country. As long as Seward talked about his "higher law," and was content to merely talk about it, he might safely be visited by the mere contempt of honorable men, but when he becomes the associate of conspirators—when he lends his influence to plots of treason, by silently acquiescing in them, his presence in the Senate chamber becomes intolerable, and he should be driven from it in ignominy and disgrace. Nor would any "higher law" be called into requisition by this eviction of Seward from the Senate. The Senate, or any other legislative body, has the right to expel from its midst any member who may be guilty of an infamous offence. The offence of cheating at cards, committed by a member of the House of Commons of this State, was, some years ago, punished by the expulsion of the offending member from that body. Subsequently a member of the Senate of this State was expelled on what was believed to be a well-grounded charge that he had committed forgery. Infamous as both these offenses are, they sink into insignificance, when compared with a connivance at a plot of blood, murder and treason, and the more especially in the case of Seward, when it is remembered that his course in the Senate and out of it, (at Rochester for instance) was well calculated, if not designed, to incite the treasonable plot, and conspiracy at which by his silence, or worse than silence, he connived. If [Colonel Hugh] Forbes [an English mercenary hired by Brown in 1868] tells the truth—if after his plans were unfolded to Seward, the latter "expressed regret that he had been told, and said that he, in his position, ought not to have been informed of the circumstances," Seward's course wears a double aspect of infamy. First, it shows his consciousness that his "position" as a Senator of the United States demanded a prompt discountenance and denunciation of the treasonable scheme, and second, it conveys a caution to Forbes not to trust his plans to others occupying a similar "position," and whose consciences might not be as convenient as his own. It matters not that Brown's exploded plot was not Forbes', it matters not that Forbes discountenanced Brown's mode of operations. He did so because he believed his own plan—the plan submitted to Seward—was more efficient than that of Brown. Forbes' plan was by force of arms to stampede, or run off parties of slaves from the frontier States, and thus continually drive slavery inwards, until it was finally extirpated at the centre, and to this plan, according to Forbes, Seward either did not object, or by his language consented.

Government by Conspiracy

C. Chauncey Burr

The Lincoln administration took a number of controversial steps during the course of the Civil War that seriously restrained civil liberties, the most famous being the suspension of habeas corpus. With wartime income taxes and a military draft as well, many began to question whether the war was worth the cost. As the 1864 elections approached, the northern Democrats, who had been viewed with suspicion by Republicans since the start of the war, came out in support of peace with the South and formal recognition of the Confederacy. In part this was driven by Lincoln's Emancipation Proclamation. Many northern Democrats, known as Copperheads, were less supportive of continuing to fight for the purpose of abolishing slavery. These Copperheads began to see a conspiracy by abolitionists to remake the nation and punish dissent. In 1863, C. Chauncey Burr (1817–83) began publishing the *Old Guard*, a journal "Dedicated to the principles of 1776 and 1787." Burr had edited anti-slavery publications in the 1840s and 1850s, and started his new journal in response to the un-American policies and legislation he perceived coming from the Republicans. (From C. Chauncey Burr, "Government by Conspiracy," *Old Guard* 1, no. 6 (June 1863): 125–27.)

America is governed by conspiracy. Conspiracy implies secrecy on the part of the conspirators, and noninformation on the part of the people conspired against. Infraction of the laws on one side, and blindness and suffering on the other. No man needs proof of this. He has but to cast his eyes backwards over the legislative and executive history of the last year, to see it all. There it stands, as awfully visible as the skulls in the temple of death. Now and then a member of Congress has been awakened to a vague half-sense of the dangers that threaten us, and has ventured to introduce a resolution calling upon the President for information, but his vigilance only brought down hisses upon his own head, without opening the sealed chambers of executive doings. One man, for introducing a resolution asking for information from the President . . . was denounced as "a traitor," "a secessionist," "a sympathizer with Jeff Davis," and he narrowly escaped being expelled from Congress. Against the only two or three members who had the virtue and the courage to attempt to discuss the doings of the administration, schemes and threats of expulsion were instantly set on foot. In one instance, over $10,000 of the public funds were expended in carrying on a gigantic conspiracy to expel a representative for daring to review the acts of the administration on the floor of Congress. A wretch who, it was afterwards proved, had served out a term in the Sing Sing State Prison, was found to invent a tale on which charges were based, and then men and papers and documents were sent for all over the country, for the purpose of "making out a case"; but, in the mean time, the conspiracy became so transparent . . . that the conspirators were forced to abandon their designs. The party accused, after he had been held up . . . as a "traitor," and after they had caused it to be published . . . that they had "positive proofs of his guilt," demanded . . . a report on his case. At almost any time of the session of the last

Congress, Macbeth's address to the witches would have been appropriate: "How now, ye secret, black, and midnight hags! What is't y do?"

And the congressional conspirators might have truly answered, with the witches: "A deed without a name!" For, never before were such scenes enacted in an American Congress. Every member who did not permit himself to be crushed down into an uncomplaining, silent tool of the abolition conspiracy, was denounced as a "traitor" and a "rebel." An abolition colonel threatened to "cut the heart out" of a congressman, while he was standing on the steps of the capitol, because he overheard him . . . dissent from the unconstitutional deeds of the conspirators. And almost every Republican newspaper . . . applauded these threats of assassination of one of the people's representatives. . . . When, at last, a resolution was engineered through the House of Representatives to ask the President for certain information . . . he refused to give it, and the Republican press everywhere came down upon the "impudence" of such an inquiry. Not only was debate struck down in Congress, but democratic newspapers were thrown out of the mails, or destroyed by the order of U. S. Marshals, and men and women were . . . dragged off to bastilles for daring to . . . question the unconstitutional deeds of Congress and the Executive. The silence that sat in the Valley of Graves, was forced upon the lips of men. The administration must not be spoken of . . . without a threat of dungeons being hurled at the head of the offender.

To a man of sense there is needed no other proof than this malignant secrecy which the administration determined should cover up its acts, that a deep laid conspiracy was going on against our Constitution and laws—against liberty—against all kinds of liberty, but negro liberty. The voices of white men must be dumb, that the mouth-pieces of the negroes alone may be heard. All who are not for liberating the negroes, must be restrained of their liberty. That is the conspiracy. Since Mr. Lincoln's advent, the country has been governed by conspiracy. It has been pronounced treason for a Judge to issue the writ of habeas corpus, as by solemn oath he is bound to do. . . . All who claim liberty for the white man, are a "sympathetic rebel crew." Wherever they hear a man speaking for the Constitution as it is and the Union as it was, they cry out at him, "rebel!" "traitor!" "sympathizer with Jeff Davis!" They pay an undeserved compliment to Jeff Davis, whose acts have shown that he is almost as bad an enemy to the Constitution as they are themselves. . . . Their conspiracy is old. The signs, by which we know it, are old, for they belong to every conspiracy which history records, since the world began. We know it by the secrecy with which it seeks to cover its deeds, and by its enforced silence upon speech and the press. No tyrant ever allowed his deeds to be discussed. . . . No conspirator ever permitted his designs to see the light. . . . Discussion and light are fatal to tyrants and conspirators. . . . Mr. Lincoln emulates the Turkish tyrant, who does not permit the sacred cities of Mecca and Medina to be polluted by the footsteps of a Christian. We shall not be astonished to see him keep on, until . . . he refuses to allow the sun to shine upon his illustrious head, because it performs the same thing for common mortals. . . .

Clergymen have been ruthlessly dragged from their pulpits . . . and plunged into filthy dungeons, for refusing to pray for Mr. Lincoln. No doubt Mr. Lincoln is sadly in need of prayer; but refusing to pray for him, however unchristian . . . is not a crime punishable by any law known to this country. "Sympathies" . . . are not crimes, according to the law. In all these cases, the administration is the criminal. It is a conspiracy against the laws, against the Constitution, against liberty. There is no softer name for it. Conspiracy! Its own discretion is the only law it tolerates. . . . To question its acts is to be a "traitor." Remember, if you dare, that white men were once free in this country, and you will be hunted down by a flock of irresponsible, gambling, drunken Provost-marshals, as unreasoning and as rapacious as wolves. Conspiracy! A free people governed by conspiracy! The laws, instead of being administered, are suspended. By an executive order, every judge . . . has been deposed, every court suspended, and the safety and liberty of the people put . . . at the mercy of provost-marshals, as ignorant as boot-blacks, and as brutal as Chinese executioners.

By the late elections the people have . . . said, that these things must cease. They will be governed no longer by conspiracy, but by laws. They will faithfully support every constitutional measure to put down rebellion in the South, but they will no longer permit constitutional liberty to be put down in the North. . . . Let the ballot speak: let the press speak. Let the ignominiously silenced voices of the people speak. Let conspiracy alone be dumb.

The Assassination of President Lincoln

John A. Bingham

In the aftermath of the assassination of President Lincoln, questions immediately arose as to whether John Wilkes Booth had acted in concert with those close to Lincoln or with other insidious groups. At various times it has been posited that Booth was the leader of the assassins, that Vice President Andrew Johnson was involved, that northern Copperheads had conceived of the plot in order to restart the war in the West, or even that international bankers conceived the plot. Mary Todd Lincoln believed that the vice president was involved, but over the years she has been suspected herself. Numerous conspiracy theories always seem to swirl around assassinations, but assassinations that occur during times of great political and social upheaval seem especially poignant. The following selection is taken from the closing argument of John A. Bingham, special judge advocate for the Military Commission sitting in judgment of Booth's co-conspirators David Herold, George Atzerodt, Lewis Payne, Mary Surratt, Edward Spangler, Samuel Mudd, Michael O'Laughlin, and Samuel Arnold. While summarizing the case against the defendants, Bingham makes the case that the defendants were Confederate agents and had been acting on behalf of Jefferson Davis with his full knowledge and consent. By putting the blame on the rebel government, the stage was set northern support for radical reconstruction in the South. (From Benn Pitman, *The Assassination of President Lincoln and the Trial of the Conspirators* [New York: Moore, Wilstach & Baldwin, 1865; reprint, Birmingham: Notable Trials Library, Gryphon Editions, Ltd., 1989], 372–80.)

May it please the Court: It only remains for me to sum up the evidence, and present my views of the law arising upon the facts in the case on trial. The questions of fact involved in the issue are: First, did the accused, or any two of them, confederate and conspire together, as charged and, second, did the accused, or any of them, in pursuance of such conspiracy, and with the intent alleged commit either or all of the several acts specified . . . ?

What is the evidence . . . that the accused . . . together with John H. Surratt, John Wilkes Booth, Jefferson Davis, George N. Sanders, Beverley Tucker, Jacob Thompson, William C. Cleary, Clement C. Clay, George Harper and George Young, did combine, confederate, and conspire, in aid of the existing rebellion . . . to kill and murder . . . Abraham Lincoln, late . . . President of the United States of America . . . Andrew Johnson, Vice-President of the United States; William H. Seward, Secretary of State of the United States; and Ulysses S. Grant, Lieutenant-General of the armies thereof, and then in command under the direction of the President?

The time, as laid in the charge and specification, when this conspiracy was entered into, is immaterial, so that it appear by the evidence that the criminal combination and agreement were formed before the commission of the acts alleged. That Jefferson Davis . . . was the acknowledged chief and leader of the existing rebellion against the Government of the United States . . . and others named in the specification, were his . . . agents, to act in the interests of the said rebellion, are facts established . . . beyond all question. That Davis, as the leader of said rebellion, gave to those agents . . . commissions in blank, bearing the official signature of his war minister . . . to be by them filled up and delivered to such agents as they might employ to act in the interests of the rebellion with the United States, and intended to be a cover and protection for any crimes they might . . . commit in the service of the rebellion, is also a fact established here, and which no man can gainsay. . . .

That the rebel chief, Jefferson Davis, sanctioned . . . crimes, committed and attempted through the instrumentality of his accredited agents in Canada . . . upon the persons and property of the people of the North, there is positive proof. . . .

No one can doubt . . . that the rebel Davis only wanted to be satisfied that this system of arson and murder could be carried on by his agents in the North successfully and without detection. With him it was not a crime to do these acts but only a crime to be detected in them. . . .

It only remains to be seen whether Davis, the procurer of arson and of the indiscriminate murder of the innocent and unoffending . . . was capable also of endeavoring to procure, the murder, by direct assassination, of the President of the United States and others charged with the duty of maintaining the Government of the United States, and of suppressing the rebellion in which this arch-traitor and conspirator was engaged.

The official papers of Davis, captured under the guns of our victorious army in his rebel capital . . . and placed upon your record, together with the declarations and acts of his co-conspirators and agents, proclaim to all the world that he was capable of attempting to accomplish his treasonable procuration of the murder of the late President . . . by the hands of hired assassins. . . .

Accomplished as this man was in all the arts of a conspirator, he was not equal to the task . . . of concealing, by any form of words, any great crime which he may have meditated or perpetrated either against his Government or his fellow-men. It was doubtless furthest from Jefferson Davis' purpose to make confession. His guilt demanded utterance; that demand he could not resist; therefore his words proclaimed his guilt, in spite of his purpose to conceal it. He said [when informed of Lincoln's assassination and the attack on Seward], "If it were to be done, it were better it were well done." Would any man, ignorant of the conspiracy, be able to devise and fashion such a form of speech as that? Had not the President been murdered? Has he not reason to believe that the Secretary of State had been mortally wounded? Yet he was not satisfied, but was compelled to say, "it were better it were well done"—that is to say, all that had been agreed to be done had not been done. . . . Whatever may be the conviction of others, my own conviction is that Jefferson Davis is as clearly proven guilty of this conspiracy as is John Wilkes Booth, by whose hand Jefferson Davis inflicted the mortal wound upon Abraham Lincoln. His words of intense hate, and rage, and disappointment, are not to be overlooked—that the assassins had not done their work well; that they had not succeeded in robbing the people altogether of their Constitutional Executive and his advisers; and hence he exclaims, "If they had killed Andy Johnson, the beast!" Neither can he conceal his chagrin and disappointment that the War Minister of the Republic . . . had escaped the knife of the hired assassins. . . .

Thus it appears by the testimony that the proposition made to Davis was to kill and murder the deadliest enemies of the Confederacy—not to kidnap them.

The Copperhead Conspiracy

Unknown

The Copperheads, or northern Democrats, were not immune from suspicion following the Lincoln assassination. Some Republicans looked to the Knights of the Golden Circle—a secret organization—as a force behind the conspiracy. Originally founded in the 1850s to support annexation of northern Mexico and the expansion of slavery, the order was enthusiastically embraced in the South and was embraced in many of the western states. In 1863 it was reorganized as the Order of American Knights and in 1864 as the Order of the Sons of Liberty. The treatment of the Knights in the selection is strikingly similar to earlier treatment of Masons. By looking for a cabal within the loyal opposition, the Republicans carried on a long tradition in American politics of casting the opposition party as wrong, disloyal, and subversive. The following selection is taken from an anonymous piece published in 1865. (From *The Assassination and History of the Conspiracy: A Complete Digest of the Whole Affair from Its Inception to Its Culmination* [Cincinnati: J. R. Hawley & Co., 1865], 30–36.)

"There can be no reasonable doubt that Lincoln and Seward have been assassinated. The crimes of these two men may make this event justifiable . . . but we do not concur with those who rejoice. Johnson has greater native ability . . . than any Northern statesman of his party. . . . The war will now assume a new phase. If confined to these States, then it is one of utter extermination. The veritable Reign of Terror has already begun in Tennessee. *It is probable . . . that the assassination of Lincoln is the work of those secret Western clubs whose mysteries have been developed in late judicial proceedings in Chicago and Ohio. If this be true, the war may begin in the Northwest. . . .* "

"He is a veritable 'plebian,' a leveler, a sans culotte [a French revolutionary]. However wedded to Johnson's theories of radicalism may have been the Republican newspapers, a few of them dared to mollify his violation of all laws of civilized decency. *Copperheadism could have inflicted upon the vanity and self-respect Puritanism no wound so deep as that which sent Lincoln to perdition and elevated Johnson to the throne.* He hastened to assume the royal purple, and despite the recent military triumphs, the pride of the North was never so humiliated as at this very hour."

The italicized portions of the above extract point unmistakably to the Knights of the Golden Circle, or, as they are latterly known, Sons of Liberty; and convey information that is anything but guess-work on the part of the author. Matter coming to us in this semi-official form is abundant confirmation . . . and we are fully assured that the damnable conspiracy that culminated in the murder of our beloved President, was incubated in the temples of this cursed league of the Circle. . . . The rapid . . . development of facts by the investigators . . . is daily offering proof in support of this theory . . . and, if the proofs are really conclusive, what further outrage by this compact with hell are our people waiting for before they arise in their might and destroy it? Has it not been treated as a myth long enough? And where its existence was known, have not its vagaries and mummery been sufficiently laughed at to allow people to give it a little serious attention just now? After this evidence of its power . . . are there any weak enough to believe it impalpable, or simply the matter for pleasantry? Such are in danger; and our country is in imminent danger until the destructive elements . . . are searched out and thoroughly expurgated from our politics!

Knights Illini, and similar quackeries, are scarcely congenial to the spirit of Republican Institutions. . . . Ben Allen, the Grand Seigneur of Copperheadism in New York, declared at the Democratic National Convention at Chicago, last year: *"The people will soon rise, and if they cannot put Lincoln out of power by the ballot, they will by the bullet."* This declaration was received with loud cheers. . . . Threats of assassination were not made vaguely, but if Copperhead chiefs meant what they publicly declared, every one of them should be indicted as accessories . . . and tried without ceremony.

The order of the Knights of the Golden Circle is not confined to the Northwest, as rebel authority would have us believe. . . . It was an invention of the Secession movement a few years ago, when Jackson forced the poisonous hydra to secrete itself in dark and unfrequented places, and deposit its slime where it would not be contagious; but copperheadism could not thrive without it, and it was imported from the South to force the growth of a Northern party with Southern sympathies. It has existed in our midst during the past four years. . . . Its oaths and penalties, its spy system and police regulations, all its murderous ingenuity and damnable crimes, should be made public, that we may know the enemy . . . and that the people may know what a mine has been planted beneath their homes. . . . It is more dangerous to our liberties today than all the armies the South have had in the field. . . . It works in secret, and we can have no notice of its intentions to sally forth to burn, pillage and murder. Its oaths are binding . . . its penalties terrible . . . its police regulations are on a large scale . . . and all the guards that ingenuity can invent are thrown out to prevent recursancy. It is sworn to support the South . . . and such has been its oath through four years of devastating war. It is sworn to kill all who oppose its designs . . . and the initiate pledges his own life to assist in murder, arson, robbery, and the carrying out of all its schemes. . . . Not a few of the sudden disappearances of people will never be heard of more in this world, may be traced to the "Knights," provided the knowing ones would uncover some of their tracks in the sand; and they will be forced to answer for the death of Abraham Lincoln!

This order . . . still exists—not only in the Northwest, but to an alarming extent throughout the North and South; and its leaders are now plotting fresh treason. . . .

When the tidings of the assassination were made public throughout the land, a few in each locality were inconsiderate enough to express gratification at the calamity of the nation! Who were they? Of what class and antecedent? Many paid the penalty for their blasphemy with their lives. . . .

In other localities, remote from telegraph stations, detailed reports of the great crime reached the people too soon, and in forms greatly exaggerated. . . . It is useless to assume that in such neighborhoods something of the matter was not foreknown,—but by whom? Evidence is plentiful enough that the conspiracy was extensive, and that its moving spirits were of the North and South, in combination.

SECTION FOUR

Conspiracy in the Industrial Age through the New Deal

Many of the conspiracy theories of the late nineteenth and early twentieth centuries echoed sentiments of previous generations, but new ones emerged as well. Another influx of Catholic immigrants renewed fears among Protestant nativists and immigration restrictionists that the Vatican in Rome was involved in a plot to seize control of Protestant America. Political corruption on the local, state, and national level led to charges of conspiracy in government by monied interests, and the emergence of labor radicalism—anarchism, socialism, and communism—brought charges of insidious conspiracies to overthrow the government.

The United States emerged in the late nineteenth century as the world's most advanced industrial power. This second industrial revolution transformed industry, manufacturing, politics, and how Americans lived and worked. In this economic transformation, huge amounts of capital were needed to finance the railroad industry, steel, petroleum refining, and manufacturing. Investment bankers such as John Pierpont Morgan raised funds through the selling of bonds and equities. Morgan's firm also became the major lending agency for the federal government. In 1895 he formed an international syndicate that effectively halted a drain of gold from the federal treasury. It was at this time that conspiracies about international Jewish bankers and financial interests found expression among farmer and labor radicals. The Jewish international conspiracy theory had its roots in early European anti-Semitism, but it gained new vibrancy in the late nineteenth century and continued to find expression throughout the twentieth century. Many farmers found themselves trapped by depressed prices for their crops and high debt. As a result many lost their land and blamed eastern financial interests and railroads for their plight. In addition, they accused international financial agents working through American banking and investment interests to maintain the gold standard, conspiring with government officials to profit off the sale of bonds, and to thwart the interest of farmers and the working men and women of America.

Conspiracy theories seeped into the radical labor movement as well, which itself was the focus of conspiracy fears. In 1886, workers went on strike against McCormick Harvester in Chicago. When the police brutally attacked strikers demonstrating outside the McCormick plant, local anarchists called a mass demonstration at Haymarket Square. As the demonstration was about to end, the police ordered the crowds to disperse. Suddenly a bomb was thrown, killing two policemen. A riot ensued. In the days that followed, eight anarchists were arrested on charges of conspiracy to commit murder. All eight anarchists were convicted, and four were executed.

Eight years after the Haymarket riot, the American Railway Union, led by Eugene Victor Debs, went on strike in support of striking workers at the Pullman Palace Car Company. This led to a national shutdown of the railroads. Believing that the nation was on the verge of anarchy, President Grover Cleveland ordered federal troops to break the strike. The government then successfully prosecuted Debs for conspiracy to restrain trade under the recently enacted Sherman Anti-Trust Act, which declared, "Every contract, combination in the form of trust or otherwise, or conspiracy, in restraint of trade or commerce among the several States, or with foreign nations, is declared to be illegal." Although "conspiracy" in this act was not well defined, manifesting the difficulties of interpreting the legal nature of conspiracy in law, the Sherman Anti-Trust Act was aimed at illegal business activity, specifically corporate monopolies, not labor. Debs's conviction under this act reinforced belief among labor radicals that the government was operating to benefit corporate and financial interests, and while in prison Debs became a radical socialist. The emergence of labor radicalism in the late nineteenth century, and later the Bolshevik Revolution in Russia in 1917, led to fears of an international communist conspiracy among those opposed to the labor movement.

The following selections reveal the prevalence of conspiracy theories found in the United States in this period. Conspiracies were promulgated by elite and popular interests, business leaders and anti-capitalist radicals, farmers and industrialists, nativists and those who welcomed the new immigrants. The acceptance of these theories by large numbers of Americans cannot be attributed to a single social or political source. Political corruption in the late nineteenth century explains some of the conspiracies, as evident in the Whiskey Ring scandal. Intense party competition and challenges to established political parties in the late nineteenth century, as evidenced in the rise of the Greenback Party in the 1870s, the Populist Party in the 1890s, and the Socialist Party in the 1900s, explains another source for conspiracy theory but does not offer a full explanation in itself. The rise of big business and corporate finance with its disproportionate influence on American politics provided another opportunity for conspiracy theories. Ethnic tensions are evident in anti-Catholic and anti-Semitic conspiracies, as well as fears among black leaders such as Marcus Garvey to suppress African Americans.

Fears of a financial conspiracy were evident in continued accusations that the creation of the Federal Reserve banking system under President Woodrow Wilson in 1913 was part of a conspiracy by bankers to promote their financial interests. Auto manufacturer Henry Ford in the 1920s espoused a virulent anti-Semitism through his belief in an international Jewish conspiracy. In the 1930s, Reverend Charles Coughlin, who attracted a national audience on his radio program, combined fears of monied interests and an international Jewish conspiracy. On the left, journalist John Spivak warned of a planned military coup, backed by Wall Street, to overthrow Franklin Roosevelt's administration and take control of government. Apparent in all of these conspiracies is the multivaried sources and the diversity of theories prevalent in this time of political, social, and economic change.

Secrets of the Great Whiskey Ring

John McDonald

In 1871, a few of President Ulysses S. Grant's supporters designed the Whiskey Ring to help raise money for his reelection campaign in 1872. The function of the Whiskey Ring was relatively unsophisticated. Whiskey distillers, Treasury Department officials, and storeowners inaccurately reported to the Treasury Department the amount of whiskey sold. The money from the unreported barrels of whiskey then filled Republican Party coffers. But after Grant's reelection, the new secretary of the treasury, Benjamin Bristow, made the exposure of the Whiskey Ring his personal crusade. He hired secret agents and conducted several investigations of distillers and revenue agents in the nation. The St. Louis Whiskey Ring was the first to be investigated. After the investigation ended in May 1875, nearly 300 people were charged with conspiracy to defraud the government. John McDonald, Supervisor of Revenue for the Missouri District and a close political ally of Grant, was one of the individuals convicted for his involvement in the Whiskey Ring. In the following selection, McDonald claims the existence of a larger conspiracy that involved Grant and Orville E. Babcock, Grant's personal secretary who was later acquitted of conspiracy charges relating to the Whiskey Ring trial. (From John McDonald, *Secrets of the Great Whiskey Ring . . .* [St. Louis: W. S. Bryan, 1880], 130–59, 200–10.)

The visit of Yaryan [revenue agent] in March and April, 1875, was the first effective step taken to lay bare the frauds of the Whiskey Ring. Yaryan had already . . . discovered enough fraud to have exposed the illicit combination, but it is perhaps doubtful whether he could have secured a conviction of any of the member, save pos[s]ibly, two or three distillers, upon the evidence he had then collected. But the circle in which the organization was now uneasily operating grew constantly smaller. . . .

My serious alarms were excited that some treachery was being practiced, and to discover the source I determined to go to Washington and confer with the President. . . . Upon my arrival there . . . I found that the President, General Babcock and Secretary [of War William A.] Belknap, were in Boston. . . .

When I went out into the hotel office, I learned that the President and General Babcock had returned from Boston; so I went directly to the White House, where I was fortunate, upon entering the Executive room, to find the President alone. I drew a chair up near him, and after passing a very few words of general remark, I proceeded directly to disclose the object of my visit.

I first explained to him that my district was being visited by revenue agents without my knowledge; that there was a veil of secrecy over the actions of Secretary [Bristow] in matters wherein I was deeply interested and in which I should be consulted, and that this secrecy also prevented the Commissioner of Internal Revenue from giving me instructions, so that there was a rapidly widening breach in the revenue service; that if the policy outlined by Secretary Bristow should be pursued, it would result in the destruction of the Republican party.

To this the President replied that he had talked with the Secretary concerning the collection of information by revenue agents, but that his idea was that the evidence thus gathered should not be used against the revenue officers, but only against the distillers and business men; that he had thought such action even a wise party act.

To this I replied, by assuring him that the officers were too intimately associated with the distillers and rectifiers to escape an exposed connection should prosecutions be begun; that these men had been the largest contributors to the campaign fund when the collections were applied to that purpose, but that for a long time past the money thus raised had gone into the pockets of individuals, as he well knew. In addition to this, I reminded him that it the prosecutions were based upon conclusive evidence, that the distillers and rectifiers would not alone suffer, but that the officers and *every one having guilty knowledge,* would be liable to the same punishment. I told him further, that these agents, in getting this evidence, would be certain, almost, to leak some of their information, which would run directly into the newspapers.

To this the President responded, that the papers were so full of scandals that, unless the proof were furnished, their reports would hardly be credited by the public. He told me that when the agents made their investigations, their reports could easily be controlled in the [Treasury] Department, and that they should be.

I argued with him that the safest plan would be to recall the agents, because, said I, if they get this evidence, it is certain, sooner or later; to obtain publicity. I also gave him my impressions concerning the intentions of Secretary Bristow, which were, that if unrestrained, the investigations would be most searching, and with a mountain of searing evidence, it could not be hidden from the public. I further told him that the Secretary had already assured me he had "a barrel" of information, sufficient to convict a large number of the distillers and rectifiers.

The President then said: "What disposition, in your judgment, should be made of this evidence?"

My reply was, that it ought to be shoved into a red-hot stove.

Said he: "Well, I hardly think it would be policy to burn it up," but, said he, "don't you think it would be a good plan to have it all sealed up securely and placed in a vault where no one could get at it?"

I answered, that would subserve present necessities, but that it would be resurrected sometime, when there was a change of officers.

He then told me that he would prevent a further accumulation of the evidence, by having the agents recalled, and that he would confer with the Secretary as to the most desirable means for preventing any of the evidence from becoming public.

I responded by saying: "Well, General, if you have an understanding with the Secretary, you can control things."

He acknowledged that he had no understanding with the Secretary, but that, at all events, the evidence would be controlled. . . .

He then asked me what effect Bristow's action would have in other districts, and upon the party.

I told him that, as he understood everything that had been going on in my district, it was only necessary for me to assure him that the same condition of affairs existed throughout the entire country and in every district; that if the matter were allowed to reach the public it could no more be stopped than the waves of the ocean before the wind; that it would expose the internal operations of the Republican party, the sources from whence its life was derived, and that the party would collapse like a balloon rent by lightning.

He manifested much anxiety, and was, indeed, sorely agitated. His response to my opinion was: "Well, it *must* be stopped. . . ."

Immediately upon my return from Washington I held a conference with all the U.S. Revenue officers in St. Louis with relation to their resignations. Colonel [John A.] Joyce [revenue agent] tendered his resignation . . . and Collector [Constantine] Maguire adopted the same course in a day or two after. I went directly to William McKee, who was still publishing the [St. Louis] *Globe*. . . . and explained the situation to him thoroughly. He manifested the greatest alarm, and begged me to see him daily and report the actions of the Government. I was then in almost daily correspondence with General Babcock, and upon receipt of his letters, I would take them down to the *Globe* office, where I usually found Mr. McKee and Collector Maguire, and together we would read them.

The draw-strings of the Government kept squeezing the Ring tighter, and we began seriously to reflect upon the probability of our own punishment. In my correspondence with General Babcock I did not neglect to acquaint him with our fears, and ask his interposition to prevent a collapse that would entail disaster. . . .

After considering my position I could not see why I should exhibit any anxiety. I knew that Grant and Babcock were, in a measure, in my power, because they were my superiors and equally guilty with myself. So my conclusion was to let the White House end of the line take care of itself and to offer no further obstacle to Bristow's foray.

My determination brought forth abundant fruit, by alarming the President and his chevalier scribe [Babcock], who, being unable to account for my nonchalance, and quite at sea as to my intentions, learning of my return to St. Louis they took the train and arrived in the city on September 24.

The visit of the President and General Babcock was made under circumstances that would disguise their real purposes from the public. . . . Arrangements were made for an annual meeting of the Grand Army of the Potomac to be held at Des Moines, Iowa, in the latter part of September. The President desired to attend this annual reunion and he could use this fact as an excuse for coming to St. Louis. . . .

My first notification of their arrival was through Major Grimes who came to me at the Planter's House [Hotel], where I was stopping, and taking me by the arm said, "There is a gentleman over the way who wishes to see you; will you go over with me now?" I crossed the street with Major Grimes and followed him up stairs to a room. . . . Upon entering the room I found General Babcock, who cordially greeted me and then informed me that he had ordered a dinner and wine expressly for me. I saw that a very sumptuous repast had been provided for two. . . . Major Grimes did not dine with us for, as I learned from General [Babcock], matters had been arranged for a strictly private conversation between us.

He began the interview by saying: "The old man [Grant] and I have come out here to see what you want done. This thing has gone far enough and must stop right here. We have taken rooms at the Lindell [Hotel], and at four o'clock this afternoon I want you to see the President privately and tell him exactly what you want. . . ." He said that there had already been scandal enough, and he declared that the trouble would not be allowed to continue if "we (the expression he used) have to dismiss every man in the Government service. . . ." He further remarked that the old man was too easy, and that he wanted me to say to him that it was time to take the bull by the horns and stop the investigations and prevent a prosecution of any of the members. He gave it as his opinion that . . . appointees of the President . . . could be restrained by the President's wishes, especially if the matter assumed the position of "quit or go"; that a prosecution of the President's friends was a serious reflection upon the President, which could in no event [be] tolerated. . . ."

I assured him, however, that the prosecutions could not extend to the President or himself except through Colonel Joyce or myself, and that he might depend upon me to carry the secrets I had like facts hidden under the mold of centuries. I advised him to return with the President, to Washington, and to take no part in averting prosecutions, which might be construed against them, and to leave the St. Louis boys [to] take care of themselves.

Somewhat surprised, he asked: "Why, General, what do you mean by that; don't you want us to do anything out here for you . . ."

I told him that I expected the President to pardon me at once, in case of my conviction, and that it was because of this and the friendly obligations I owed him that I proposed to stand and take the full brunt of the law, in order that my fidelity might be proven.

He next asked me if I were not under a heavy expense, and upon receiving an affirmative reply he assured me that all my expenses including loss of time, lawyers fees, etc., should be refunded and not only that, but after the trouble had been settled and Grant was reelected, that my nerve and devotion would have passed the crucible of test and that I could have any office in the gift of the President, by the mere asking. . . . Before leaving he said that the President, while approving of my course thoroughly, yet he was very desirous of meeting me privately to that he might have a lengthy conversation, and assure me of his high regard and warm attachment. I asked him to inform the President that I would call at the Lindell Hotel . . . and would be in the parlor corridor . . . to meet him publicly. . . .

Our conversation lasted only a few minutes for I told the President that a lengthy interview would excite comment, so he bade me a very reluctant adieu, assuring with his last words that under any and all circumstances I should be protected as I had pledged myself to protect him.

Financial Conspiracies

Sarah E. V. Emery

In the 1880s the emergence of the People's or Populist Party in response to economic downturns signaled the growing discontent in the South and West with the domination of the nation by eastern money interests. Harkening back to a mythical time when the farmer and laborer were preeminent in American life, the Populists sought to reform the government by providing "the people" with more direct control: direct election of senators; referenda and recalls; and free coinage of silver or greenbacks—all initiatives to remove the influence of Eastern money. In the following selection, Sarah E. V. Emery, a Michigan populist, argues that money interests—"Shylocks"—had sought to embroil the nation in the Civil War to enrich themselves. Failing this, Emery argues, they then began to insinuate themselves into the government and passed legislation hostile to farmers and laborers. It should be noted that "Shylock" is drawn from the Jewish moneylender in Shakespeare's *The Merchant of Venice;* though the use of the name in this context can be seen as anti-Semitic, her exact intentions are not clear. (From Sarah E. V. Emery, *Seven Financial Conspiracies Which Have Enslaved the American People* [Lansing: Robert Smith and Co., 1887; revised 1894; reprint, Westport: Hyperion Press, 1975], 7–17; 66–70.)

The Earl of Chatham, England's great Statesman, once said, "Show me the laws of a country and I will show you the condition of its people."

Starting upon this proposition, we are led to the conclusion that the laws of our country are not in accordance with the principles of justice and equality, for there is nothing in the condition of the masses that denotes prosperity, but rather a tendency to poverty and demoralization. No period of our history has been marked by such general dissatisfaction. . . .

Thirty years ago the American laborer was a prospective lord. . . . The condition of the American people less than half a century ago is graphically portrayed by [Charles] Dickens, who, visiting in this country in 1842, wrote from Boston to a friend in London: "There is not a man in this town nor in this State who has not a blazing fire, and meat every day for dinner, nor would a flaming sword in the air attract more attention than a beggar in the streets." But today what is the outlook for the wage-workers of this country? He sees before him only toil. . . .

We are now led to the question, wherefore this amazing change in the condition of the working classes of this country? There is a solution to this problem. As I have . . . stated the American system of government afforded little . . . opportunity for robbery and oppression, but the vast plains and teeming valleys of this grand republic, with its innumerable sources of wealth . . . was a coveted prize long sought by civilized brigandage. To obtain . . . this vast wealth and reduce an intelligent people to the position of slaves, was by no means an easy task. But the promptings of avarice were not to be silenced, and greed was on the alert for an opportunity to seize the coveted prize. The fatal opportunity at last presented itself. African slavery had been a source of contention from the very foundation of the republic, and its agitation finally culminated in the secession of a majority of the slave holding states. The war cloud was gathering and the mutterings . . . were portentous of a coming storm. Old men ominously shook their heads; young men stoutly declared that "the Union must be preserved"; and mothers . . . prayed God that the storm cloud of war might pass. But above all the prayers, wailings and forebodings, the attentive listener could hear from Wall Street the echoes of jubilant satisfaction, and harmonious preparations for an onslaught upon the industry and prosperity of the country. Nor was Wall Street along in this exultation over a prospective civil war; all along the line were ringing notes of exultation, even our beloved Michigan swelled the cry "to arms!" led on by that great leader [Senator Zach Chandler, Republican of Michigan] who startled the entire Christian world with his infamous declaration, "That a nation is not worth a curse without blood-letting." A declaration that must forever dishonor the name of its illustrious author.

Now do you ask why this exultation over a prospective civil war? Do you ask why the money-kings of Wall Street and the great political chieftain of Michigan were so anxious . . . when the guns were turned upon Fort Sumter and the declaration of war sent its thrilling notes throughout . . . our land? . . . Reader, do you imagine it was because of their great love for the dusky toilers in the cotton fields of Mississippi, or because the finer instincts of their nature revolted against the cruel system of African slavery? Do you suppose the story of Uncle Tom and Little Eva had touched their hearts and they had sworn vengeance upon the perpetrators of such cruelty? No, no; the money kings of Wall Street . . . were not the men whose hearts were touched with pity by the cries of distress. Their love of gain had stifled . . . their nature, and they rejoiced because they saw in the preparation for war their long-coveted opportunity for plunder. . . . To accomplish this it became necessary to obtain possession of the national finances. As blood . . . is the life of the body, so they knew that money . . . was the life of the country. Its industry, its education, its morality, in truth, its very life depended upon its medium of exchange. Controlling it, they could inflate or depress the business of the country at pleasure. . . . They knew their opportunity was at hand, and the tidings of war . . . was to their ears sweeter than the music of the spheres.

Scarcely had the war cloud broken ere the gold and silver money of the country disappeared. True to the history of metallic money in all ages, in the hour of peril, of a country's greatest need, her gold and silver money always takes flight. What had become of it? Why Shylock had obtained possession of it, for what purposes we shall see hereafter.

The necessities of the war required vast sums of money; but the treasury was empty, the gold and silver money of the country had fled. What was to be done? The government was in duty bound to suppress the rebellion. . . . But where should she derive means for this vast expenditure, where . . . should she look for succor and support? Where . . . could the government look except her own moneyed classes? Did not Wall Street rejoice in the declaration of war, and loudly protest against the secession of the slave States? Surely, Wall Street would come to the rescue, and pour out her treasure in the defense of the government. So said justice, so said patriotism, but history tells us quite another story. Neither American nor foreign capitalists would loan money to the government upon any reasonable terms. True the banks would loan their notes at 20 percent discount, that is, they would exchange eighty dollars of their notes for one hundred dollars in government bonds, bearing a high rate of interest, payable in gold. . . .

. . . Why, sirs, the South itself was not more formidable and determined in the preservation of her slave property than were these Shylocks in their determination to wrench from the government . . . such usury as would have put to shame their world renowned ancestor. On the one hand . . . the enemy; on the other, disguised as a friend and urging on the war, stood Shylock clutching his gold. . . .

But what was Shylock to do? The gold and silver of the country were in his possession, and they would not serve his purposes unless he could loan them to the government at exorbitant rates of interest. Knowing the necessities of the government these Shylocks determined to persist in their demands, for they had planned through the misfortune of the government to enrich and aggrandize themselves. . . . By hoarding the gold and silver of the country they thought to compel the government to accede to their demands, and while the soldier was giving his life on the battlefield they would gather to themselves riches and power.

But the great leader, Lincoln, was not to be baffled; he loved the people better than Shylock, and justice better than oppression. From the constitution he read, "Congress shall have power to declare war." Again he read, "Congress shall have power to coin money." Then to the world he declared that Congress would coin money, and that the government . . . would not submit to the infamous demands of Shylock. . . .

But Shylock was sullen and disconsolate, having failed in his scheme . . . he immediately entered upon another scheme of brigandage. . . . Having hoarded the gold and silver of the country, it was through this channel, if at all, he must despoil the country. Now, since Congress had made provision to supply the government money, there was no longer a demand for Shylock's hoarded gold. . . . But greed neither slumbers nor sleeps, nor did Shylock rest until his bandits had an appointed rendezvous. We find that only four days after the passage of the legal tender act . . . a bankers' convention was held in Washington. . . . Shylock was alarmed; he saw in the . . . act a friend to the people, that it would transfer the monopoly of the money from his hands to the control of the people . . . a precedent which . . . would forever after enable the government to relieve itself and the people without submitting to this usurous extortions. . . . This, then, was plainly the object of that notable bankers' convention, to create a demand for Shylock's hoarded gold. . . .

The record of the American Congress from February 24, 1862, to January 24, 1875, is a record of the blackest and most heartless crimes. But kind reader, do not for one moment deceive yourself with the thought that this corrupt legislation ceased on that memorable day. Ah no; the act of resumption simply completed the infernal machinery by which the money power is crushing out the liberty and lives of the American people. By controlling the finances of the country they have been enabled to form trusts and syndicates which have reduced the people to a wage-slavery more abject and heartless than any chattel slavery that ever cursed God's earth.

The people having slept until this machinery was perfected, have . . . awakened . . . to find their liberties fettered, and themselves in the grasp of a system of monopolies whose Titanic enginery is crushing out not only liberty, but life itself. And when we consider the fact that the representatives of these monopolies sit in our congressional halls and practically control the United States Senate, that highest law-making power in the land, who does not tremble for the safety . . . of our civilization. . . .

Yes, the people are awakened, but the money power is on guard . . . and are now clamoring for an appropriation to establish a military power. Let us not be deceived; this cry for an established militia is not to defend ourselves against a foreign foe; the enemy is within our gates, sitting in the high places of our country. They tell us "the wealth of the country must be protected." Ah, the wealth of the country requires protection. It is not labor they would protect; it is not the oppressed they would have go free, it is not the burden of toil they would lighten, but the wealth of the country demands protection. But what is this wealth that cannot be protected without military force? Ah, sirs, it is that wealth of which the people have been robbed; it is the ill-gotten gain of a moneyed oligarchy. It is not the fear of foreign invaders, not the fear that the masses will violate law, but that they will repeal unjust statutes, and restore to the people the inheritance of which they have been so outrageously robbed. . . .

But spurred on by his appetite for plunder, Shylock still dares to raise his murderous hand against the people. Greed is never satisfied, its ill-gotten gains only serve to sharpen its appetite. . . . Cunning hands, scheming brains, degenerate souls still plot the destruction of this Republic. Their next plan is to destroy the $346,000,000 of greenbacks, which have only been preserved thus far through . . . untiring vigilance in . . . Congress. . . .

Besides the destruction of the greenbacks it is their settled policy to rob us of the silver dollar and place our currency upon a single gold basis. This is another diabolic scheme solely in the interest of the creditor class.

There is not, there cannot be a greater enemy to American producers than [Senator] John Sherman and that class of men who are devoting all their energies to the destruction of silver as money. With gold as a basis and the banks to issue the paper currency of the country, the people would be entirely at the mercy of Shylock. Indeed, are we not already at the feet of the money power?

The New York *Tribune,* under the management of Whitelaw Reid, said: "The time is near when they (the banks) will feel compelled to act strongly. Meanwhile a very good thing has been done. The machinery is now furnished by which, in any emergency, the financial corporations of the east can act together on a single day's notice with such power that no act of Congress can overcome or resist their decision."

Shades of Horace Greeley! Can it be possible that the New York *Tribune,* that once powerful advocate of justice, has become so perverted as to call it "a very good thing," that the financial corporations . . . are furnished with the machinery whereby they can control Congress. Where are we, then? Is it the financial corporations . . . or the United States Congress, that govern this country? The New York *Tribune* . . . says it is "the financial corporations of the east," and rejoices in it as "a very good thing."

What then, avail the words of Horace Greeley, or the blood of a million martyred soldiers, or the expenditure of five billions of treasure? Have we not today fifty millions of people under the bondage of financial corporations? A bondage more galling and heartless than that beneath the lash of southern slavery—more galling because perpetrated in the name of liberty, more heartless because there is none to heed the cries of the starving white slaves. . . . The shackles were dropped from . . . black slaves, not to make them free, but to enslave the whole producing industries of the country, through this infernal bond and bank scheme.

History proves that nothing has been so disastrous . . . as the enactment of laws which favor the few. . . . And history proves that such legislation destroys nations, degrades humanity, and is a mockery against . . . God. Against the Eternal Judge who will not hold guiltless him who lends a voice to such . . . legislation. A legislation that destroys both soul and body of the toiling millions.

Anarchy and Anarchists: Petticoated Ugliness and Betrayed by Beauty

Michael Schaack

After the violent events at the Haymarket Affair on May 4, 1886, and the resulting trial of eight anarchists, many Americans in the late nineteenth

"The 'Red' Sisterhood," from Michael Schaack's *Anarchy and Anarchists* (1889), depicts plotting anarchist women. Note the death mask in the background and the mannish figure of the women in the coven.

and early twentieth centuries believed anarchists were plotting a conspiracy to overthrow the American government. These fears appeared justified given that anarchists had vocally advocated the overthrow of the capitalist system and justified assassination as means of doing so. Directly in response to these fears, Michael J. Schaack, a captain of the Chicago police, published a scathing attack on anarchists in 1889. Similar to others who despised anarchism, Schaack goes to great lengths to prove his contention that anarchists were intent on overthrowing the government and would use any means necessary to achieve that goal. Perhaps the most dangerous anarchists, Schaack argued, were women. The following excerpt illustrates the striking connection that Schaack made between gender and the anarchist conspiracy. In his view, anarchist women could be mannish and cruel or beautiful and manipulative. Despite their contrasting appearances, he argued that both types of anarchist women were extremely dangerous. (From Michael Schaack, *Anarchy and Anarchists: A History . . .* [Chicago: F. J. Schulte & Company, 1889], 206–9, 213–15.)

From the many meetings I learned that the Anarchists were discussing plans to revenge themselves on the police, but in each case, as soon as they were about to take some definite action, some one would move an adjournment or suggest the appointment of a committee to work out the plan in some better shape. When the next meeting was held the fellows who had done the loudest shouting would be absent, and then those who happened to be on hand would vent their wrath upon the absentees by calling them cowards. In many of the smaller meetings held on Milwaukee Avenue [Chicago] or in that vicinity, a lot of crazy women were usually present, and whenever a proposition arose to kill some one or blow up the city with dynamite, these "squaws" proved the most bloodthirsty. In fact, if any man laid out a plan to perpetrate mischief, they would show themselves much more eager to carry it out than the men, and it always seemed a pleasure to the Anarchists to have them present. They were always invited to the "war dances." Judge [Joseph E.] Gary, [Illinois State Attorney Julius] Grinnell, [Chicago Police Captain John] Bonfield, and myself were usually remembered at these gatherings, and they fairly went wild whenever bloodthirsty sentiments were uttered against us. The reporters and the so-called capitalistic press also shared in the general denunciations. At one meeting . . . there were thirteen of these creatures in petticoats present, the most hideous-looking females that could possibly be found. If a reward of money had been offered for an uglier set, no one could have profited upon the collection. Some of them were pockmarked, others freckle-faced and red-haired, and others again held their snuff-boxes in their hands while the congress was in session. One female appeared at one of these meetings with her husband's boots on, and there was another one about six feet tall. She was a beauty! She was rawboned, had a turn-up nose, and looked as though she might have carried the red flag in Paris during the reign of the Commune.

This meeting continued all right for about two hours. Then a rap came on the locked door. The guard reported that one of their cause desired admittance, giving his name at the same time—and the new arrival was permitted to enter. He was a large man with a black beard and large eyes, and very shabbily dressed. . . . As soon as he reached the interior of the hall he blurted out hastily, in a loud voice:

"Ladies and brothers of our cause! Please stop all proceedings. . . . I was informed that you were holding a meeting here this evening, and that there is a spy in your midst."

He looked around for a moment and finally said, pointing to the man addressed:

"If I am not damnably mistaken, you are the man . . . !"

The officer then pulled out of his pocket a large revolver, and, brandishing, it in the air, asked:

"Shall I kill that bloodhound?"

The women cried out in a chorus: "Yes, yes; kill him!"

The turn of affairs completely surprised the stranger, and he became so frightened that he could not speak. No one in the meeting knew him and he was powerless to speak in his own defense. The officer held his revolver directed at the man's face and kept toying with it in the vicinity of his nose. . . .

At last the women again broke in, with a demand that the intruder be immediately ejected, and the men responded promptly by kicking him out of the door. He had not sooner reached the outside than he started on a keen run, in momentary dread of his life, and he kept up his rapid gait until he thought he was at a safe distance. . . .

On the 5th of August I received a communication from the Coroner of Lake County, Indiana, asking me if I had a man named Charles Brown working for me as a detective. . . .

Three days after, I learned that this was the same man I had employed, and I placed Officer Schuettler on the case to unravel, if possible, the mystery surrounding his death. The officer in a few days reported that it was exceedingly difficult to obtain a clue, as no one seemed disposed to give any information as to foul play; but enough was learned in a general way to warrant the conclusion that underhanded methods had been used to accomplish the man's death.

I recalled certain incidents in connection with the man's work as a detective, and, placing them by the side of the seemingly accidental drowning, I became convinced that a deliberate crime had been committed.

One day this private asked me if I would allow him to tell a young lady what he was working at. I told him that he must do nothing of the kind; that if he did so I would have no further use for him. He then begged me to permit him to use my name as his friend, and I told him I had no objection to that. But I found out later that he had said more to the young lady than I had consented to, and I believe his indiscretion in that respect is what cost him his life.

From the moment that the girl ascertained his secret occupation he was a doomed man. She let other Anarchists into the secret, and they at once set about devising means for ending his life.

The information I received later was that it had been decided upon that the young woman should tempt him to Cedar Lake, and then, when he was in her power, to do away with him. The two left the city together, and were followed by the others in the conspiracy to the place were his body was found. Before taking the trip on the water, she was seen talking with some mysterious-looking individuals, and they then and there decided upon the details of the plan. She was to get him to row out into deep water, and, when they were fairly started, her friends were to follow in another rowboat at a convenient distance. When they reached the middle of the lake she was to keep a close watch on the other boat, and as they neared her boat she was to suddenly throw herself on one side and tip the boat over so that both occupants would be thrown into the water. Her friends were then to be close at hand, pick her up and save her from drowning. The program was carried out so far as related to the capsizing of the boat, but the men did not get near enough in time to save her. She went down with her companion and was drowned with him.

There is no doubt as to the truth of this plot. It was in entire keeping with Anarchist methods; and parties who were at the lake at the time state that they saw the young lady get up in the boat, and that while thus standing she swung it over, precipitating herself and her lover into the water. I had men engaged on the case for some time, but the investigation always ended in the same way—an undoubted conclusion that the detective's life was taken by reason of a plot, but no evidence to establish the guilt of the conspirators. From the information I received, I am satisfied that the whole matter was carefully planned and carried out by the woman.

The Gold Standard and Foreign Influence

William M. Stewart

Republican senator William M. Stewart of Nevada was one of the longest-serving senators in the upper house's history. Originally a Democrat prior to the Civil War, he joined the Republican Party in order to preserve the Union. In 1896, however, he increasingly became hostile to what he viewed as the dominance of the Republican Party by eastern financiers and businessmen who supported the gold standard. Stewart, along with several other western Republicans, declared his independence from the party during its national convention in St. Louis in June 1896. This group, commonly known as the Silver Republicans, advocated the free coinage of silver. Increasingly, the Silver Republicans viewed eastern

Illustration from the periodical *Sound Money* (1896) shows English financier Nathaniel Mayer Rothschild exerting influence over American fiscal policy and subjecting American labor to poverty.

business interests and Great Britain as agents of a conspiracy to control the money supply of the United States and relegate the economy of the western states to a subordinate position. In January 1896, Stewart articulated these views during a debate to limit the sale of government bonds. (From William Stewart, *Congressional Record,* 54th Cong., 1st sess., January 9, 1896, 531–36.)

As to the question of the amount of gold in the country, nobody knows that any worth naming exists outside of the banks and the Treasury, except on the Pacific Coast, where there may be twenty or thirty million dollars in actual circulation. But there is no gold whatever in circulation east of the Rocky Mountains; whatever there is in the banks, and undoubtedly the pool understands that.

When this call [for bonds] was issued, what did the syndicate do? It will be remembered that there was a syndicate formed to take this entire loan, and that was composed of Europeans. Did they encourage a popular loan in the United States? I have in my hand telegrams from Europe showing how they boomed out popular loan. They were cooperating to destroy it, with the intention of having a pretended coercion upon the President [Grover Cleveland], a sham coercion to make him give the bonds. . . .

There were a number of other telegrams by other bankers, endorsing the Rothschilds [international banking family with ties in Great Britain]. Of course they had to endorse the Rothschilds and sustain their position. . . . A few days previous to this offer to the public, the agent of the Rothschilds who formed the other syndicate, [John] Pierpont Morgan, was in this city, as all the papers announced, with [Francis Lynde] Stetson, the same attorney who helped manage the other pool. Rothschild & Sons tell us they were part of the other pool. It was announced in the press that a new pool had been formed to take this loan, but it was the old pool, the old syndicate somewhat enlarged, a few more American bankers being taken in, and here were . . . Rothschild & Sons with a pool already formed, and with the gold all cornered.

When this offer was published—which, if I might express my opinion without being impolite, I would call a "sham offer"—in order to defeat it, the members of this syndicate telegraphed from London that the bonds could not be sold, that they would not take them under existing circumstances, when their agent had been in this city and had made arrangements to take them and expected to get them, and still expects to get them, and get them cheap, when the force of a popular loan has failed.

They wanted to discourage the American people. It seems to me that such a message coming from a syndicate which was proposing to buy bonds for less than their value shows a conspiracy against the finances and honor of this country that should make us pause; and it is time to stop selling bonds until there is some mode provided for their issuance by law and some regulation, so that a syndicate cannot fool with the Government in this way.

The Rothschilds are in a syndicate to buy the bonds, and when the offer is put out, in order to discourage the American people and to damage the finances and credit of this country, then come telegrams from members of the syndicate, disparaging American credit; and our papers have been teeming with laudation of the patriotism of the syndicate—the syndicate saved the country!—and the commercial press throughout the land has been commending the syndicate for the last year. Now come these same individuals applying for $100,000,000 of bonds, after they have collected the gold which nobody else can get. This proposal, pretending to be a popular loan, is trammeled by the necessity of bidders having gold. Then come telegrams from the same banking syndicate disparaging the credit of the United States. . . .

The President is now offering these bonds. The people are hungry for them, but they cannot reach them. The President will withdraw them and give them to his pet syndicate. The evidence is accumulating that the people are not going to get any of them. . . .

Nobody doubts that the country is perfectly secure, now that it is underwritten by Morgan! The failure of the offer would be an excuse for selling bonds at a remarkably low figure. Then we shall hear Rothschild lauded as the only patriotic American anywhere. We have to go to the other side of the water [Atlantic Ocean] to get patriotism. . . .

There is now $178,000,000 cash balance in the Treasury, nearly $150,000,000 of which is legal-tender notes. If we put out another $100,000,000, the syndicate can buy up all those notes and make more contraction. It is undoubtedly the object to continue to buy them up and pile them in the Treasury for the purpose of depriving the people of what little money is in circulation. The President says he does not need any more revenue, but he needs this money to sustain the honor of the Government. He has got to deal with this Rothschild syndicate, which is disparaging our credit and is speculating off the Government, getting bonds 10 or 15 percent less than their actual value, piling up debt on us, and we must do this to sustain the honor of the Government! How long will this Government have honor or credit if these outrageous speculations and peculations are allowed to proceed? We cannot imitate the press, which says it is patriotism for Rothschild to disparage our credit and buy bonds for less than their value. We should not be intimidated by the Executive power, which offers these bonds in such a way that the people cannot get them. We should stop these wicked transactions, and stop them now.

The Conspiracy of the East St. Louis Riots

Marcus Garvey

Marcus Garvey, born in Jamaica on August 17, 1887, was one of the earliest proponents of black nationalism. He founded the Universal Negro Improvement Association (UNIA) in Jamaica in 1914 to uplift and unite the various groups of Africans in the world, and he formed the first UNIA chapter in the United States in New York City in 1916. In order to achieve black unity and uplift, Garvey pursued various business ventures such as the Black Star Line, a shipping company that was largely unsuccessful, and the Negro Factories Corporation that encouraged the building of black-owned and -operated factories. Garvey delivered many lectures in the United States promoting the UNIA. After spending a little over a year in the United States, Garvey delivered a speech at Lafayette Hall, New York, on July 8, 1917, in response to the race riots in East St. Louis, Illinois, a booming industrial city on the eastern shore of the Mississippi River. The riots had erupted on July 2 because many white laborers feared that they would lose their jobs to the massive influx of African Americans emigrating from the South in search of work. The riots devastated the community of East St. Louis and resulted in the deaths of thirty-nine African Americans and nine whites. In the following excerpt, Garvey outlines his belief that the East St. Louis riot was the product of conspiracy led by the city's leadership to prevent the displacement of white immigrant laborers and to dissuade African Americans from migrating to the city. (From Marcus Garvey, *Conspiracy of the East St. Louis Riot Speech by Marcus Garvey Delivered at Lafayette Hall, New York, Sunday, July 8th, 1917* [n.p., n.d.], in the collections of the Moorland-Springarn Research Center, Howard University.)

The East St. Louis Riot, or rather massacre . . . will go down in history as one of the bloodiest outrages against mankind for which any class of people could be held guilty. This is no time for fine words, but a time to lift one's voice against the savagery of a people who claim to be the dispensers of democracy. I do not know what special meaning the people who slaughtered the Negroes of East St. Louis have for democracy of which they are custodians, but I do know that it has no literal meaning for me as used and applied by these same lawless people. America, that has been ringing the bells of the world, proclaiming to the nations and the peoples thereof that she has democracy to give to all sundry, America that has denounced Germany for the deportations of the Belgians into Germany, American that has arraigned Turkey at the bar of public opinion and public justice against the massacres of the Armenians, has herself no satisfaction of a farcical inquiry that will end where it begun, over the brutal murder of men, women and children for no other reason than that they are black people seeking an industrial chance in a country that they have labored for three hundred years to make great. For three hundred years the Negroes of America have given their life blood to make the Republic the first among the nations of the world, and all along this time there has never been even one year of justice but on the contrary a continuous round of oppression. At one time it was slavery, at another time lynching and burning, and up to date it is wholesale butchering. This is a crime against the laws of humanity; it is a crime against the laws of the nation, it is a crime against Nature and a crime against the God of all mankind. . . .

Yet, for all his services he receives the reward of lynching, burning, and wholesale slaughter. It is even strange to see how the real American white people, the people who are direct de[s]cendants from the Pilgrim Fathers, allow the alien German, Pole, Italian, and other Europeans who came here but yesterday to lead them in the bloody onslaught against the Negroes who have lived here for over three hundred years. When I say that the Aliens are leading the descendants of the Pilgrim Fathers against the Negroes of this country I mean to support it with as much facts as possible.

Mayor [Fred] Mollman [elected in 1915] of East St. Louis if [no]t himself a German, is a descendant of German immigrants, he is the man to be blamed for the recent riot in East St. Louis. I say so because I am convinced that he fostered a well arranged conspiracy to prevent black men migrating from the South much to the loss of Southern Farmers who for months have been moving heaven itself to prevent the exodus of the labor serfs of the South into the North.

Two months ago I was in New Orleans completing a lecture tour of the United States, and on the 26th of April Mayor Mollman arrived in the city on a trip from St. Louis. In New Orleans he was met by Mayor [Martin] Behrman and the New Orleans Board of Trade. For months the Farmers of Louisiana were frightened out of their wits over the every day migration of Negroes from great farming centers of the State. They wrote to the papers, they appealed to the Governor, the Mayor and the Legislature and the Board of Trade to stop the Negroes going away, but up to the 26th of April nothing was done to stop the people excepting the Railway Companies promising to use certain restraint on the ruse of people obtaining passages on the trains by Railway orders sent to them from the North. At this time Mayor Mollman arrived and the Farmers and Board of Trade met him and asked his help in discouraging the Negroes from going North and especially to East St. Louis. In an interview given out to the New Orleans press he said that the Negroes from the South were reaching St. Louis at the rate of 2,000 per week, and that they were creating a problem there. He said that some of the largest industries in the country were established in East St. Louis and there were strikes [in the meat-packing plants and metal-works factories] for the last few months. He believed the labor conditions in East St. Louis were responsible for the number of Negro laborers going to that city. When the strikes started, he said, United States District Judge Wright issued an injunction restraining the strikers from intimidating the laborers who took their places. This order prevented uprisings and riots. . . . His interview did not make pleasant reading for the Farmers and others interested in labor in New Orleans and Louisiana so that the very next day he appeared at the Board of Trade where he met the Farmers and others and in discussing the labor exodus with them, he promised that he would do all he could to discourage the Negroes from Louisiana going into East St. Louis as the city did not want them. . . . His remarks to the people whom he met were published under big headlines in the newspapers, so that the Negroes could read that they were not wanted in East St. Louis, but that did not deter the blackmen of Louisiana who were looking for better opportunities than the South offered with lynching and Jim Crowism. The Negroes still continued their migration North. The Mayor of East St. Louis returned to the city after making his promise to the Farmers, Board of Trade and others who were interested in Negro labor. On the 5th of May the New Orleans Board of Trade elected Mr. M. J. Sanders its president, and Mr. W. P. Ross as delegates to attend a transportation conference at St. Louis to be held on May 8–9. You will remember that Ma[y]or Mollman appeared before the Board of Trade on Friday the 27th April where he made his statement of promise. . . . It isn't for me to suggest the Mayor Mollman met these gentlemen again; it is for you to imagine what further transpired while these gentlemen from the South who were so deeply interested in keeping the Negro below the Mason and Dixon line said and did among themselves while in that vicinity where Mayor Mollman held sway so much so as to be able to make a promise to keep out citizens of the United States who were not born in Germany, but in the Southland. One thing I do now know; the first riot started on May 28 after a conference of labor leaders with Mayor Mollman. On that day . . . crowds of white men after leaving the City Council stopped street cars and dragged Negroes off and beat them. Then the night following three Negroes and two white men were shot. An investigation of the affair resulted in the finding that labor agents had induced Negroes to come from the South. I can hardly see the relevance of such a report with the dragging of men from cars and shooting them. The City authorities did nothing to demonstrate to the unreasonable labor leaders that they would be firmly dealt with should they maltreat and kill blackmen. No threat was offered to these men because Mayor Mollman himself had promised to do all he could to drive the Negroes out of East St. Louis, and to instill fear in the hearts of the people in the South so as to prevent them coming North. . . .

The mob and white populace of East St. Louis had a Roman holiday. They feasted on the blood of the Negro, encouraged as they were by the German[-]American Mayor who two months ago when to New Orleans and promised to keep the Negroes out of East St. Louis. . . .

I can hardly see why blackmen should be debarred from going where they choose in the land of their birth. I cannot see wherefrom Mayor Mollman got the authority to discourage blackmen going into East St. Louis, when there was work for them, except he got that authority from mob sentiment and mob law. It was because he knew that he could gain a following and support on the issue of race why he was bold enough to promise the white people of Louisiana that he would keep Negroes out of East St. Louis. He has succeeded in driving fully 10,000 in one day out of the city, and the South has gone wild over the splendid performance in so much so that the very next day after the massacre the Legislature of Georgia sent out the message that their good Negroes must come home as they will treat them better than East St. Louis did. Can you wonder at the conspiracy of the whole affair? White people are taking advantage of blackmen today because blackmen all over the world are disunited.

Angles of Jewish Influence

Henry Ford

Henry Ford, founder of the Ford Motor Company and father of mass-assembly manufacturing, gained fame and wealth through his Model T Ford automobile. Ford's politics were an odd mixture of anti-finance capitalism, anti-labor unionism, isolationism, and anti-Semitism. In 1918, Ford purchased the *Dearborn Independent*, which became a vehicle for his anti-Semitism. Anti-Jewish articles appearing in the newspaper were released in four separately bound volumes under the title *The International Jew, the World's Foremost Problem*. The articles gained widespread influence, including in Nazi Germany. Under threat of a libel suit, Ford closed his paper in December 1927, but material from *The International Jew* continues to appear on anti-Semitic and neo-Nazi web sites today, which reveals the insidious nature of Ford's bigotry. (From Henry Ford, "Angles of Jewish Influence," *Aspects of the Jewish Power in the United States, Four Volumes* [Dearborn: Dearborn Publishing Company, 1920], 41–53.)

The Jewish Question exists wherever Jews appear. . . . because they bring it with them. It is not their numbers that create the Question, for there is in almost every country a larger number of other aliens than of Jews. It is not their much-boasted ability, for it is now coming to be understood that, give the Jew an equal start and hold him to the rules of the game, and he is not smarter than anyone else; indeed, in one great class of Jews the zeal is quenched when opportunity for intrigue is removed.

The Jewish Question is not the number of Jews who reside here. . . . it is in something else, and that something else is the fact of Jewish influence on the life of the country where Jews dwell; in the United States it is the Jewish influence on American life.

That the Jews exert an influence, they themselves loudly proclaim. The Jews claim, indeed, that the fundamentals of the United States are Jewish and not Christian, and that the entire history of this country should be re-written to make proper acknowledgment of the prior glory due to Judah. . . .

It is not the Jewish people but the Jewish idea, and the people only as vehicles of the idea, that is the point at issue. In this investigation of the Jewish Question, it is Jewish influence and the Jewish Idea that are being discovered and defined.

The Jews are propagandists. This was originally their mission. But they were to propagate the central tenet of their religion. This they failed to do. By failing in this they, according to their own Scriptures, failed everywhere. They are now without a mission of blessing. Few of their leaders even claim a spiritual mission. But the mission idea is still with them in a degenerate form; it represents the grossest materialism of the day; it has become a means of sordid acquisition instead of a channel of service.

Labor and Jewry

The essence of the Jewish Idea to its influence on the labor world is the same as in all other departments—the destruction of real values in favor of fictitious values. The Jewish philosophy of money is not to "make money," but to "get money." The distinction between these two is fundamental. That explains Jews being "financiers" instead of "captains of industry." It is the difference between "getting" and "making."

Now, previous to the advent of Jewish socialistic and subversive ideas, the predominant thought in the labor world was to "make" things and thus "make" money. There was a pride among mechanics. Men who made things were a sturdy, honest race because they dealt with ideas of skill and quality, and their very characters were formed by the satisfaction of having performed useful functions in society. They were the Makers. And society was solid so long as they were solid. Men made shoes as exhibitions of their skill. Farmers raised crops for the inherent love of crops, not with reference to far-off money-markets. Everywhere THE JOB was the main thing and the rest was incidental.

With the required manipulation of the money and food markets, enough pressure could be brought to bear on the ultimate consumers to give point to the idea of "get," and it was not long before the internal relations of American business were totally upset, with Jews at the head of the banking system, and Jews at the head of both the conservative and radical elements of the Labor Movement, and, most potent of all, the Jewish Idea sowed through the minds of workingmen. What Idea? The idea of "get" instead of "make."

All over the United States, in many branches of trade, Communist colleges are maintained, officered and taught by Jews. These so-called colleges exist in Chicago, Detroit, Cleveland, Rochester, Pittsburgh, New York, Philadelphia and other cities, the whole intent being to put all American labor on a "get" basis, which must prove the economic damnation of the country. That is the end sought, as in Russia.

Until Jews can show that the infiltration of foreign Jews and the Jewish Idea into the American labor movement has made for the betterment in character and estate, in citizenship and economic statesmanship, the charge of being an alien, destructive and treasonable influence will have to stand.

The Churches and Jewry

The last place the uninstructed observer would look for traces of Jewish influence is in the Christian Church, yet if he fails to look there he will miss much. If the libraries of our theological seminaries were equipped with complete files of Jewish literary effort during recent decades, and if the theological students were required to read these Jewish utterances there would be less silly talk and fewer "easy marks" for Jewish propaganda in the American pulpit. For the next 25 years every theological seminary should support a chair for the study of Modern Jewish influence and the Protocols. . . .

The Church is now victim of a second attack against her, in the rampant Socialism and Sovietism that have been thrust upon her in the name of flabby and unmoral theories of "brotherhood" and in an appeal to her "fairness." The church has been made to believe that she is a forum for discussion and not a high place for annunciation.

Jews have actually invaded, in person and in program, hundreds of American churches, with their subversive and impossible social ideals, and at last became so cocksure of their domination of the situation that they were met with the inevitable check.

The Jew has got hold of the Church in doctrine, in liberalism, so-called, and in the feverish and feeble sociological diversions of many classes. If there is any place where a straight study of the Jewish Question should be made it is in the modern Church which is unconsciously giving allegiance to a mass of Jewish propaganda.

Jewry in Schools and Colleges

Colleges are being constantly invaded by the Jewish Idea. The sons of the Anglo-Saxons are being attacked in their very heredity. The sons of the Builders, the Makers, are being subverted to the philosophy of the destroyers. . . . They find that "freelove" doctrines make exhilarating club topics, but that the Family—the old-fashioned loyalty of one man and one woman to each other and their children—is the basis not only of society, but of all personal character and progress. They find that Revolution, while a delightful subject for fiery debates and an excellent stimulant to the feeling of superman-likeness, is nevertheless not the process of progress. . . .

It is idle to attack the "radicalism" of college student—these are the qualities of immaturity. But it is not idle to show that social radicalism ("radicalism" being a very good word very sadly misused) comes from a Jewish source. The central group of Red philosophers in every university is a Jewish group, with often enough a "Gentile front" in the shape of a deluded professor. Some of these professors are in the pay of outside Red organizations. There are Intercollegiate Socialist Societies, swarming with Jews and Jewish influences, and toting Jewish professors around the country, addressing fraternities under the patronage of the best civic and university auspices. Student lecture courses are fine pasture for this propaganda, the purpose being to give the students the thrill of believing that they are taking part in the beginning of a new great movement, comparable to the winning of Independence.

The revolutionary forces which head up in Jewry rely very heavily on the respectability which is given their movement by the adhesion of students and a few professors. . . .

Nab The Enemy!

The warning has already gone out through the colleges. The system of Jewish procedure is already fully known. How simple it is! First, you secularize the public schools—"secularize" is the precise word the Jews use for the process. You prepare the mind of the public school child by enforcing the rule that no mention shall ever be made to indicate that culture or patriotism is in any way connected with the deeper principles of the Anglo-Saxon religion. Keep it out, every sight and sound of it! Keep out also every word that will aid any child to identify the

Jewish race. Then, when you have thus prepared the soil, you can go into the universities and colleges and enter upon the double program of pouring contempt on all the Anglo-Saxon landmarks, at the same time filling the void with Jewish revolutionary ideas.

The influence of the common people is driven out of the schools, where common people's influence can go; but Jewish influence is allowed to run rampant in the higher institutions where the common people's influence cannot go. Secularize the schools, and you can then Judaize the universities.

This is the "liberalism" which Jewish spokesmen so much applaud. In labor unions, in churches, in universities, it has tainted the principles of work, faith and society. The proof of it is written thickly over all Jewish activities and utterances. It is in exerting these very influences that Jewry convinces itself that it is fulfilling its "mission" to the world. . . . It is not a fair fight when in the movies, in the schools, in the Judaized churches, in the universities, the Anglo-Saxon idea is kept away from the Anglo-Saxons on the plea that it is "sectarian" or "clannish" or "obsolete" or something else, say, reaction.

It is not a fair fight when Jewish ideas are offered as Anglo-Saxon ideas, because offered under Anglo-Saxon auspices. Let the heritage of our Anglo-Saxon fathers have free course among their Anglo-Saxon sons, and the Jewish idea can never triumph over it, in the university forum or in the marts of trade. The Jewish idea never triumphs until first the people over whom it triumphs are denied the nurture of their native culture.

Judah has begun the struggle. Judah has made the invasion. Let it come. Let no man fear it. But let every man insist that the fight be fair. Let college students and leaders of thought know that the objective is the regency of the ideas and the race that have built all the civilization we see and that promises all the civilization of the future; let them also know that the attacking force is Jewish.

Internationalism

Rev. Charles Coughlin

Father Charles Edward Coughlin gained a national following in the late 1920s through his weekly radio program that was broadcast from his parish church, the Little Shrine of the Flower, in a suburb of Detroit. In 1932, he endorsed Franklin Roosevelt for president, but he turned against the Roosevelt administration when it refused to accept Coughlin's proposals for monetary reform. Coughlin denounced Roosevelt as a tool of international bankers and Jewish conspirators. His newspaper, *Social Justice,* reprinted the vilely anti-Semitic *The Protocols of the Elders of Zion,* that had been forged by Czarist agents in the First World War. An ardent nationalist, Coughlin opposed Roosevelt's policy of aiding England under attack from Nazi Germany. Following his support for an unsuccessful third-party candidate in 1936, Coughlin became associated with the pro-Nazi Christian Front. In 1942, the bishop of Detroit ordered Coughlin to stop his radio broadcasts. He retired in 1966 but continued to write anticommunist and anti-Vatican II pamphlets until his death in 1979. In this selection Coughlin links an international Jewish and communist conspiracy to internationalism and Satanism. (From Charles Coughlin, Father Coughlin's Radio Sermons, October 1930–April 1931 [Baltimore: Knox and O'Leary, 1931], 99–111.)

Patriotism and internationalism! The one born of Godliness and Christliness; the other, the offspring of atheism and greed. . . !

In the United States of America at this moment we have two separate kinds of radicals. To the first class belong those men who have sworn allegiance to the red flag of Russia and whose sole ambition is the overthrown of our government and the subjugation of our people. These unmolested revolutionists, in one sense, are to be congratulated because of their open honesty and straightforwardness.

The other class of radicals who throw up their hands in unholy horror of the red flag, carry no card which proclaims their identity with the Third [Soviet Communist] International. Unlike their Russian cousins they do not preach sabotage, neither do they proclaim openly against religion nor scoff at patriotism. Both are desirous, however, of building up a world-wide rule of class ascendancy. Both are international. The former are less feared than the latter because, due to their power and wealth, they are the greater menace to the American public's prosperity. . . .

What is this called communism? According to its founder, Adam Weishaupt [founder of the Bavarian Illuminati in the eighteenth century] from whom Karl Marx drew his inspiration, communism is necessarily identified with atheism. "Destroy Christianity and civilization," said he, "and we will be happy." Following his master, Karl Marx emphasized the fact that "religion is the opiate of the people." This accounts for the fact that every form of religion has been practically banned from Russia. Hundreds of its churches have been converted into theatres or factories. Catechism is forbidden to be taught to children. . . .

This is the first tenet of communism, because as its founders have said, "Christianity has failed." No wonder the unspeakable Lenin [the father of Soviet communism] once boasted: "We have rid the earth of its false kings. Now let us rid the sky of its false God."

The second general belief of communism is expressed by the word "internationalism." As a matter of fact, the founders of this new communism are neither Russian, nor English, nor American. As a matter of fact, it was the Imperial German Government in 1917 which sent into Russia the revolutionary leaders who had been gathered from the gutters of every nation. It is international in that it hopes to amalgamate the workers of the world in one great nation known as the human race. Trotsky from New York, Lenin from Germany, Bela Kun from Hungary—men from every nation who long since devoted themselves to the anarchy, the atheism and the treachery preached by the German Hebrew, Karl Marx. As Lenin himself writes on page sixty-one, volume XVI, of his *Complete Works:* "The complete world revolution will be obtained only when the proletariat has won victory in the majority of advanced countries. . . . The existence of the Soviet Republic alongside imperialist states cannot long continue."

And lastly, as its name suggests, communism strikes at the right of private ownership. All property, all children, all men and women, all intellectual and material goods are the possession of the State.

As you observe, my friends, the first word in the vocabulary of the communist is "down": "Down with God and religion!" "Down with country and patriotism!" Because it is negative you cannot define it. Communism is the negation of God, or morality and of nationalism. It is a fester of negatives. One might describe it as a maggot which feeds on the ulcers of civilization. Wherever society has decomposed communism appears. When the bulwarks of religion breakdown the slimy thing grows fat on the doctrines of atheism. When rulers become oppressors the followers of Marx and Lenin are multiplied on the open sores of tyranny. Where the greed of capitalism and mass production beget idleness and hunger and discontent, the doctrine of "down with private ownership" becomes the doctrine of the laborer. Yes, and I might also add that wherever the integrity and fidelity of matrimony is treated like a scrap of paper, vows become a parody on truth, the free love of communism becomes the bible of unleashed passions of every man. Behold the maggot and upon what it feeds! No wonder it waxes fat in America. Last year more than one-hundred- and ninety-five thousand divorces or licenses for infidelity were granted. All about us the oppression of the poor almost on a parallel with that which oppressed the peasants of czarist Russia. . . .

Undoubtedly, one of the first doctrines of communism is political internationalism. Alexander the Great was imbued with it when he desired to Persianize the entire world and wept by the banks of an oriental river because there were no more nations to conquer. So was Augustus Caesar. So was Napoleon whose secret ambition was to make the world his footstool and France his throne.

The most loathsome after-birth of the World War has been the revival of this internationalism which in its last analysis is nothing more than universal class rule. On the one hand the Soviet desires to control the entire world by the military arm of an enslaved laboring class. And on the part of certain captains of industry and finance there seems to be a determination to rule the universe through the agency of wealth.

If Russia established its Third International, conservative Europe kept step with it in the establishment of a League of Nations. If Russia clumsily renounced its foreign obligations, the League of Nations adroitly accomplished the same thing through its establishment of a League Court which claims the authority to legislate for all its members on matters of immigration, of tariff and of other affairs of international character. This internationalism is a greater menace to our prosperity than is the type advocated by the Soviets.

Identified both with the League of Nations and with the World Court, whose correct name, bear in mind, is "The Permanent Court of International Justice of the League of Nations," is this new Colossus called the International Bank, which to all advertised purposes exists to facilitate the payment of war debts.

But in the minds of many there is another story behind its illegitimate birth. It is a story in which are woven the name of the J. P. Morgan Banking Company, the company who are the fiscal agents of Great Britain, of France, of Belgium and of Italy; the name of Montague Norman, Governor of the Bank of England; the names of certain gentlemen in our Federal Reserve Bank which is a depository for practically eight thousand smaller banks throughout the United States. Acting in collusion, these men succeeded in lowering the American money to three-and-one-half-per-cent; then exported more than five-hundred-million dollars in gold to Europe despite the fact that the Honorable Louis T. McFadden, the Chairman of the Committee on Banking and Currency of the United States of Representatives, calls this last transaction very questionable insofar as it appears to be beyond the spirit of the law which created the Federal Reserve System.

If victory belonged to one man, it is due to Montague Norman, the Governor of the Bank of England. He has served his country well. He has succeeded in having our bankers establish the international bank at the back door of Great Britain.

Now that our gold has been poured into Europe, these same international bankers of Wall Street and of Washington are anxious that our nation shall surrender its independence by becoming a member of "The Permanent Court of International Justice of the League of Nations." This means that we become identified with that same useless tool during whose brief existence we have experienced so many revolutions and so much unrest. I refer to the League of Nations, whose future is very questionable.

My friends, this internationalism leads only to one thing. It means that the laboring class of this country will be reduced to the same status as that of the worn out European nations. Our ancestors came to these shores to be rid of the persecutions both financial and political and religious which were so common before the XVIII Century. Under brighter skies and with hearts filled with new hopes we and our forefathers built up a standard of living where poverty had practically ceased; where cheap charity was not required and where every man was guaranteed sufficient honest labor and such far-reaching opportunity for advancement that it surpassed the wildest dreams of the peasant class and the middle class of Europe. So today, we are on the verge through a decade of internationalistic philosophy of lowering our standard to meet those of war-torn Europe. The organized effort to accomplish this has been in no little sense responsible for the sadness and sorrow and misery in which we now find ourselves.

Wall Street's Fascist Conspiracy

John L. Spivak

In this selection, published in the Communist Party newspaper the *New Masses* in 1935, John L. Spivak warns of a plot by American bankers, including J. P. Morgan and Company, Kuhn, Loeb, and Company, and Felix Warburg, to engineer a military takeover of America. This conspiracy was investigated by a congressional committee headed by Samuel Dickstein, a New York Democratic congressman. One of the ironies of the Spivak essay was that it was later revealed in documents found in the archives of the Soviet Union in the 1990s that Samuel Dickstein was in the pay of the NKVD, the Soviet spy agency, from 1937 to early 1940. Dickstein was not a communist but a corrupt congressman willing to share information gathered by the Select Committee on Un-American Activities investigating fascist and Nazi groups in the United States. Dickstein later served as a justice of the New York Supreme Court until his death in 1954. John Spivak (1897–1981) was a left-wing journalist whose book on southern chain gangs, *Georgia Nigger*, caused a sensation upon its publication in 1932. He investigated fascist groups in the *United States and Europe in America's Pogroms* (1934), *Europe Under Terror* (1936), and *The Shrine of the Silver Dollar* (1940). His autobiography, *A Man in His Time* (1967), reprinted two of his essays published in the *New Masses* alleging a fascist takeover plot. Evidence for this plot was thin and based on hearsay, but it reveals that conspiracy theory was not a monopoly of right-wing extremists. (From John L. Spivak, "Wall Street's Fascist Conspiracy: Testimony that the Dickstein Committee Suppressed," *New Masses*, January 29, 1935, 9–15.)

An organized conspiracy exists to seize the government by a fascist coup. The Congressional Committee appointed to investigate just such activities has not only failed to follow the trail of evidence to its fountain head—Wall Street—but has deliberately suppressed evidence pointing in that direction. . . .

The suggestion of the existence of Wall Street's fascist conspiracy was made public in November [1934]. The Dickstein Committee then was forced to call General Smedley D. Butler [a retired marine general known as the "Fighting Quaker"], one of those who made the charges to testify. And that was the end of the Committee's interest in proving the charges. . . .

The suppression of evidence by the Dickstein Committee reveals the Committee's real character: With an ostensive mission to uncover fascist activities, the Committee actually turned out to be a close collaborator with the would-be fascist rulers of the country; it covered up the conspiracy by suppressing evidence which led too high up in those financial and industrial groups which run Congress, advise the President, and dominate the country.

It will be shown that financial and economic considerations rise above every other kind, including racial and religious ones. The anti-Semitic character of Nazism has been abundantly demonstrated in these pages; nevertheless this article . . . will reveal Jewish financiers working with fascist groups which, if successful, would unquestionably heighten the wave of Hate-the-Jew propaganda. . . .

Shortly after the Dickstein Committee was empowered by Congress to investigate "subversive" activities, leaders of the American Jewish Committee began to steer the Congressional Committee's investigation. In the course of this steering, information was suppressed which reflected upon leading bankers, as well as information of fascist organizations in which they were interested.

Instead of actually seeking evidence of fascist organizations and who are behind them, the Congressional Committee ignored Fascism until its menace was thrust upon them; and then suppressed vital evidence regarding it. The reason: Wall Street interests such as Morgan's were involved which are tied up with the Warburg interests—which dominate the American Jewish Committee without the knowledge of the overwhelming majority of its membership. . . .

I will show:

1. That the Dickstein Committee refuses to explain why it suppressed evidence for fascist organizations and fascist movements.

2. That the Dickstein Committee knew of an offer made to Gen. Smedley Butler to organize a fascist army of 500,000 men, but ignored this information until it was forced to call Butler.
3. That having called him, the Committee issues a garbled statement of what he said and not until the national furor died down and it issued [only] parts of his testimony.
4. That General Butler named a fascist organization in which some leaders of the American Jewish Committee are active—and that this testimony was suppressed.
5. That a Nazi agent worked in Warburg's Bank of Manhattan and that Felix Warburg was never called upon to explain how he got there. . . .
6. That Warburg financial interests have heavy investments in Nazi Germany. The American Jewish Committee has steadfastly opposed the boycotts of German goods.
7. That the most powerful fascist organizations are controlled by J. P. Morgan's interests.
8. That the Warburg financial interests are tied up with Morgan. . . .
9. That Grayson M. P. Murphy, involved in the plot to organize a fascist army, is a Morgan man and one of those who originally financed the starting of the American Legion for "Big Business" and who supports dissemination of anti-Semitic propaganda. . . .
10. That a Hearst [a newspaper chain] man tied up with Morgan interests captured control of the American Legion, which Butler was asked lead a fascist army. . . .
11. That the American Liberty League [an anti-Roosevelt group] was named by Butler. . . . The League is controlled by Morgan-duPont interests as well as having Warburg representation on it.
12. That the Remington Arms Co., controlled by Morgan-duPont, was named as the body which would supply arms and equipment to the fascist army. . . .

Let us first consider Butler's testimony that he was offered $3,000,000 to organize a fascist army with the promise of $300,000,000 more if it became necessary. . . .

Gen. Smedley Butler testified that he was approached by Gerald C. MacGuire, a "100 a week bond saleman" with an offer of $18,000 in one thousand dollar bills to go to the American Legion convention in Chicago in 1933 to make a speech in favor of the gold standard; it was after this connection was established that MacGuire suggested organizing the fascist army. MacGuire at the time said he was working for Robert S. Clark, who inherited millions of the Singer Sewing Machine fortune. While working for Clark, MacGuire was kept on the payroll of Grayson M. P. Murphy, a Wall Street broker. During the period when these negotiations were going on, MacGuire, who had never owned more than a few thousand dollars, suddenly began to handle large sums of money far beyond $100,000. . . .

What Butler Really Said. . . .

"There was something said in one of the conversations that I had either with Macguire or with Flagg [a fictitious name who could not be traced] whom I met in Indianapolis. . . . He said 'When I was in Paris, my headquarters were Morgan and Hodges. We had a meeting over there. I might as well tell you that our group is for you, for the head of this organization [secret army]. Morgan & Hodges are against you. The Morgan interests say that you cannot be trusted, that you are too radical, and so forth, that you are too much on the side of the little fellow; you cannot be trusted. They are for [General] Douglas MacArthur [chief of staff of the U.S. Army] as head of it. Douglas MacArthur's term expires in November, and if he is not reappointed it is to be presumed that he will be disappointed and sore and they are for getting him to head it.'

"I said, I do not think that you will get the soldiers to follow him, Jerry. He is in bad odor, because he put on a uniform with medal to march down the street in Washington. I know the soldiers. . . ."

There are other portions of the suppressed testimony such as Butler's story of the conversation he had in Indianapolis with a man named Flagg who knew all about the fascist plot to organize an army directed by Wall Street financiers. I have been unable to locate a man by the name who is an Indianapolis publisher, as he was introduced to Butler, and I am inclined to think he was masquerading under a different name and had been sent there to feel out Butler. Because of my inability to locate any such person I am not quoting the testimony.

The most significant part of all this suppressed evidence is that the Dickstein committee dropped it like a hot coal though there was plenty of evidence of a fascist-militarist plot. Nevertheless, when the Congressional Committee had MacGuire on the stand repeatedly, it questioned him about his finances but not one single question was directed at him regarding the American Liberty League, controlled by the du Pont interests (which are tied up with Morgan interests and Morgan interests are tied up with Warburg interests and Warburg interests control the American Jewish Committee which in turn guided this Congressional body) nor of the discussion sworn to under oath about the Remington Arms Co. supplying arms and equipment for the fascist army. . . .

Not a single du Pont or Remington Arms official was called. No—not a single official of the Liberty League on whose body are members of the American Jewish Committee. . . .

If the Congress of the United States really wants to investigate fascist activities why does it not ask this Committee why this testimony was suppressed?

SECTION FIVE

Conspiracy in the Cold War Era

Conspiratorial thinking undoubtedly increased in the wake of World War II and the onset of the Cold War between the Soviet Union and the United States. But the conspiracy theories of the 1950s and 1960s had antecedents in the aftermath of World War I. The strikes in many industries across the United States and the Bolshevik Revolution in Russia accelerated a fear of communism—dubbed the Red Scare—that led to a series of investigations by President Woodrow Wilson's attorney general, A. Mitchell Palmer, from 1918 to 1921. In the 1930s and 1940s, some Americans worried about President Franklin D. Roosevelt's seemingly wayward path to socialism through the New Deal, and fascists and communists in the government. Led by Texas congressman Martin Dies, the House Un-American Activities Committee (HUAC) conducted searches for communists and fascists beginning in 1938. Drawing on these themes, conspiracists in the 1950s and 1960s saw communist conspiracies lurking in the shadows of government, educational institutions, and international organizations. But unlike in the previous Red Scare, conspiracists increasingly linked communism to themes of race, public policy, religion, and popular culture. Their broad conspiracy theories undoubtedly fed a general mistrust of government and a belief in government cover-ups, including a cover-up of the existence of UFOs and, later, government participation in the assassinations of President John F. Kennedy in November 1963 and Dr. Martin Luther King Jr. in April 1968.

One of the most common theories to emerge from this was the belief that the United States and its membership in the United Nations was a precursor to America's enslavement in a one-world government by communists or other insidious subversive organizations working behind the scenes. Conspiracists also believed that communists had infiltrated public health facilities to introduce fluoride into the water supply of the United States to weaken the minds and bodies of Americans and thus lessen their resistance to a communist takeover. Other conspiracists of the period believed that communists occupied high-level government positions in order to overthrow the government. There were, in fact, communist spies who had infiltrated the government on many levels and who had received their orders from the Soviet Union, as revealed by the Venona documents—Soviet diplomatic messages from World War II that were decoded by the federal government. Nonetheless, some conspiracists saw communist influence in nearly every aspect of American foreign and domestic policy. They also linked communist conspiracy theories to race. These theories, articulated most prominently by ex-communist and preacher Kenneth Goff, held that the National Association for the Advancement of Colored People (NAACP) was under the influence of the Soviet Union with the goal of causing racial strife to usher in a revolution.

Conspiracy theories regarding a government cover-up of the existence of alien life first gained popularity in July 1947 when several people reported sighting an Unidentified Flying Object (UFO) crash in Roswell, New Mexico. Numerous other reported sightings followed, and interest in alien life skyrocketed. In response, the U.S. Air Force launched Operation Blue Book in 1947 to catalog and investigate reported sightings of UFOs. There were thousands of such reports, but the Air Force deemed them either hoaxes or the result of mass hysteria. Meanwhile, literature of the 1950s reflected a growing belief, or at least interest, in alien life. Popular works included Frank Scully's *Behind the Flying Saucers* (1950), Donald Keyhoe's *Flying Saucers from Outer Space* (1953), and Harold Wilkins's *Flying Saucers on the Attack* (1954). Scully, as well as Keyhoe in his later book *The Flying Saucer Conspiracy* (1955), charged that government officials were covering up the existence of alien life and evidence of alien spacecraft that had crashed within the country. It was not until the 1970s and the efforts of nuclear physicist Stanton Friedman that conspiratorial thinking about Roswell and alien life became popular. Movies such as *Close Encounters of the Third Kind* (1977) furthered the idea in its portrayal of the military evacuating the area of an alien landing sitr under false pretense.

Assassinations during the 1960s, most notably that of John F. Kennedy and Martin Luther King Jr., have also been the focus of various conspiracy theories. After Kennedy was assassinated in Dallas, Texas, on November 22, 1963, by Lee Harvey Oswald, various conspiracy theories arose. Conspiracists have argued that prominent political groups and organizations were behind the assassination, including communists, members of the Central Intelligence Agency unsatisfied with the results of the Bay of Pigs invasion of Cuba in 1961, and organized crime. The most popular theories pointing to the involvement of communists in Kennedy's death were by Revilo P. Oliver in "Marxmanship in Dallas" (1963) and Carlos Bringuier in *Red Friday: November 22, 1963*. Conspiracists have even pointed to the possibility that Vice President Lyndon B. Johnson, with connections in his home state of Texas, planned Kennedy's death in order to reach the presidency. Other theories have tried to dissect the assassination, contending that

Oswald did not act alone in killing Kennedy. This speculation was fueled by Oswald's murder three days later by nightclub owner Jack Ruby, which appeared to conspiracy theorists to be an attempt to silence Oswald. The unexplained mysteries and coincidences in the case certainly have given credence to some theories, but each collapses under scrutiny, as journalist Gerald Posner has ably shown in his book *Case Closed* (1993).

The sheer number of conspiracy theories about JFK's assassination is mind-boggling, and no other conspiracy theory has occupied the American imagination more. This is strikingly evident in five public opinion polls conducted by Gallup in 1963, 1976, 1983, 1993, and 2003, which have consistently revealed that over half of all Americans believe that Oswald was part of a conspiracy. The lowest figure of Americans believing in a conspiracy was 52 percent in 1963; the highest was 81 percent in 1976. The latter figure was probably influenced by the Watergate cover-up and President Richard M. Nixon's resignation under pressure in 1974. The last three polls have remained constant at 75 percent. The overall increase in the popularity of a conspiracy theory over these forty years can be attributed to the increased availability of literature and web sites evaluating Kennedy's death, as well as the success of filmmaker Oliver Stone's conspiratorial docudrama, *JFK,* in 1993.

Although not as popular as the Kennedy assassination conspiracy theories, the assassination of Dr. Martin Luther King Jr. has educed a similar response. Conspiracy theorists have posited that James Earl Ray did not act alone and that the federal government orchestrated King's assassination because of his increasing criticism of the Vietnam War and anticommunism in 1968. This interpretation of King's assassination was further ingrained into the American consciousness with the airing of an episode of the popular television series "The X-Files" entitled "Musings of a Cigarette Smoking Man" (1996), which portrayed a government agent killing King. But more important, the conspiracy theories about King's assassination clearly illustrate the impact conspiracy theory has played in fueling racial tensions in the United States.

The question of "who" or "what" organization controls the mechanisms of the U.S. government has also elicited many conspiracy theories. Conspiracists contend that organizations such as the Bilderbergers, the Trilateral Commission, and the Council on Foreign Relations (CFR) are the puppet masters and actively plan the direction of American foreign, economic, and political policy to serve their own devious interests. Indeed, many members of these organizations are among the most powerful and influential in American society. Nevertheless, the charge that they control the government is dubious and probably more reflective of the great social, cultural, and political divisions in society. Indeed, the belief in an all-powerful and controlling elite has proven a constant theme in the conspiratorial literature that still resonates today.

The Roosevelt Death: Suicide, Assassination, or Natural Death?

Gerald L. K. Smith

On April 12, 1945, President Franklin D. Roosevelt died at his resort in Warm Springs, Georgia. In the wake of his death, conspiracy theories emerged surrounding the manner in which the president died and was buried. Gerald L. K. Smith, preacher, political activist, vociferous anti-Semite, and supporter of Louisiana senator Huey P. Long in the 1930s, articulated a theory in a pamphlet published by his organization, the Christian National Crusade (1947). In his magazine *The Cross and the Flag* (1947–52), Smith pointed to an international conspiracy led by a coalition of communists and Jews. Not only does Smith personally attack the Roosevelt family, but he also implies that FDR belonged to a Jewish cabal of some sort. (From Gerald L. K. Smith, *The Roosevelt Death: Suicide, Assassination, Natural Death?* [Los Angeles: Christian Nationalist Crusade, 1947], 3, 9–10, 13–17.)

Until Eleanor Roosevelt explains to the world why the casket, containing the remains of Franklin D. Roosevelt, was not opened to be viewed by the public, the death of her husband . . . will remain an unsolved mystery. Not only must Mrs. Roosevelt . . . explain this matter, but it must be explained satisfactorily. Glib answers will not suffice. Ordinary yarns told in the ordinary New Deal fashion will not satisfy a suspecting and suspicious and even a superstitious public.

Every prominent figure who has passed away in modern times has left behind him a responsible group of friends and relatives who have insisted that his body "lie in state" to be viewed by the public prior to burial. This custom was not only violated by the Roosevelt family and the White House palace guard as pertains to the public, but in the case of the eldest son, Jimmy, who barely arrived in time to see the casket lowered into the ground at Hyde Park [the New York residence of the Roosevelt family].

It has been a custom among American families to open the casket even in the cemetery when a member of the family through some unavoidable circumstance was unable to return to the family home or the church in time for the funeral service. James Roosevelt at the time of his father's death was on duty in the South Seas. He was unable to reach the White House in time for the service. . . .

If the Roosevelt family and their political coordinates were of a modest and retiring nature, this might be understood as being merely a natural display of modesty. But the Roosevelt family talks about everything. Nothing seems sacred as far as domestic problems are concerned. Divorce scandals, profiteering scandals, money-making enterprises indulged in by Eleanor Roosevelt and the children, seem to cause them no anxiety or chagrin. Eleanor Roosevelt in her column has discussed everything from the mating dates of the household dogs on up to how much an American girl should drink. She has advocated the intimate and social mixture of black and white. She has entertained Communists in the White House. She has addressed, encouraged, and inspired practically every left wing, pro-Stalin, pro-Communist organization in the United States. The Roosevelt sons have indulged in all the more crude forms of conduct necessary to establish themselves as brazen extroverts. Franklin, Jr., while in Paris, squirted champagne in a diplomat's face. Elliott obtained air passage priority, in time of war, for a dog belonging to his second wife (an actress) at a time when it was necessary to leave military personnel stranded in order to care for this dog belonging to a wife of a "prince." In the midst of a blare of trumpets the Roosevelt daughter, Anna, divorced the father of her children and remarried. The antics of the elder son [James] are too numerous to mention. . . .

Thus, even a superficial survey of the conduct of the Roosevelt family should convince any person with ordinary intelligence that the Roosevelts are not modest, retiring or timid. The casket was left closed because somebody had something to hide. What is was we may never know exactly but some of us have some well-founded suspicions.

Following the death of the president, it was announced that the Roosevelt papers, the Roosevelt letters—in fact, all of the Roosevelt correspondence—would be sent to Hyde Park, but it wasn't that simple. "Sammy the Rose" [Samuel Roseman, Roosevelt's private secretary] assumed complete authority over the files, and went through them letter by letter, paper by paper, pencil note by pencil note, and removed everything that, in his opinion, the public should never see. Were these papers destroyed? If so, who destroyed them? If not, where are they? Who was given authority over the official correspondence of a man who was our president? Why should this ghost writer have ever been given authority to delete the official files of a president of the United States? What is being hidden from the American people? Much, much, much—too much! Not only is much being hidden now, but much was hidden prior to his death. . . .

Various stories have been told about the actual death of Roosevelt. No details were made available to the public. It is believed that when he died the only person with him was a Russian artist, whose name was Elizabeth Shoumatoff [a Jewish immigrant who became a famous portrait artist of the wealthy]. The picture that this artist was making of the president was incomplete. The nurse was not present. No member of the family was in Warm Springs. There is no eye-witness to his death as far as public conventional information is concerned. It is alleged that he was alone at least two hours. Some say that these two hours of solitude took place in the Little White House. Others say that he drove into the mountains and there requested that he be left absolutely alone.

Those who hold to the suicide theory insist that he withdrew from the Secret Service men, his servants, and other associates, put a pistol to his head and pulled the trigger.

The writer knows some people, whose judgment he respects, who are not satisfied with the accounting that has been given of the movements, the conduct, and the motives of the Russian artist. The story of the Russian artist is yet to be told. Time and space do not permit that even the speculations be reviewed in this manuscript.

Those who hold to the murder theory insist that Roosevelt was the tool of a terrible international cabal. They felt that he had fulfilled his purpose. They knew he was in bad health and they feared the he might make some horrible blunder growing out of delirium or senility that might expose their hand and spoil years of successful and satanic plotting. All through history it has been the custom of international conspirators to either murder their tools or condition them, by the power of suggestion, for suicide.

The death of Roosevelt took place one week after he was quoted as saying, "I learned more about Palestine in five minutes from Ibn Saud [King Abdul Aziz of Saudia Arabia on February 14, 1945] than I had known in my entire life previous." Since Roosevelt's death Ibn Saud has been quoted as saying, "He [Roosevelt] assured me that Palestine would never be taken away from the Arabs."

Did Franklin D. Roosevelt commit suicide? Did he draw a weapon on himself which so defaced him or marred his physiognomy that his family and the White House authorities dared not permit him to lie in state for public view?

There sat Franklin Roosevelt, the man, broken in health, with more world secrets on his mind than any living creature, with the possible exception of certain unnamed politicians, who, like their predecessors in centuries past, have played the ambitious politicians like chessmen in the dreadful game of power and authority. These international manipulators have no regard for the comfort and the welfare of the human race. They start and stop wars. The create panics. They promote booms. They pour the blood of millions on the ground. They reduce human beings to slavery and bondage without concern. They are the most powerful men on earth. They are the international bankers. . . . Those of us whose opinions are not formed by superficial radio comment or newspaper headlines believe that Roosevelt occupied a paradoxical position in the international cabal. He played the role of both tool and master, and fulfilled his responsibility in the role of a saint with the motives of a sinner. . . .

If Franklin D. Roosevelt's mind was clear and rational when he sat in Warm Springs, Georgia, in April 1945, he knew that he was about to be overtaken by his conscience, by the peoples of the world, by his own fellow citizens, and by public sentiment in general. He loved nothing as much as praise, glory and power. He knew that the discovery of the truth by the public in general would rob him of everything he held dear. From a materialistic standpoint, he had nothing for which to live. He may have died from shock. He could have committed suicide, and even though he died a natural death, brought on by physical deterioration, it is easy to believe that even this physical deterioration was brought about by a circumstance which cornered this man and forced him to face repudiation in the eyes of the world, because he could no longer divert the attention of the people by a promise, a glib speech, a new emergency, or a world catastrophe. There was no more money to spend, no blood to spill, no promises to make. The end had come.

The sonless mothers, the bankrupt nations, the legless veterans, the battle dead, and the inevitable world chaos remain as monuments and the memorials to this man who wanted to rule the world and failed.

The United States as a Satellite Nation . . . Under Which Flag?

Austin T. Flett

In the early 1950s, Austin T. Flett, an insurance broker from Chicago, believed that a worldwide conspiracy led by the International Cooperative Alliance (ICA), based in London, had been hatched to strip the United States of its sovereignty. The ICA was founded on August 9, 1895, with the expressed intention to encourage ownership and community among employees and international trade in the world. Cooperatives from the countries of Argentina, Australia, Belgium, England, Denmark, France, Germany, Hungary, India, Italy, the Netherlands, Russia, Serbia, and the United States were charter members of the ICA. The ICA still exists today and has 230 member organizations from 92 countries. For years, Flett had contacted members of the Department of Justice and policymakers in Washington, D.C., about what he perceived as a threat to the United States. He poured most of his money from his insurance business into promoting his conspiracy theory about the ICA through lectures and publications, which received much attention from the media across the nation. On March 4, 1958, Flett testified at hearings held by the Senate Subcommittee to Investigate the Administration of the Internal Security Act, and Other Internal Security Laws. Flett provided factual data that he claimed to have culled from ICA publications outlining the conspiracy. A common technique of conspiracists is to take legitimate factual material out of context. Flett charged that the League of Nations and President Franklin D. Roosevelt's administration played a fundamental role in perpetuating the conspiracy to establish a one-world government. According to Flett, the United Nations would be the last step in this transition to a one-world government. (From Austin T. Flett, *The United States as a Satellite Nation* [Chicago: n.p., 1958], 7–18.)

Eighteen years ago, when I started a sales analysis of my competition, known as mutual fire and casualty insurance, I had no idea this analysis would terminate in exposing the main root of an international conspiracy to destroy the social, economic, and political structure and sovereignty of the United States of America via the teachings of internationalism and cooperation, otherwise known in the worldwide cooperative movement or cause as collectivism, socialism or communism.

This testimony is the result of my studying more than 10,000 pages of yearbooks as published by the Cooperative League of the United States of America, 1930–1954, inclusive; reports of the congresses of the International Cooperative Alliance of London, England, 1902–1957, inclusive; and other books and publications I own which are accepted in the worldwide cooperative movement as official or authentic.

The United States tentacle of this movement or cause is a part of, and subservient to, an International conspiracy whose stated goal is to communize national and international trade and commerce, individual, corporate, and national wealth and private property, farmlands, natural resources, the people and governments of all capitalistic nations, and establish a one-world, collectivized, nonprofit, cooperative commonwealth in which the United States of America is to become a participating state policed by foreign troops who will enforce the liquidation of the executive, legislative, and judicial branches of our Government, immigration and trade barriers, our educational, religious, labor, and profit systems, national defense, our flag, and the sovereignty of the United States.

This one-world cooperative commonwealth of nations is to supersede the United Nations . . . successor to the defunct capitalistic dominated League of Nations [founded in 1919, which the United States did not join].

Since 1921 cooperative and Communist leaders affiliated with the Cooperative League of the United States of America have represented the highly organized, politically powerful, tax and legislative favored cooperative movement in our country at international headquarters of this conspiracy, which is known as the International Cooperative Alliance of London, England . . .

Great Britain is considered the motherland of the cooperative and labor movement. British leaders sowed the first seeds of cooperation in Russia about 1900; where it has developed to present day magnitude and threat to our national security. British efforts to organized this movement in the United States were considered a dismal but not a hopeless failure until the advent of the Roosevelt administration in 1933.

As of today, headquarters of the dominating influences in this plot against the people of the United States are (1) London, England (2) Washington, D.C. (3) Moscow, U.S.S.R., (4) Paris, France (5) Rome, Italy.

After leading Asiatics into this movement via technical assistance programs of the United Nations and specialized agencies, Red China is stated to become one of the five great powers in the Communist-dominated cooperative commonwealth of nations.

The two major prongs or fronts used in this movement to attain their objectives are:

1. Peaceful infiltration of the economic, educational, labor, political, religious, and social structures of a nation via the teachings of internationalism, peace and disarmament crusades, self-help, mutual aid, a nonprofit economy, democracy, and the democratic way of life and finally, "Cooperation."
2. The use of force and violence, strikes, sabotage, rebellions and civil war and other means of legal or illegal resistance to capitalistic industry or governments. . . .

The bloodless revolution which took place in our country at the elections of 1932 swept into political power a President and other high government officials who were sympathetic to promoting this conspiracy against the people of the United States with the result the full financial and political resources of the executive, legislative, and judicial branches of the U.S. government, including the armed services in World War II, have been and are being used to promote and finance this conspiracy, internally and, via foreign aid programs, in other nations throughout the world.

The following statement published in 1936 Yearbook of the Cooperative League of the United States speaks for itself: "The Roosevelt administration gave us much help and also showed a more than friendly attitude toward the cooperative movement. It protected cooperation and set up many agencies for assistance to the cooperatives. This is the first Federal Administration this country has ever had that aggressively promoted cooperation and continued to favor cooperation in the face of the hostility of the special interests. . . . The Cooperative League has been consulted, referred to, and assisted up to the present time by many departments of the Government. . . ."

The President of the United States was issuing executive orders for leaders in the cooperative movement to instruct high officials of the United States Government in the teachings of "cooperation." As a result of some of these Executive orders the Tennessee Valley Authority was organized by co-op International Worker's of the World (IWW) [labor union] leaders. . . .

Analysis of the pattern used in the international cooperative Communist movement to capture trade and commerce and the peoples and governments of other nations in Europe, Asia, Africa, and Latin America indicates a rebellion in the United States is now being organized.

A study of this plot indicates that if a rebellion in the United States is a success, our country is to be divided into four police districts and the Southern States may become a colored republic or State in one-world government and will be policed by Soviet troops stationed at Mobile, Alabama. . . .

My study of this conspiracy indicates that contributions of the United States' taxpayers' money to the United Nations Educational, Scientific, and Cultural Organization (UNESCO), the International Labor Office and other specialized agencies of the United Nations promoting a one-world government, is not only [a] violation of the internal security laws of the United States but it is also financing the destruction of our national security.

The disintegration of our assets, our homes, our business, the future of our families, our flag and our country is taking place and unless drastic action is taken immediately by officials of the Government including Members of Congress to protect our national security, the United States of America will become a vassal state in a one-world, communist dominated empire and this . . . the rainbow flag of the cooperative commonwealth will supersede the flags of all nations including the Stars and Stripes.

The Flying Saucer Conspiracy

Donald E. Keyhoe

Since the supposed crash landing of an alien spacecraft at Roswell, New Mexico, in 1947 and the dramatic number of Unidentified Flying Object (UFO) sightings in the early 1950s, conspiracy theorists have been obsessed over unearthing facts relating to the existence of extraterrestrial life. Conspiracists have argued that the government has been the principal roadblock in achieving this goal and has actively pursued an agenda to cover up the truth. One of the first conspiracists to make these accusations was former U. S. Marine Major Donald E. Keyhoe. Keyhoe's first book *Flying Saucers from Outer Space* (1953) was an innocuous indictment against the government, in comparison to subsequent conspiracist literature that accused the government of suppressing valuable information regarding the existence of UFOs. Two years later, Keyhoe took a stronger position in *The Flying Saucer Conspiracy* (1955): the United States had developed protocols in dealing with UFOs and actively undertook measures to silence critics and hide the existence of extraterrestrial life. (From Donald E. Keyhoe, *The Flying Saucer Conspiracy* [New York: Henry Holt, 1955], 13, 24–26.)

For several years the censorship of flying-saucer reports has been increasingly tightened. In the United States, this top-level blackout is backed by two strict orders.

I learned of the first order, a Joint-Chiefs-of-Staff document in the fall of 1953. Known as JANAP 146 (Joint-Army-Navy-Air Publication), this order sets up a top-priority radio system for the most urgent Intelligence reports. Pilots are directed to report from all parts of the world, using this emergency system—and to keep these sightings *secret.*

Under Section III [of JANAP 46] any pilot who reveals an official UFO report can be imprisoned for one to ten years and fined up to $10,000. *(Title 18, U.S. Code, 793)*. . . .

Several fellow Marines, Annapolis classmates, and friends in the other services had given me UFO leads, when security was not involved. Checking with some of them, I soon found that AFR 200–2 was withheld from the public; but after days' digging I had most of the key points.

Classed as "Restricted," AFR 200–2 was issued on August 26, 1953, by order of the Secretary of the Air Force, Harold E. Talbott [President Dwight D. Eisenhower's administration].

Even though I knew some of the facts, this hidden order was a revelation in its apparent distrust of the American people.

Under paragraph 9, ironically called "Release of Facts," it was provided that only *hoaxes, practical jokes, and erroneous UFO reports can be given to the press.*

All genuine UFO reports received by the Air Force must be kept from the public. These include thousands of verified sightings from military pilots, radar men, guided-missile trackers, and other trained observers under government control.

Under AFR 200–2, all confirmed flying-saucer reports must be rushed to Intelligence by teletype or radio. When possible, all tangible evidence must be flown immediately to ATIC (Air Technical Intelligence Center) at Dayton. Such evidence includes:

1. Parts of flying saucers—actual or "suspected"
2. Photos of radarscopes showing "saucer" maneuvers and speeds.
3. Genuine pictures of flying saucers

To conceal flying-saucer discoveries, AFR 200–2 confines the actual UFO investigation to three super-secret groups:

The Directorate of Air Force Intelligence at the Pentagon: the 4602d Air Intelligence Service Squadron, which has special investigators at all Air Defense bases; the ATIC.

Even top-ranking Air Force officers are warned not to probe beyond the first state—securing UFO reports for the three groups.

Because of JANAP 146 and AFR 200–2, hundreds of new, dramatic encounters have been kept under cover.

Some reports, of course, are bound to leak out, especially when saucers are sighted near cities. But even when local papers run front-page stories, the UFO censors often deny the reports or quickly explain them away. One such incident occurred in August 1954.

At 8:30 P.M. on August 28, 1954, a formation of 15 flying saucers approached Oklahoma City. Picked up by radar, the strange machines were spotted from Tinker Air Force Base.

Within seconds, by standing orders of the Air Defense Command, a flight of jets was dispatched.

Under AFR 200–2, emergency teletype messages were flashed to Air Defense Command [ADC] Headquarters, to ATIC, and to the Pentagon.

At the same time, warning alerts were phoned to Will Rogers Airport, the Oklahoma State Police, and to Ground Observer Corps (GOC) posts in a radius of 200 miles.

Meanwhile, in precise triangular formation, the 15 saucers had raced over the edge of the city. The jets, guns set to fire, hurtled after them at full power. Abruptly the formation broke. Changing into a semicircle, the saucers speeded up and vanished into the west.

Immediately, additional alerts were flashed to western Air Filter Centers. When the Tinker Field pilots landed, after a fruitless chase, they were bombarded with questions by a team of Intelligence officers. Then the teletypes clattered again, with urgent follow-up reports.

But though the saucer chase had been seen by hundreds in the city, and the alert was confirmed by the State Police, Tinker Field officers refused to admit the sighting.

Time and again, in the past year, Air Defense fighters have streaked up into the night, trying to force down saucers hovering over our cities. Yet few of these incidents are officially admitted.

From abroad hundreds of reports indicate that this new surveillance covers the entire globe. In 1954 low-flying UFO's set off panic in several countries, among them France, Italy, Morocco, and Venezuela. On September 15, at Bihar, India, a flying saucer suddenly descended to a height of 500 feet and hovered over an Atomic Energy Commission mine. Eight hundred Biharas fled their homes, as a *sadhu* [an ascetic Hindu] warned them the object was "something from Heaven." After its close-range observation of the mine, the disc-shaped machine disappeared in a swift, vertical climb.

Since the fall of 1954, secret investigations have been made in 21 countries, including England, France, Italy, Brazil, Venezuela, and South Africa. After strange reports by hundreds of foreign airmen, several new, mysterious developments have been linked with the so-called UFO's. But in most countries strict government censorship hides these dramatic discoveries.

Roman Catholicism Un-American

O. C. Lambert

Roman Catholicism has been a continual theme in conspiracy theory throughout American history. In a thirty-one-page pamphlet excerpted below, O. C. Lambert links the Roman Catholic Church to a worldwide plan to undermine governments throughout the world, especially the United States, where, he claims, documents show that the Vatican has plans for the violent overthrow of the government. As legal scholar Philip Hamburger shows in *Separation of Church and State* (2002), anti-Catholicism was a major force in the shaping of legislation and court decisions in the late nineteenth and twentieth centuries involving church-state relations. Anti-Catholicism found expression in the postwar period in the writings of journalist Paul Blanshard (1892–1980), an ordained Congregational minister. Although Blanshard was not a conspiracist per se, he maintained that the Catholic Church had an undue influence in politics and was undemocratic. Lambert (1890–1962), a Protestant minister based in Alabama, devoted his career to warning of a conspiracy to subvert American democracy. He spoke to hundreds of churches disclaiming Roman Catholics and authored four books denouncing the Catholic conspiracy, including the two-volume *Catholicism Against Itself.* (From O. C. Lambert, *Roman Catholicism Un-America* [Winfield, Ala.: O. C. Lambert Publisher, 1956].)

In our day the Catholic Church overthrew the government of Spain "violently" less than fifteen years ago. A few weeks ago she overthrew the government of Argentine [*sic*] in the same way. A few months ago they attempted to overthrow the government of Belgium but was unsuccessful.

You may think that they never attempted to overthrow any but Catholic governments, but just remember that all governments of Europe were overthrown and made Catholic. In fact, they boast that the Catholic Church is the only church that has converted whole nations. Well, other churches might do that if they used the same means as the Catholics and Mohammedans! But the gentle religion of Jesus of Nazareth cannot be propagated by force. The truth is that the Catholic Church has attempted to overthrow just as many non-Catholic nations as Catholics. Since she claims authority over "every human creature," she would make no distinction. Just a few years ago, the Pope and Mussolini overthrew the government of Ethiopia "violently." It, you remember, was a Protestant country.

No one can any longer claim that the Catholic Pope and the hierarchy do not advocate the "violent overthrow of government." . . .

There is much talk today about the Communist infiltrating our government, when the fact is, the frightening fact, that the Catholic Church has infiltrated every department of our government, executive, legislative, and judicial. There is in every department of our government a person at the right place at the right time to do the right thing for the Catholic Church. You may have wondered why, as our brethren have been persecuted in Italy [reference is unclear], that our State Department did not immediately demand that the billions of our dollars flowing into Italy stop until our nationals were allowed the freedom in Italy that Catholics enjoy here. Why did the State Department in referring the matter characterize it as a "misunderstanding between the Church of Christ and the Police of Italy? Why did they not tell the truth and charge the government of Italy with breaking their solemn treaty with the United States which guarantees religious freedom to all? Why did they have to be prodded by thousands from all Protestant bodies before they gave a feeble and belated protest? The truth is, and I am sure that it was not accidental, that Clare Booth Luce, a Roman Catholic, has been appointed Ambassador to Italy. It might help also to know that John Foster Dulles [Secretary of State, 1953–59] has a son who is a Catholic priest! The Communists number less than twenty-five thousand in the United States, but Catholics claim more than thirty-one million, therefore I am convinced that the Catholic Church is more than a hundred times as great a menance as Communists!

Not only is government dominated by Catholics in this country, but they are taking over everything; the hospitals, the chaplaincy of the armed services, newspapers, radio, television, schools and business. But the methods and means that are being employed to take over America will have to be a subject of another lesson.

The language of Catholic writers is interesting. A number of quotations given have spoken of "exterminating" Protestants. Protestant people speak sometimes of "exterminating" bed bugs and rats!

I want to emphasize again that nearly all these statements which I have read are by members of the American hierarchy and the books printed here in America. With this fact we will be saved from the blunder of imagining that the Catholic Church in America is different from the Catholic Church in Italy, Spain or Columbia, or South America. They have the same Pope, the same hierarchy, the same Canon Law, and as we have seen the same un-American beliefs. . . .

While the Catholic hierarchy talks glibly about Our Way of Life, and they like to wave the American flag, the frightening truth remains that the hierarchy of Rome is the gravest threat to America and everything we hold dear. Her falsification of history, (admitted falsification,) her doctrine of Mental Reservation, which is a license to lie to promote their diabolical system, marks them as the wolves in sheep's clothing which the Lord warned us against!. . . .

I feel that this lesson would not be complete without throwing the spotlight on Catholic justice exhibited in that frightening Catholic court known as the Inquisition. This will give us a clear picture of what will happen to Americanism if the Catholic Church takes over our country. It will also show clearly why the wise founders of our country placed those wonderful provisions in our Declaration of Independence, our Constitution, and our Bill of Rights. Catholic tyranny was burned so indelibly into their minds that they were endeavoring to fence the Catholic Church and the Inquisition out. Here are some basic American principles. When a person is accused he always has the right to face his accusers; he has the right to call all the witnesses he wishes; the accused stands innocent before the law until he is proven guilty; an accused person always has a right to legal counsel; he cannot be compelled to testify against himself. . . .

Let us now compare the Catholic arrangement. The person who decided whether an accused was innocent or guilty was an "inquisitor" appointed by the Pope—a bishop, an archbishop or a cardinal; the accused was never allowed to know who his accusers were. . . . For eight hundred years this diabolical court burned millions at the stake, and instead of disowning this, present-day ecclesiastics speak of it as the most lenient court ever devised, and insist that this was not cruel. Catholic writers tell us that the Inquisitors were tender hearted and than many of them are enrolled among the "saints"! Burning at the stake was only suspended when the people of Europe rebelled in every country when its terrors could be endured no longer. It should not be forgotten that the Inquisition is now masquerading under the alias as "The Holy Office" [the Vatican], to keep the people from knowing that it is still one of the most cherished parts of the satanic system known as Catholicism. Do we want this in America?

Flouridation: The Crime against All of Civilization

Rev. Lyle F. Sheen

Fears of a conspiracy to put fluoride in municipal water supplies drew wide opposition in many communities in the 1950s. Fears of fluoridation combined expressions of anticommunism, big business, and health concerns. Hundreds of communities voted against fluoridating their municipal water supplies, even though the American Dentistry Association officially recommended fluoridation as a treatment for tooth decay. The fluoridation conspiracy was satirized in the 1964 movie *Dr. Strangelove* in which a character, General Jack D. Ripper (played by Sterling Hayden), launches an American nuclear strike against the Soviet Union after he decides that fluoridation is part of a communist plot that made him impotent. In the 1990s, some environmental and green activists have seen fluoridation as a corporate conspiracy to gain profits. There is no substantial body of scientific evidence that fluoridation of water causes adverse health and there is no evidence of a communist or corporate conspiracy to introduce fluoridation into the water supply. This selection is from a ten-page fold-out pamphlet written by a Catholic priest in Genesco, Illinois, who argues that public health officials promoting fluoridation are not communist agents per se, but they are unwittingly serving the interests of a communist conspiracy. There were dozens of other such pamphlets produced in the decade of the 1950s. (From Rev. Lyle F. Sheen, *Fluoridation: The Crime against All Civilization* [Toledo: Research Publishing Company, 1956?].)

I wish to add my voice to the constantly increasing claim or protest against the completely devilish and un-American plot to fluoridate the water of American cities. . . .

Sodium Fluoride in the water supply is used in Communist countries to keep people in subjection. It attacks the nervous system producing a dullness of mind and a weird sense of weariness. It has been used in asylums to keep patients quiet, and in circuses to keep beasts tame. Years ago it was used to cause abortion. It would not only prevent caries in the teeth of children; it would prevent children completely!

J. Edgar Hoover, chief of the FBI, in a nation-wide statement against possible sabotage, warned us of the "Poisoning of water supplies." He no doubt referred to men who were traitors, who would furnish their own poison, and dump it into reservoirs. Adoption of fluoridation by any community would provide our enemies with a perfect weapon. A turn of a value, and the city is at their mercy. Fantastic? It is happening all over the world, but appears most common in America. Why should Communists spend millions of men and billions in money to conqueror us, if they can persuade us to commit suicide? The men who push this cruel practice may not be themselves Communists, but what is the difference if they accomplish the same thing? Communists at least admit that they are trying to wreck our once great nation. . . .

Only a few years ago American doctors spent millions to defeat the socialized medicine law [legislation supported by the Truman legislation]. How is it that today, they risk their lives, their fortunes and their sacred honor to promote Communized medicine? If fluoride is medicine, we have mass-medication, compulsory at that. But since it is not medicine, but poison, what else have we but mass-poisoning? And promoted by the guardians of our health! To me the whole procedure has all the elements of a nightmare in a madhouse!

Apparently the law which punishes with ten years in prison and a fine anyone who "puts poison into a well, spring, or reservoir of water" is still on the Federal, State and City books. I have never heard of the law being repealed. What, then, has happened to law enforcement in America? Do we still have a Government,—or does the Government have us? By Divine and Civil law, the act of shortening human life by as little as ten minutes is classed as murder. Scientists worthy of the name insist that fluoridation of drinking water can shorten life by ten years! Why are the vital statistics . . . so carefully covered up? Why do newspapers refuse to print material that carries any real argument against fluoridation? Do we not have freedom of the press? Is not the blackmail of editors immoral. . . ?

In conclusion, let me say that a 500 page book would not contain all the objections in detail to this hideous attack upon the health of Americans, made by the Fluoridators. There is so little health left, due to refining of foods, sterilizing and poisoning of foods with sprays that few Americans could pass a microscopic health examination. Rotten teeth are all the proof a good dentist needs of poor health. Until the American Medical Association moves against the processing of foods in real earnest, M.D. will signify Miserable Diet, the source of so much "unearned income."

I know my words will cause enmity—they already have done so. But my concern is not primarily with men, but with God. I am aware that St. John the Baptist had his head cut off for less—but what wonderful company to be in on Judgment Day.

Reds Promote Racial War

Kenneth Goff

Kenneth Goff was a communist from 1936 to 1939 and claimed to have operated under the alias John Keats. In 1939, he testified to the House Un-American Activities Committee (HUAC), under the leadership of Representative Martin Dies, Republican of Texas, about his involvement in the Communist Party. A few years after the end of World War II, he became an evangelical minister and befriended well-known evangelist Billy Graham. In the late 1940s or early 1950s, Hoff made it his personal crusade to preach against communism and warn the public about the communist conspiracy through pamphlets and books. In 1948, he privately published his autobiography, *This Is My Story: Confessions of Stalin's Agent,* and an anticommunist tract, *The Red Betrayal of Youth.* Six years later, he followed with another anticommunist book, *Strange Fire.* In that same year, Goff claimed to have been the principal editor of the popular anticommunist tract *Brain-Washing: A Synthesis of the Russian Textbook of Psychopolitics,* which was purportedly based on the writings of Lavrenti Beria, the Soviet Union's chief of secret police from 1946 to his death in 1953. It has been speculated that L. Ron Hubbard, science fiction writer and founder of Scientology, actually wrote the book. Nevertheless, Goff continued writing various pamphlets, some of which tied various conspiracy theories of the 1950s, such as the existence of alien spacecraft and fluoridation, to the Soviet Union. Increasingly, Goff's writings became more anti-Semitic and racist. In the following excerpt, Goff's racism and anticommunism become dangerously linked. He argues that African American organizations such as the National Association for the Advancement of Colored People (NAACP) were taking direct orders from communists and were important tools in the facilitation of the communist revolution in the United States. Nowhere was this more evident, Goff argued, than the Communist Party's direct participation in challenging segregation in the United States. Goff also perceived the dating and marriages of African American men and white women as precipitating a conspiracy to create one world through one race. Goff believed that cult leader Reverend Major Jealous Divine, otherwise known as George Baker Jr., was a primary culprit in this conspiracy. (From Kenneth Goff, *Reds Promote Racial War* [Englewood, Calif.: Soldiers of the Cross, 1958], 15–64.)

As early as 1936, when I was a member of the Communist Party, I could already see the handwriting on the wall; Earl Browder [general secretary of the Communist Party of the United States of America, 1930–44] and Eugene Dennis [general secretary of the Communist Party of the United States of America, 1944–51, 1956–59] told us in our Plenum meetings, that the proud capitalistic inspired white civilization was the only real remaining obstacle in the path of the final triumph of world Communism. They boasted that once its back was broken by war, depression, and mongrelization, we could see the Red Flag flying over the parliaments of men. Every white member of the Party was taught that chauvinism was a crime. No white girl dared refuse the advances of a black comrade. Her sleeping with a black man was looked on by other members as a badge of honor. On one occasion in 1937, I hear Ella Bloor [a Communist organizer] address over a hundred young girls in the Party, as an underground rally in New York. Many of these girls came from fine homes. They were students in eastern colleges and universities. They were the daughters of judges, lawyers, preachers, and political leaders. Mother Bloor, as she was known in the Party, called upon these girls to sleep with negro longshoremen, so as to win their favor, thereby making them prospects for membership and helpers in East Coast Strikes to halt shipments of goods to Europe. She gave them a list of taverns, cheap waterfront rooming houses and hotels, and restaurants where these longshoremen hung out. Having been given their orders, they were challenged to go into action—as daughters of the revolution, and to remember they would go down into history as the true emancipators of the working class. . . .

The Communist Party has for years concentrated their propaganda on the black population of the United States. We were told in Party circles that the black man was to be robbed of his religion . . . organized into shock troops to do the dirty work and bear the brunt of the street fighting, when the revolution came. In the Party, great stress was laid on using the negroes in the revolution. They were to be armed and turned loose into the streets of our larger cities to carry on mass rape and murder, thereby terrorizing the populace. . . .

While in the Communist Party . . . both my wife . . . and I were assigned to work in the NAACP, which is an arm of the Communist Party. I led a drive to admit Negroes to the dances at the Eagles Hall in Milwaukee, Wisconsin. We promoted trouble in restaurants, by sending in picked blacks with whites to follow as witnesses. The Communist Party was in control of the NAACP from coast to coast. . . .

The spirit of Antichrist is sweeping the world today through materialistic Communism. Their aims are a one-world government, a one-world church and one race of mankind.

It is interesting to note that the one individual who has more to do with desegregation and the mongrelization of the races in America, is a man who is acclaimed by over three million followers as "God Almighty." To the public he is known as Major Divine or Father [Jealous] Divine [George Baker].

My interest concerning him was greatly aroused as far back as the 1930s when I was still a member of the Communist Party. In those days I was conscious of the fact that if he was not a member of the Communist Party, he was at least closely allied with us, and was a strong arm of movement among the blacks. On several occasions when he appeared in his limousine bedecked with gold and silver and surrounded by his black secretaries, he was hailed by many of the black Communists as "God."

Since that time I have watched his activities very closely, and have noted that he has built up a powerful spy ring, which reaches into the homes of our outstanding American leaders—not only in the field of politics, but in military affairs. Through the maids, the baby sitters, houseboys and handymen who belong to his organization, he has thousands of ears alerted to everything that is going on in our nation. . . .

I made it my duty while in New Jersey and Pennsylvania to visit several of his "heavens" and also to attend his blasphemous "Marriage Supper of the Bride and Lamb." . . .

On my arrival in Philadelphia, I hired a cab and set out for the international headquarters of Divine. . . .

On my arrival I entered the hallway, and there on both sides were crude benches upon which both Negro and white women were sitting and singing praises unto Father Divine [a black activist]. . . .

As the morning drew on and the singing continued I became restless and decided that my best bet was to corner the lion in his den. . . .

For a minute he was both shocked an surprised, but I believe he was amused over my abrupt entrance. He sat behind a desk surrounded by 11 beautiful secretaries, both white and black, and it looked as if he had picked the choice of both races with which to surround himself. . . .

In a few minutes the bell rang in the dining room and the "angels" by the hundreds rushed forward. . . . I knew that there would be no chance of getting through this hysterical mob, and I felt that my visit there had come to a conclusion. . . .

As I moved forward, the crowd parted so that I could pass through, and I was placed at the head of the table facing Father Divine and his beautiful white wife, who sat at his right hand. As soon as we were seated two of his young black secretaries were placed on both sides of me, to serve the food and to instruct me. Immediately the crowds on the side began singing and clapping their hands. . . . They sang songs about racial equality, and one went like this:

> *"Father Divine is my Father, Father Divine is walking in the land. Father got the world in a jug, and the stopper in his hand."*

All the singing seemed to be led by the beautiful white woman whom they worshipped as Mother Divine, and she continually looked upon him as one with whom she was deeply in love. Yet one could see in her someone who desires to rule, and one who hated anyone who did not approve of their marriage. She sang a little ditty to him and her eyes sparkled:

"I want the whole world to love you, just as I say I do."

This seemed to please her black daddy [to] no end. . . .
Standing around the table were white and black women who never once took their eyes off of Father Divine. Every once in awhile a white woman would brighten up like a street lamp and begin screaming, "Oh God, I love thy beautiful body—every part of they beautiful body oh God. I love thee oh God." Many of them, after screaming out like this, would fall on the floor and lay prostrate under the table at his feet. . . .

Through all this Divine kept smiling, and every once in awhile he would look at me and shake his head as if to say, "You see they know it, even if you can't believe." On two occasions I caught him winking at his chauffeur as if they were enjoying a good joke or something secret between themselves. . . .

It goes without dispute that they [Communists] are not sincere . . . but are using it [the racial question] as another cunning device to divide the nation and to foster hatred and bloodshed, all in the hopes of accomplishing their one desire—the establishment of a World Communist State.

Parents are Puppets of the Parent-Teacher Association

Tarrant County, Texas Public Affairs Forum

During the Cold War, many conspiracists viewed the power exerted by national organizations in influencing national policy as harbingers of a vast conspiracy. Those involved in American educational institutions and policy making were even more insidious because it was believed that they could indoctrinate America's youth. The movement to establish a national education organization started in 1897 through the efforts of Alice McLellan Birney, Phoebe Apperson Hearst, and the National Congress of Mothers. In 1907, the Parent-Teachers Association was founded as part of the National Congress of Mothers.

In the following selection, the Tarrant County (Texas) Public Affairs Forum outlined its belief that the Parent-Teachers Association (P-TA), which indeed did partially influence the direction of U.S. education policy, was one such organization. Through its removal of parental control in education policy, support of the United Nations, mental health reform, and fluoridation of water, the members of the Tarrant County Forum argued that the P-TA was supporting a conspiracy to establish a one-world government. Parents, the authors of the pamphlet ultimately resolved, should not let an organization that supported such policies control the future—through education—of their children. (From Tarrant County Public Affairs Forum, *Parents are Puppets of the P-TA* [Fort Worth, Tex.: Tarrant County Public Affairs Forum, 1963], 3–23.)

A group composed of parents and teachers is an important part of the educational program. The vast majority of P-TA members join simply because they have children in school. They join because they are interested in what and how their children are taught, physical facilities and what the teachers look like. Parents can find out all of these things. If they should, for some good reason, happen to disagree with curriculum, methods, textbooks, or educators they might assume that their local P-TA unit would be a forum for airing grievances and for possible organized action to correct abuses or deficiencies.

Parents who may have entertained such "controversial" thoughts are rudely awakened. There is no place in P-TA for a non-conformist who wishes to "interfere" with school administration, methods, or curriculum. There is no place in P-TA where a parent may truly be represented. Once a parent joins P-TA, his name and money are used to promote objectives and policies which he cannot choose and in which he has no representation. . . .

No local P-TA, affiliated with the State and National Congresses, can have members who do not belong to the two upper groups. State and National by-laws require joint membership, which includes full approval of all programs, policies and philosophies of the top strata. This condition is not known to the average P-TA member. Many members are unfamiliar with these programs. As long as they belong to the State and National Congresses, members of affiliated local P-TA units are counted as supporting all the schemes of the State and National legislative body.

It is almost impossible to alter any part of the State or National program from the grassroots level.

The standard practice of the P-TA is to forbid any discussions in P-TA meetings which are contrary to P-TA policy on specific issues. Take "pro" and "con" for example. Pro-policy discussions are "proper" matters for P-TA meetings; con-policy discussions are "controversial."

The state handbook warns: "Local associations may not sponsor state legislation that has not been endorsed by the Texas Congress." In other words, a local association is forbidden to think for itself.

As stated in National By-laws local associations are permitted to support "only such international or national organizations as may be approved by the National Board of Managers." Thus, National P-TA can endorse any organization it chooses without consideration for the wishes of 12,000,000 dues paying members, many of whom might object but are forbidden to do so.

The national organization is so far removed from local units that it is difficult for local members to detect or voice disapproval of their actions. . . .

The national P-TA states in its Manual that it believes in the "interdependence of the nations of the world." Further as one of its policies, P-TA says, "The UN should be supported as the best available instrument for world peace."

What is the UN? Will the UN stop war and bring peace? The UN promises much but can it keep those promises? Or is it a trap which promises all things to all men, but which imprisons, maims and destroys. . . ?

The central theme of the UN and one-worldism is general is this: disarmament or controlled armament under and effective international government will bring peace to the world: a UN with an international army to enforce its decisions will mean the end of large-scale wars.

The United States is now disarming. We are doing it unilaterally to "set an example" to "Shame the Russians" into doing likewise. . . .

Under the disarmament plan [,] the United States would (1) stop nuclear test[s], (2) reduce nuclear stock piles, dismantle military bases, (3) turn over our army, navy, and air force to United Nations command. Thus, a "peace" force would be established strong enough to over power any nation or combination of nations. There is no guarantee of "Peace." . . .

With an all powerful military force, the UN would be unquestionably a superstate quite capable of interfering in the internal affairs of all nations. Free elections would disappear, the Constitution would be scrapped, human freedom and property rights would vanish. . . .

The UN Charter being ratified as a treaty has thus suspended our Republican form of government and supplanted it with a world government. Until our participation is ended, the Federal and State governments and the people are ruled not by our Constitution but by the United Nations Charter and all its self-executing involvements as the supreme law of the land. . . .

The National P-TA by their insistence that each member promote understanding of "our world responsibilities" may be acting in good faith under the world law concept but is promoting one-world government which is definitely not to the best interests of the United States. . . .

By its support of [the] UN Educational, Scientific, and Cultural Organization (UNESCO), P-TA agrees . . . to destroy the patriotism and the influence of the homes in the lives of American youth. Why should any world agency decide what and how our American children should be taught? Why should we rewrite our histories to suit UNESCO?

UNESCO's proposed treaty known as the "Convention Against Discrimination in Education" is now before the State Department. Bulgaria, communist Cuba, Czechoslovakia, Hungary, Poland, Byelorussian Soviet Socialist Republic, Ukrainian Soviet Socialist Republic, and the Union of Soviet Socialist Republics participated fully in the drafting of the Convention. Making education the subject of a treaty automatically removes education from under "domestic" law and control. This treaty encompasses every phase and facet of American education, from a definition of what "education" must consist of, down to dictation as to the physical facilities and equipment under which schools may continue to function without being disclosed by UNESCO as "discriminatory." The treaty would deliver the entire American educational system into UNESCO international control. It could close every private, public, and parochial school at will. It could abolish local school boards and professional teachers' organizations. . . .

Under UNESCO control would there be a National P-TA . . . ?

According to the P-TA Manual each local P-TA should have a Mental Health Committee and present programs on Mental Health. . . .

The Mental Health movement seeks to compel conformity in an individual's political beliefs, social attitudes, and personal tastes. The mental health movement is an ever increasing threat to the Church and viciously attacks Christian concepts. In the Mental Health Annals, page 159, we are told that "all concepts of right and wrong must be abolished." The knowledge of the difference of right and wrong is as old as religion as religion itself. To know what is right and to do wrong is to sin. Without the knowledge of right or wrong people everywhere would be as extremely happy as idiots, imbeciles, and nitwits. . . .

Public Law 830, 84th Congress, 2nd session, 1956 is now as the Alaska Mental Health Act. It provides that persons can be transported out of their state and put in insane asylums in other areas of the United States. Numerous states including Texas passed similar laws. . . .

A mentally ill person is defined in the Alaska Mental Health Bill as "an individual having a psychiatric or other disease which substantially impairs his mental health." This is such a broad definition as to include anything form dandruff, toothaches, or fallen arches. . . . No written authorization is necessary, no notice need be given to relatives or friends and "rules of evidence need not apply." The Texas Mental Health Law is equally damaging to the rights of the individual as the National Mental Health Law.

Charges of "mental instability" are increasingly being made in cases where the victim disagrees with policy in which he becomes involved. Americans who openly attack the United Nations have been confined to mental institutions as lunatics. . . .

The aim of the Mental Health movement is unmistakable: nonconformists are in actual peril of being judged insane. . . .

If the American peoples value their freedom of thought and expression, they will do well to regard as suspect very legislative proposal bearing the "mental health" label. . . .

The following statement appears on page 92 of the 1962–1963 Parent-Teacher Manual:

"Since fluoridation of the water supply one part in a million, has been shown to reduce dental decay by one half, local parent-teacher groups should be encouraged to interest themselves in making this health measure available to children in their communities."

Artificial fluoridation has been a widely discussed subject in American medicine and dentistry. Most people know very little about it except that fluorides are supposed to decrease cavities in children. This approach appeals to emotions—no one could be against stopping tooth decay! However, after making a thorough study of the subject parents, teachers, doctors, and dentists will find the following statements are true:

1. Sodium fluoride is a deadly poison, toxic in any part per million. . . .
4. Artificial fluoridation is politically inspired. . . .
7. Artificial fluoridation is mass compulsory medication with a deadly poison. . . .
23. Sodium fluoride has been used for years as a rat and roach poison. . . .
24. Flourine is the identifying element in the fatal nerve and madness gases of chemical warfare.
25. Flouridation has been used in countries taken over by dictators to immobilize the people's will and ability to think. It has been used in Russia for this purpose. . . .

We have seen how a study of the National Legislative Policies of the National Congress of Parents and Teachers can be very revealing. Naturally, any organization claiming to speak for the welfare of children is bound to carry great weight. Criticism of these policies or activities can instantly be smashed down with the charge "enemy of education" or "an attack on the American school system. . . ."

The National P-TA should be dissolved—probably the State Congress, too, if those groups cannot put their house in order. In some parts of the country individual units have withdrawn. Some local units in Fort Worth have taken a stand and withdrawn. However, unless there is a dramatic mass exodus withdrawals might not be effective as a concerted educational program to combat the apathy of parents and teachers who have allowed the situation to assume its present proportions.

Cover of Matt Cvetic, *Conspiracy!*, published by The Big Decision Press in Hollywood, California. The claw of Soviet Communism dangerously looms.

Communism, Hypnotism, and the Beatles

David A. Noebel

The cultural changes of the 1960s—apparent in rock music, drugs, and youth culture—led some conspiracists to explain these changes as part of a communist conspiracy to weaken traditional values. Rev. David Noebel offers such an explanation in his pamplet *Communism, Hypnotism, and the Beatles*, published in 1965 by the well-financed Christian Crusade Against Communism, headed by Billy Hargis in Tulsa, Oklahoma. By the third edition of this pamphlet, over 50,000 copies had been distributed. Before joining the Christian Crusade as Associate Evangelist, Noebel was pastor of the Bible Church in Madison, Wisconsin, where he was also working on his doctorate in philosophy at the University of Wisconsin. This twenty-six-page pamphlet has 168 footnotes, giving it the appearance of a scholarly dissertation. (From David A. Noebel, *Communism, Hypnotism, and the Beatles* [Tulsa: Christian Crusade Publications, 1965].)

It is no secret that the communists have determined in their innermost councils to destroy the United States of America. The methods to obtain our destruction have varied from time to time, but the goal has never changed. One of the methods concocted to bring about the demise of the United States is a weapon know as menticide: a lethal psychological process that produces a literal suicide of the mind. . . !

The communists, through their scientists, educators, and entertainers, have contrived an elaborate, calculating, and scientific technique directed at rendering a generation of American youth useless through nerve-jamming, mental deterioration and retardation. The plan involves conditioned reflexes, hypnotism, and certain kinds of music. The result, destined to destroy our nation, are precise and exacting. . . .

In the years, 1924–1929, A. R. Luria conducted extensive experiments with children in the areas of hypnotism and rhythm. His book, published in 1932, was entitled *The Nature of Human Conflict*. It was subtitled, "An Objective Study of Disorganization and Control of Human Behavior." This communist explains in great detail the nerve jamming of children and how younger children can be retarded mentally and even animalized. . . .

Following the laboratory experiments the communists contracted educators and procured entertainers to convert this devilish scheme into a program scientifically designed to destroy American youth—mentally and emotionally! The intermediary between the scientist, educators and entertainers was a man by the name of Norman Corwin [a well-known scriptwriter and producer for radio in the 1930s and 1940s]. This psycho-political plot was hatched in the United States of America in 1946.

"In July of 1946 a 'cultural' congress was held in Moscow. Norman Corwin, a writer and radio commentator, was the 'honored guest.' He presented the Moscow International Convention with two recordings from the American-Soviet Music Society. Following the convention in Moscow, renewed activity in the recording field for communist causes and objectives became apparent. A few of the fronts which resulted are as follows . . . Young People's Records . . . People's Songs" [original ellipses quoting from "Fourth Report of Un-American Activities," State of California, 1949].

The personnel involved in the make up of these communist recording companies include such well-known personalities as Peter Seeger, Earl Robinson, and Tom Glazer [folk song performers]. . . .

But our younger children are not the only ones being tampered with by the communists. Our teenager is also being exploited. Exploited for at least three reasons: a) his own demoralization; b) to create in him mental illness through artificial neurosis; and c) to prepare him for riot and ultimately revolution in order to destroy our American form of government and the basic Christian principles governing our way of life.

Four young men, noted for their tonsils and tonsure, are helping to bring about the above. When the Beatles conducted their "concert" in Vancouver, British Columbia, 100 persons were stomped, gouged, elbowed, and otherwise assaulted during the 29-minute performance.

Nearly 1,000 were injured in Melbourne, Australia; in Beirut, Lebanon five hoses were needed to disperse hysterical fans. In the grip of Beatles fever, we are told the teenagers weep, wail, and experience ecstasy-ridden hysteria that has to be seen to be believed. Also, we are told teenagers "bite their lips until they bleed and they even get over-excited and take off their clothes." To understand what rock and roll in general and the Beatles in particular are doing to our teenagers, it is necessary to return to Pavlov's laboratory [referring to a Russian psychologist known for his behavioral experiments with dogs]. The Beatles' ability to make teenagers take off their clothes and riot is laboratory tested and approved. It is scientifically labeled mass hypnosis and artificial neurosis. . . .

Attending a Beatle "concert," these young people already possess a built-in inhibitory reflex. This has been placed within them by their parents and society. This reflex includes such things as decent behavior; prohibiting the coed from taking off her dress in public; tearing up the auditorium and wreaking destruction.

However, within 29 minutes the Beatles have these young people doing these very things. The destructive music of the Beatles merely reinforces the excitatory reflex of the youth to the point where it crosses the built-in inhibitory reflex. This in turn weakens the nervous system to the state where the youth actually suffers a case of artificial neurosis. And the frightening, even fatal, aspect of this mental breakdown process is the fact that these teenagers, in this excitatory, hypnotic state can be told anything—and they will. . . .

The Beatles were sponsored in Milwaukee, Wisconsin, by Mr. Nicholas Topping. Nick described his operations (he runs the Topping & Co. International House on 2nd Street) as "making life interesting. . . ." Nick also admits he is active in "freedom marches" [civil rights demonstrations] in Milwaukee.

A personal friend of this writer went to the International House, run by Topping and found not only pacifist literature, but communist literature as well. "Folk Song" books by Peter Seeger and Paul Robeson [a black entertainer involved in Communist party popular front activity in the 1930s and 1940s] were for sale. Mr. Seeger was involved in communist music companies set up in this country in 1946. . . .

The Beatles were in Seattle, Washington for a "concert" in August 1964. "At 8:07 o'clock the show began. First came the Bill Black Combo, then the Exciters, and after them the Righteous Brothers. Next on the program was Jackie de Shannon, who sang 'Needles and Pins' and several other songs, as well as having the audience sing 'Happy Birthday' to her" [quoting *Seattle Post Intelligencer*, August 22, 1964, p. 6]. . . .

In conclusion, it seems rather evident to this writer that the communists have a master music plan for all age brackets of American youth. . . . Although some may disagree, at least *The Worker*, the official publication of the Communist Party agrees with our deduction. "Don't Throw Rocks at Rock n Roll" agrees with our deduction. "Don't Throw Rocks at Rock 'n' Roll" was an official headline of a recent issue of *The Worker* [Noebel cites March 9, 1965, p. 7]. The writer, Gene Williams, believes "it's time that we set out to develop a more positive evaluation of the styles, roots and future" of rock 'n' roll. He contends that "beneath all the juke-box jive there exists an idiom capable of narrating the millions of young lives confined to the ghettos of our cities" and concludes by warning that "no one should disparage the importance of Rock 'n' Roll in today's young people." . . .

We are in the fight our lives of our children. Action taken now by concerned Christians and patriotic Americans is of the utmost importance.

Make sure your homes, churches, record shops, and television stations are not playing or selling Young People's Records, Children's Record Guild records or Pram Records. Make sure your schools are not using these communist records.

Cybernetic warfare is the ultimate weapon and we can't afford one nerve-jammed child!

Throw your Beatle and rock and roll records in the city dump. We have been unashamed of being labeled a Christian nation; let's make sure four mop-headed anti-Christ beatniks don't destroy our children's emotional and mental stability and ultimately destroy our nation. . . .

It is also inexplicably important that you inform your friends, neighbors, preachers, educators—in short—the whole nation. Circulate copies of this report!

The Soviet-Israelite Class Strangles the Arabs

Louis Bielsky

This selection is drawn from a fifty-page pamphlet originally published in Paris in 1965 and later translated into English and Spanish by a Mexican publisher, Ediciones UDECAN (the translator's command of English is obviously limited). Little is known of the author, Louis Bielsky, other than that he was Polish. His anti-Semitism is typical of the neo-Nazi Right in its projection of a Jewish conspiracy to dominate the world. He presents an insidious case that Israel and the Soviet Union were seeking to defeat Arabs as part of a design for world government. The pamphlet reveals how anti-Semitic conspiracists were drawn to Middle Eastern extremism and their difficulty explaining Soviet support of Arab nationalism against Israel and the Sino-Soviet split following Stalin's death. Bielsky's assertions that Stalin, Khrushchev, Roosevelt, and Truman were Jews are complete fabrications, and his views are so fantastic that they warrant inclusion in this volume only because his publications were widely circulated in Western Europe, Latin America, and North America throughout a loose network of neo-Nazi and anti-Semitic extremist organizations.

Preface

The only purpose of this edition is to divulge the historic truth about great political secrets and vital events now happening in the world. For that reason, copies of this edition are distributed in a gratuitous way, and we thank the philanthropists in Mexico City who financed this edition with the only wish of benefiting humanity.

Zionism and Communism. . . .

The First World War, 1914–1918, offered an opportunity for Judaism to take a giant step toward the creation in Palestine of the State of Israel. The projected disintegration of the Ottoman Empire by Judaism was to give the opportunity to conquer Palestine. England was then governored by a Masonic and crypto-Jewish government in 1916, in the midst of the world war, the British War Cabinet, composed of freemason officials, promised to help establish a "Jewish National Home in Palestine." . . .

It was very significant that the Soviet Union was the first to recognize the State of Israel and the one that proposed its admission in the United Nations Organization. . . . The Communist support of Zionism could not be clearer and more decisive. . . .

The struggle between Stalin and the State of Israel, which he had enthusiastically supported, came about in the following way. After the underground Jews Roosevelt and Harry Salomon Truman delivered Eastern Europe and China to their Israelite brother Stalin, according to Hebrew plans to establish communist dictatorships all over the world, Stalin's paranoic aspirations of power made him fell almost as if he was the master of the world, desiring to become . . . the supreme leader of International Judaism. This provoked, at the end of 1948, a rupture between Stalin and the Stalinist Jewish communities on the one hand and the rest of International Judaism on the other.

In this case the differences between Stalin and Stalinist Judaism, which were being discussed and resolved for some time in the parliamentary way it had been usual for many centuries, in the Jewish secret Universal Rabbinical Synodus came to the extreme of totally breaking the institutional unity of International Israel. Stalin and his secret sect disregarded the authority of the World Jewish Congress and of Bernard Baruch [an American financier and Democrat Party supporter], over the Israelite communities of the Soviet Union and the red satellite states in Eastern Europe. Baruch used Zionism—which had received great support from the Jewish Soviet leaders—, as a weapon against them, thus pushing the Israelite leaders of the Kremlin to start a ferocious war against Zionism, against the state of Israel, the World Jewish Congress of New York, the B'Nai B'Brith Order, and against the hidden leader of all this, Bernard Baruch. At the same time, Stalin and his Hebrew followers also started in the Soviet Union as well as in the Socialist dictatorship, a brutal prosecution, not only against Zionists, but rabbis and Jewish community leaders, who were suppose to be loyal to the New York Jewish command. . . .

Truman and the Hebrew gang that had handed Eastern Europe and China over to Stalin, now headed the struggle to prevent him from achieving control of the world. . . .

Although the majority of the leaders of international Judaism directed from New York wanted to prevent Stalin from achieving world control, they did not want to destroy communism at all, because that would mean the destruction of their own work and the loss of everything that the Jewish world revolution had gained in 32 years. Therefore, the policy of Judaism, directed from New York, was purely defensive both in the political and military aspects trying to recover Russia, China, and the satellite states by means of the destruction of Stalin and Stalinism in general, substituting them with Communist Jews loyal to the Jewish power from New York. . . .

The Jew Nikita Saloman Khrushchev finally gained control of the situation; his real name was Salomon Pearl Mutter, but like the rest of Soviet Jews he changed it in order to hide his Judaism and to appear as an authentic Russian. . . . However, the New York Jewish powers continued to distrust him, because he was a creation of Stalin. Annoyed because of this distrust Khrushchev, in one of his well-know outbursts of anger, supported the action taken by President Nasser of Egypt to take over the Suez Canal [in 1956] . . . but he felt sure that the Jewish power in Moscow could recover it in the future by means of paratroopers and the advance of the Soviet tanks and armies over the Suez Canal, or by turning Egypt into a satellite state progressively controlled by the Soviet Union.

Anyway, this incident caused even more anguish in Jewish communities of all the world, among the Hebrews of both rival bands, and all the institution of internal reunification that I mentioned before, increased with success the attempts of reconciliation that were finally able to finish the disastrous schism which had slowed down the overwhelming advances of Communism. . . .

Soon after this, the government of Eisenhower would help Fidel Castro [who came to power in Cuba in 1959] reach power and President Kennedy would prevent every effective action to overthrow him. In order to complete this betrayal, the crypto-communist John F. Kennedy planned secretly with Nikita Salomon Khrushchev a way to justify, before the opinion of the American people, a vile treaty that would pledge the United States government to support the red government of Fidel Castro against any invasion, thus guaranteeing the consolidation of the communist regime in the enslaved Cuba. . . .

The Jews went to China more or less two thousand years ago. Due to mixed marriages with the Chinese, to climate conditions and the food regime, a community of Chinese Jews was formed through the centuries. . . . These Chinese Jewish "marranos" were the ones who organized the Chinese masonry first, and later they took very important part in the organization of the Communist Party in China. . . . Mao Tse-Tung [the leader of the Chinese Communist Party that came to power in 1949] was already, after Stalin, the most powerful leader of world communism. Therefore, it was natural that Mao and his followers thought Mao . . . should inherit Stalin's place as the Supreme leader of communism. This thing will never be accepted by International Judaism, which wants to have Jews in the leadership of communism. . . . [T]he Jewish powers in no way want—through their dispute with Mao Tse-Tung—the destruction of communism in China, as that would mean a catastrophic step back in Hebrew plans to communize the world. What they want is to promote the revolt against Mao and his gang to overthrow and substitute them by communists . . . loyal to Moscow. . . .

In a common agreement, the leaders of World Judaism both from New York and Moscow, approved the following policy with regard to the Arabs and the State of Israel. . . . The Soviet government would be instructed to offer all kinds of military and economic aid to the Arabs, but this would force them, whether they want it or not, to fall into the hands of the Soviet Union. . . . Thus, Islam, which would be hard to be conquered by atheistic communism, has been penetrated in this skillful manner, and it will be gradually conquered if the powers of the Free World do not arrive to stop it. . . . It is obvious . . . that Jewish imperialism and the communist revolution have [plans] for the conquest of the Arab states and the Islamic world.

Paris, February 1965

Red Friday: November 22, 1963

Carlos Bringuier

The assassination of President John F. Kennedy on November 22, 1963, by Lee Harvey Oswald has been a continual subject of conspiracy theories. In this selection, Cuban expatriate and lawyer Carlos Bringuier claimed that Cuban leader Fidel Castro and communism were responsible for Kennedy's assassination. Bringuier bases his opinion on two facts: his direct experience under Castro's regime and his encounters with Oswald in New Orleans. In the early 1960s, Oswald founded the Fair Play for Cuba Committee (FPCC) chapter in New Orleans, a pro-Castro organization. One of the first tasks Oswald tried to achieve was the infiltration of Bringuier's anti-Castro organization in New Orleans, the Student Revolutionary Directorate. Oswald met with Bringuier and told him that he wanted to join his organization to fight Castro. Later he gave him his Guidebook for the Marines. While distributing FPCC flyers in August 1963, Oswald was confronted by Bringuier for his duplicity. A few days later after their confrontation, Bringuier, Oswald, and anticommunist

Edward Butler squared off on a New Orleans radio station to debate the merits of communism. Butler portrayed Oswald as a traitor and mentioned his defection to Russia. It appears that this event was the turning point for Oswald. In the wake of Kennedy's assassination, Bringuier testified before the Warren Commission about his encounters with Oswald. In 1993 he was portrayed in Oliver Stone's docudrama *JFK*. (From Carlos Bringuier, *Red Friday: November 22, 1963* [Chicago: Charles Hallberg, 1969], 3, 4, 14, 108, 112–15, 116, 119, 121.)

For several years after the assassination I dedicated part of my time to studying the 26 volumes of the President's Commission on the Assassination of President Kennedy, knowing that the only way scavengers and propagandists could be exposed is by presenting the truth as I know it from my experience and testimony.

The Government of the United States has made not only one mistake, but many. And when someone makes a mistake, he has to pay the price. The Government is paying dearly for its mistakes.

The Government gathered evidence proving that Lee Harvey Oswald was the assassin and then turned the report over to the people of the United States with the thought that the people would believe it. The report, however, was written by a staff that was suspect in the people's mind for many reasons: It was, for example, integrated by persons who at one time or other defended the travel of students to Communist Cuba, or opposed anti-Communist laws in their respective states. I don't mean that these persons are not honest, but the Commission certainly was not wise in hiring them. How could they hire a man to investigate Oswald's activities and motivations who had been publicly in favor of allowing young students to go to Castro's Cuba and be indoctrinated in communism?

Immediately after the publication of the "*Warren Report*," several books were published presenting diverse theories but almost all of them contradicted the findings of the Commission. The many theories presented caused confusion and made it difficult to counter their effect. If they would have presented one or two theories, then it would have been easy to prove their falsehood but in this way you have hundreds of theories and it is almost impossible to expose each one of them.

From the moment the "*Warren Report*" was published until now there has been a lack of communication between the Government and the people of the United States, a lack that has served the Communist efforts to undermine the prestige of some of the institutions of this country. . . .

In this book I have tried to present the truth, and nothing but the truth as given to us by reliable witnesses such as the dedicated members of the Federal

Bureau of Investigation, the Secret Service, the physicians, the reporters and other eye witnesses to the assassination of President John Fitzgerald Kennedy on November 22, 1963, the day that will go down in history as Red Friday. . . .

There have been many theories in regard to Oswald's motivations. After an intensive study of Oswald's personality, I can reach only the conclusion that Oswald killed President John Fitzgerald Kennedy by reason of his communistic ideals, as previously explained.

If a conspiracy to assassinate JFK originated in Havana, Moscow, or among subversives somewhere in the United States, this is something we cannot prove, but there is evidence to suspect that a Communist conspiracy involving several persons besides Lee Harvey Oswald is a distinct possibility. . . .

To understand exactly what circumstances triggered the assassination, we cannot look at world problems as they are today, but must look at them as they were in 1963 to realize the titanic struggle that was going on in this hemisphere. On one side, Fidel Castro and his followers were trying to bring about a violent bloody, communistic revolution in Latin America. They knew that their's was a battle for the survival of the only Communist base in America: Cuba.

On the other hand, a young, intellectual President, John F. Kennedy, was trying to bring about a peaceful democratic Revolution for social, political, and economic reform in Latin America.

The American continent was too small for both giants. Only one could be the leader of the masses of people hungry for a chance to improve their living conditions. It was obvious, Kennedy, with all his possible mistakes, was the most dangerous enemy that Castro had to confront.

Castro saw his popularity among the liberal, intellectual, leftist and moderate Latin Americans slipping from him to favor Kennedy, as Cuba failed to live up to her promise of a "workers Paradise." John F. Kennedy became the most popular United States President in history to the masses of people in Central and South America. His name was magic south of the border. . . .

In December 1962, at the Orange Bowl in Miami, Florida, President Kennedy received the flag of the Cuban Brigade 2506 (defeated at the Bay of Pigs on April 17, 1961). During the ceremony, Jacqueline Kennedy praised the courage of those brave men and the President promised to return their flag, in person, to a free Havana. Fidel Castro knew . . . Kennedy meant it.

The only major defeat JFK ever received in his life was the defeat of the American sponsored Bay of Pigs invasion. Until he could avenge that mistake, he could not look to other foreign problems with confidence. On July 22, 1963, in a letter to me Senator Edward Kennedy stated vigorous support for a policy which will rid our hemisphere of Communism and restore freedom in Cuba. He also pointed out that the U. S. Government has continued a firm policy which includes no assurances against the invasion [of Cuba] in the absence of on-site inspections and which in no way modifies out Inter-American treaty commitments [the Inter-American Reciprocal and Assistance (Act of Chapultepec) signed in 1945 and the Inter-American Treaty of Reciprocal Assistance (Rio Pact) signed in 1947]. . . .

On November 18, 1963, President Kennedy delivered an address in Miami, KENNEDY VIRTUALLY INVITES CUBAN COUP. . . .

Five days later, President Kennedy's life was cut short by bullets fired by Lee Harvey Oswald from that sixth floor window in the Book Depository Building in Dallas, Texas. His promise to return the Cuban freedom fighters['] flag to a free Havana could not now be fulfilled and Fidel Castro remains in power. The giants met and Communism won. . . .

One of the mistakes made by Castro after the assassination was his anxious desire to confuse the investigative agencies of the United States. A clear example of this is contained in a letter intercepted by the Secret Service on December 5, 1963, postmarked Havana, Cuba and addressed to Oswald in Dallas, and dated November 10, 1963. It was signed Pedro Charles and was written in such a way as to indicate . . . Oswald had been paid by Charles to carry out an unidentified mission which involved accurate shooting.

In the meantime, on November 28, 1963, another letter postmarked in Havana and addressed to . . . Robert Kennedy . . . was turned over to the FBI. This letter, dated November 27, 1963 and signed Mario del Rosario Molina, alleged that Oswald assassinated President Kennedy at the direction of one Pedro Charles, a Cuban agent who had traveled to the U. S. under various aliases and who met with Oswald in Miami to pay him $7000.00.

An examination of both these letters was conducted by the FBI and it disclosed that they were both typed on the same typewriter, both envelopes came from the same batch, both postmarks contained similar irregularities, and the same type pen and ink was used to sign both. The FBI concluded: "Based on these circumstances, including the postmark on the first letter (six days after the assassination) and the fact that both letters were prepared on the same typewriter, it appears this matter represents an attempted hoax."

Who can honestly believe that the Castro government did not aid in [the] perpetration of this hoax? Anyone familiar with the censors in a communistic country is aware that neither letter could have left Cuba had not the government wanted it that way, to confuse the American investigative agencies into blaming the hoax on the anti-Castro Cubans who were trying to frame Oswald and Castro. There is no other possible explanation in light of the fact that Castro was trying desperately to avoid any connection with the President's assassination.

It was a pity that Oswald could not have been brought to trial. Then, it may have been possible to know many things as absolute facts that today we believe to be true but cannot prove. If Oswald had not been murdered, Oswald would not have been the lone defendant on trial for the assassination of President Kennedy.

International Communism and Fidel Castro would have been on trial with Oswald and they knew it. . . .

There is no question in my mind that the best gift Castro and his comrades have ever received was the killing of . . . Oswald at the hands of Jack Ruby. . . . But, let us never forget the one indisputable fact, President John Fitzgerald Kennedy was assassinated by Communists and in naming Oswald as the assassin, the *Report of The President's Commission on the Assassination of President John F. Kennedy* is absolutely correct. . . .

One day, sooner or later, I expect to have the hard facts to prove that it was Castro's "line" inside the Communist movement that pulled the trigger of Oswald's rifle. In the meantime, I want my four children to walk with their heads up, looking straight into the eyes of their friends and neighbors. I want that all Cubans in exile can be proud of themselves rather than ashamed by the smear campaign brought against us, the anti-Castro, anti-Communist Cubans and I want all freedom-loving human beings, honest conservatives and honest liberals to be proud of a system of government which allows liberty and freedom even to those who work every day to destroy it. Maybe for that very reason, the United States is so strong and maybe for that reason, its enemies must appeal to violence, hate and assassination.

Blacks Seek Assassins of King

The Black Liberator

This selection reflects a belief that the assassination of civil rights leader Martin Luther King Jr. by James Earl Ray on April 4, 1968, was part of a larger conspiracy. Theories about the King assassination gained momentum when King's son Dexter met with his father's convicted murderer in prison in 1997. At the meeting Dexter King announced that he was convinced of Ray's innocence. Conspiracy theorists gained further momentum in 1999 when a Memphis jury in a wrongful death suit awarded the King family a symbolic $100 and declared that the assassination was a larger conspiracy involving bar owner Lloyd Jowers and several unknown conspirators. Although there was clear evidence that Ray was the shooter and little substantial proof that he was involved in a conspiracy, Ray continued to deny that he was guilty. His death in 1998 did not end talk of a conspiracy involving white supremacists, the FBI, Army intelligence, and the Mafia. This selection, from a short-lived black radical newspaper, the *Black Liberator*, based in Chicago in the late 1960s, asserts that the King assassination involved the U.S. government. (From "Blacks Seek Assassins of King," *Black Liberator*, April 1969, p. 4.)

The convicted assassin of Dr. Martin Luther King, Jr., James Earl Ray has been sentenced to a 99-year prison term by the Memphis court, after a ludicrous trial which ended in Ray's confession that he murdered Dr. King and his allusion to the court that he was part of a conspiracy.

The deal that was made between defense attorney Percy Foreman and the prosecuting attorney Phil M. Canale to swiftly place Ray in solitude to avoid scrutiny by an extended court trial, reveals infamous undermining by the Memphis court to smother the truth about King's assassination.

It is obvious that James Earl Ray, a petty criminal who has spent one-third of his 41 years in jail, could not have masterminded the King murder. How could he have expertly eluded the Memphis Police Department, the FBI, and escaped to Canada and Lisbon? Where did he get $15,000 [allegedly found on his possession at the time of his arrest]?

We agree with the statements made by Reverend Ralph Abernathy [an associate of King]. . . . that Ray was involved in a conspiracy and probably served as the "Fall Guy." By making a deal to avoid a full court investigation, the racist Memphis court and federal government are seeking to avoid any thrust of BLACK OUTRAGE if the trial reveals POLITICAL COLLUSION.

The black community demands that President Nixon reopens investigation into the King assassination by appointing a black commission to direct the inquiry. Such a commission should be composed of black men who understand the meaning of justice, since they have been unjustly intimidated by the racist court system. . . .

If the White Establishment thinks that by quietly throwing dust over the King assassination by convicting a scapegoat such as James Earl Ray, it has certainly miscalculated. Black people will remain outraged until all conspirators are tried for their will be no law and order without justice!

Kissinger—The Council on Foreign Relation's Man in the White House

Phoebe Courtney

In her second book examining the Council on Foreign Relations (CFR), Phoebe Courtney, a conservative activist and author, outlined an immense conspiracy to dictate American foreign policy through powerful forces associated with the CFR. She found this influence evident in the Eisenhower, Kennedy, and Johnson administrations. She argued that the Nixon administration's foreign policy was controlled by the CFR through Henry Kissinger, Nixon's first national security advisor and later his secretary of state. (From Phoebe Courtney, *An Exposé—Nixon and the CFR* [New Orleans: Free Men Speak, 1971], 21–43.)

Background on Kissinger

On December 2, 1968, Nixon announced that he had appointed Harvard Professor Henry A. Kissinger as his assistant for national security affairs to oversee the foreign and defense policy machinery of the White House. . . . By setting up Kissinger as the key foreign policy advisor . . . the CFR now has its man at the pinnacle of government, overseeing the activities of both the State Department and the Defense Department.

That the slot of chief White House policy advisor on national security is controlled by the CFR, regardless of which party is in power, is obvious from the fact that the man Kissinger replaced—Walt R. Rostow, President Lyndon B. Johnson's special assistant for national security affairs—was. . . . also a high-ranking member of the CFR. . . .

Kissinger's Views on Foreign Policy

It is not President Nixon who makes the foreign policy of this nation. It is the CFR, acting through Henry A. Kissinger, who makes the foreign policy of the Nixon Administration. . . .

Kissinger shares the Liberal intellectual commitment to "peace through law" and "reasoned dialogue" with the Soviet Union. In words spoken and unspoken, Kissinger clings to the Liberal illusion that our differences with Communism are negotiable, refusing to accept the fact that the only "reasonable dialogue" which results in treaties advantage of the Soviet Union and the disadvantage of the United States. . . .

There has been some confusion regarding Kissinger's real views. Kissinger is the author of several books on the subject of nuclear strategy and foreign policy. However, during the period of 1957 to 1960, Kissinger changed his views—a fact overlooked by some political analysts.

In 1957, Kissinger wrote *Nuclear Weapons and Foreign Policy,* which was published for the CFR. In that book, Kissinger had argued that the most effective deterrent to any substantial Communist aggression was the knowledge that the United States would employ nuclear weapons from the very outset.

Four years later in his book, *The Necessity for Choice, Prospects of American Foreign Policy,* Kissinger stated that he had rethought the theory and decided that it was wrong. . . . Kissinger stated: "This is the measure of the task ahead: Simultaneously with building up our capability for limited war and our conventional forces, we will be embarked on arms-control negotiation of crucial import." In other words, it would appear that the future foreign policy of the United States, based on Kissinger's advice and influence, will be endless no-win wars against Communist aggression in areas throughout the world selected by the international Communist conspiracy headquartered in the Kremlin, while at the same time negotiating with the Communists on disarmament of the United States. . . .

Nixon Administration Defends Communist Cuba

It will be recalled that when campaigning for the presidency in Key Biscayne, Florida on October 12, 1968, Nixon declared that communist Cuba "cannot remain forever a sanctuary for aggressions and a base for the export of terror to other lands." During his campaign, Nixon also stated regarding Communist Cuba that "U.S. foreign policy requires. . . . this kind of government be quarantined; quarantined for the sake of peace." . . .

And this, in spite of the fact . . . as of May 30, 1969, Castro was continuing to build up his military forces on the island. . . . U.S. intelligence authorities stated that more than 8,000 Russian military advisors and combat soldiers were stationed in Cuba. In addition to this, several hundred Cuban anti-aircraft missile experts returned in 1969 from North Vietnam after being trained on SAM, ground-to-air rocket launchers. . . .

Acting as the President's chief foreign policy advisor, Kissinger has barred all other agencies of the government from asking Cuban policy studies without his advance approval.

This veto power gives Kissinger tight control over what Cuban policy papers are to be presented to the National Security Council for President Nixon's consideration—clear evidence again of the influence and control exercised over the President by the CFR man. . . .

Is it, therefore, any mystery why the CFR's man, Henry A. Kissinger, is promoting his soft-on-Castro line? And should it be born in mind, the official soft-on-Communist Castro line of the Nixon Administration is being pursued at a time when Cuba presents a clear threat to the national security of the United States. . . .

Kissinger Promotes "Sufficiency" in Weapons for U.S.—Not "Superiority"

At Nixon's January 27, 1969, press conference, in answer to a question regarding his previous position advocating "superiority" and Kissinger's view of "sufficiency," Nixon stated, "I think the term sufficiency is a better term, actually, than either 'superiority or 'parity.'"

There could hardly be a more controversial word in relation to national defense that the word "sufficiency." Military generals—unlike grammarians—rarely define "sufficiency" to mean "enough."

Because of the obvious and ominous control which Kissinger exerts over President Nixon, it can certainly be assumed that if any question arises as to the definition of the world 'sufficiency' in national defense, it will be Henry Kissinger, a member of the Communist appeasing CFR, who will determine what sufficiency means. And, because of his views . . . Kissinger's definition of sufficiency in national defense can only mean that the United States will—under such policies—degenerate into a second-rate nation.

SECTION SIX

Conspiracy in Contemporary America

Political scandals, economic turmoil, and war have allowed conspiracy theories to flourish in modern America. The break-in at the Democratic National Committee's headquarters at the Watergate office complex in 1972 that ultimately implicated members of President Richard M. Nixon's administration, leading to Nixon's resignation in 1974, eroded American confidence in the government. Shocks to the economy led to conspiracy theories that blamed various cabals for allegedly controlling the nation's political leaders. The Vietnam War and police infiltration into radical groups also fostered an environment of political paranoia. All these examples share a common thread: whereas conspiracists during an earlier era had viewed communism and external threats as the most dangerous problems facing America, conspiracy theorists since the Watergate scandal have increasingly pointed to the government of the United States as integral to conspiracy. In this sense, government became the enemy.

Many of the most popular conspiracy theories in recent times have focused on the CIA, the FBI, and the National Security Administration. For example, some conspiracists have accused the CIA of conducting medical experiments on American citizens in Jonestown, Guyana. Additionally, conspiracists have charged that the CIA has protected Nicaraguan anti-Sandinistas who allegedly exported cocaine into the United States to undermine the underclass in urban America. The Federal Emergency Management Agency (FEMA) has also been accused of intentionally sparking a disaster in the United States in order to gain emergency powers, and then take control of the government and precipitate the establishment of a one-world government or "New World Order."

The establishment of such a "New World Order" has also found expression among the militia movement in the United States. According to the FBI, the militia movement first gained momentum in the early 1990s. Mostly found in western states, militia members have justified their organization because they are opposed to the ability of the government to tax and regulate society. The militia movement received national attention when two members of a militia family were killed in a confrontation with federal officials in Ruby Ridge, Idaho, in 1992 and when a government confrontation with a Christian cult, the Branch Davidians, in Waco, Texas, left dozens of followers dead in 1993. As a response to these events, militiamen increasingly viewed the government as an enemy conspiring against American liberty.

The emergence of the human immunodeficiency virus (HIV) and acquired immunodeficiency disease syndrome (AIDS) have prompted some conspiracists to conclude that the United States government created the virus as a biological weapon. A study conducted by the Rand Corporation and Oregon State University in 2005 revealed that nearly half of African Americans surveyed believed that HIV was manmade. More than a quarter of blacks believed that HIV was produced in a government laboratory, and 12 percent believed it was created and spread by the CIA. A slight majority believed that a cure for AIDS was being withheld from the poor. Dr. Alan Cantwell, in *AIDS and the Doctors of Death* (1986), articulated one of the first theories to emerge about the purpose of AIDS: that it was introduced in the gay community across the United States under the guise of Hepatitis B testing. Others such as Haki Madhubuti, Dr. William C. Douglas, and Dr. Gary Glum have elaborated on this theory, arguing that AIDS was devised in order to prevent an increase in the population of African Americans, Asians, and homosexuals.

Since the terrorist attacks on September 11, 2001, conspiracists have formulated several theories alleging the involvement of the federal government in the terrorist attacks. The majority of these theories purport that the administration of President George W. Bush plotted the terrorist attacks to provide *casus belli* for the wars that followed in Afghanistan and Iraq. Conspiracists such as David Ray Griffin and Steven E. Jones have based this information on detailed analysis of photographs and videotape of airliners crashing into the World Trade Center and the Pentagon. They claim that the Twin Towers collapsed because of explosives planted by the government, not because of burning jet fuel. Conspiracists have also claimed that the Pentagon was attacked by a missile, not American Airlines Flight 77. One conspiracist, Carol A. Valentine, has argued that the emergency teams responding to the Pentagon used water rather than foam to keep the fires burning longer and cause more destruction. Each of these theories was evaluated and debunked in an issue of *Popular Mechanics* (March 2005) but nevertheless continue to have a receptive audience, particularly on the internet. Thirty-six percent of the 1,010 Americans polled by the Scripps Survey Research Center at Ohio University in 2006 believed that the government planned the September 11 attacks in order to go to war in the Middle East. But as the pollsters pointed out, this sentiment may reflect the findings of another 2006 poll, in which 54 percent of Americans expressed discontent with the government, a stark contrast with the 10 percent of Americans who expressed a similar view in 2001.

Public outcry over the seeming failure of the local, state, and federal governments after Hurricane Katrina, which obliterated the Gulf Coast in the fall of

2005, spurred further conspiracy theories. Almost immediately, some African American residents of New Orleans and Nation of Islam leader Louis Farrakhan claimed that the Bush administration employed secret agents to destroy the levees surrounding the city. Other conspiracists charged that the government created the monster hurricane using weather machines developed during the Cold War. They argued that the creation of a destructive hurricane in the gulf was intended to drive up oil prices and prevent the disclosure of scandals about the Iraq War.

The following selections are representative of the conspiratorial literature that is available today in various segments of American society. What is not clear is the nature or source of conspiratorial thinking in general. Perhaps the amount of conspiracy theories available today is reflective of the dissonance between American citizens and the government. Perhaps it can be argued that conspiratorial thinking is intrinsic to the human condition. Whatever the source of conspiratorial thinking in contemporary America, one constant remains: some Americans remain as conspiratorial-minded as their forefathers.

Was Jonestown a CIA Medical Experiment?

Michael Meiers

The Peoples Temple, led by cult leader Jim Jones, was established in the 1950s in Indianapolis and later moved to San Francisco to better evade a nuclear attack. In 1974, following several conflicts with local and state officials in California, Jones leased 3,000 acres from the government of Guyana in South America. He established Jonestown there in 1977 and moved his congregation to the new location in early 1978. At the same time, family members of congregants became increasingly concerned with Jones's teachings, the living conditions in the Guyana complex, and Jones's erratic behavior. This led California congressman Leo Ryan, who represented part of San Francisco and who chaired a House subcommittee with jurisdiction over Americans living abroad, to fly to Guyana with a group of reporters in November 1978. As the delegation was preparing to leave the airstrip outside Jonestown, Ryan and six of the reporters were murdered by cult followers; soon after, Jones ordered his followers to commit mass suicide. Over 900 people in the Jonestown complex either did so or were killed. In the following selection, Michael Meiers outlines his belief that the medical mind-control and HIV experiments conducted at Jonestown, the assassination of Ryan, and the mass suicides were orchestrated by the Central Intelligence Agency and its agent—Jim Jones. (From Michael Meiers, *Was Jonestown a CIA Medical Experiment? A Review of the Evidence* [Lewiston, N.Y.: Edwin Mellen Press, 1989], 385–459.)

Jim Jones was an expert in the psychic science of coercive persuasion, behavior modification, mind control and brainwashing. It was his favorite subject ever since the early days in Indianapolis, when he studied and altered primate behavior. . . . The CIA employed hundreds of scientists and behavioral experts in over 149 different projects located in laboratories throughout the world. This multimillion dollar, super secret project was given the code name MK ULTRA. Their psychic research encompassed hypnosis, sensory deprivation, electroshock, ESP, subliminal projection, sleep deprivation, sleep teaching, and the development of hundreds of mind altering drugs. By the early 1960s, most of the work had progressed as far as it could in a laboratory and the CIA gathered the results of the lab experiments to compile a comprehensive study in the psychic sciences. The compiled data was then given to their agent, Jim Jones, who was assigned the task of conducting an actual field test to verify and improve upon the results of the lab tests. Considering the vast amount of knowledge he possessed, both from his personal research and from the MK ULTRA project, Jim Jones was the foremost authority on the psychic sciences in the world.

When Jones moved his Peoples Temple to the Ukiah, California area in 1965, the group immediately infiltrated the Mendocino State Mental Hospital which would provide, not only test persons . . . for his preliminary experiments, but also a training ground for the many medical technicians he needed for the ultimate experiment. Within a very short period of time, every employee of the hospital was a member of the Peoples Temple. From nurses, to therapists, to counselors, to cleaning women, every worker in the facility was replaced by a Temple member. California virtually gave the Mendocino State Mental Hospital to Jim Jones. . . .

Eventually, most of the patients at Mendocino . . . were released in the charge of the Peoples Temple. The public funds previously allocated to Jim Jones via the hospital's budget, the staff's salaries and their subsequent donations, now came directly from the state to Jones, who reportedly bled the program by providing a minimum of patient care for patients at Mendocino State Hospital prompted then Governor Ronald Reagan to close the facility which, after all, was the desired intent of the Mendocino Plan. Jones protested the closing, but, in truth, it mattered little to him. The hospital had outlived its usefulness as a training center for the Temple's medical staff. . . .

With his research in the psychic sciences and ethnic diseases as background, Jones was prepared for the next phase of his work; the development of weapons that would affect only specific racial groups, namely Blacks and Native Americans. . . . He claimed that fascism was simply "capitalism gone mean" and that the United States was already preparing to wage a race war in which the targeted groups would be interned in concentration camps, enslaved, and eventually exterminated. . . .

One could write volumes on the deceitful nature of Jim Jones but . . . he did not lie. The CIA was developing ethnic weapons and their largest project was a field test called Jonestown.

Between 1973 and 1975, foreign management, employed by the CIA used Jonestown as a training base for mercenaries bound for Angola, but by 1975 the site was under complete control of the Peoples Temple and was known, not as an agricultural project, but as a "medical mission." It was a medical mission, but, for obvious security reasons, all references to "medical" were dropped and the community was renamed Jonestown and billed as an agricultural project.

At the height of the experiment, the Jonestown medical staff numbered seventy. Most were psychiatrists, psychologists, behavioral scientists, therapists, pharmacologists, and an army of nurses. . . .

There were additional medical experiments conducted in Jonestown and one of these, the most frightening of all possibilities, was concerned with the virus responsible for . . . AIDS. . . .

All the elements that would have been necessary to conduct a field test in the transmission and implementation of the epidemic were present in Jonestown. As evidenced by their own published articles, the Peoples Temple was very concerned about the development of racial weapons. They had the medical expertise, the required lab monkeys, and even a group of supposedly "reformed" homosexuals and drug addicts who made up a disproportionately large number of Jonestown residents. . . .

In the fall of 1978, Jones sent a few of his infected homosexual followers on a paid vacation to nearby Haiti, a frequent port of call for the Temple's ship and a popular winter resort for New York City gays. While in Haiti, they infected a number of male prostitutes just prior to the tourist season. This was the origin of the AIDS epidemic in the gay community. It first surfaced in the Haitian homosexual whorehouses in December of 1978 and in New York City in January 1979. . . .

This was the nature of the Jonestown medical experiments. Had they remained simple, they might have gone undetected but the CIA proceeded to add so many other desired results to the project as to make their sponsorship all too obvious. . . .

The assassination of Congressman Ryan and the mass suicide/murder that followed was not the flippant reaction of a crazed preacher but a calculated political assassination and medical field test that had been planned. . . .

[Reporter Gordon] Lindsay learned of . . . Ryan's congressional inquiry into Jonestown and suggested the Congressman invite the press to accompany him for some degree of protection on what could be a dangerous mission. Ryan, who always played to the cameras, agreed and Lindsay took it upon himself to invite the newsmen he wanted to attend. . . .

By the time that the newsmen and relatives finally reached Jamestown, it was about seven o'clock and the sun was setting. Clearly, their visit was intended to be a night encounter. They soon joined . . . in the open-air pavilion for a welcome and reportedly delicious barbequed pork dinner. . . .

It was about 11:00 P.M. when the crowd dispersed in unison like so many fish in a school responding to some mysterious mass communication. It was obvious that the evening encounter had drawn to a close. As the residents made their way back to their cabins, Jones concluded the interview with reporters, complaining of a conspiracy to destroy the Peoples Temple. When asked who was plotting his demise, Jones responded, "Who conspired to kill Dr. Martin Luther King, Malcolm X, and John Kennedy? Every agency of the whole government is giving us a hard time. Somebody doesn't like socialism." It was another calculated statement from the master of deceit. In so few words he gave the reporters the impression of a paranoid man with delusions of grandeur who was persecuted by the U.S. government for his socialistic beliefs. . . . Actually, Jones was working for the CIA which had issued a "hands off" order to the other agencies of the government permitting him to perpetuate his many crimes in the U.S. unabated. . . .

Obviously, it was not the intention of the Temple assault team to kill everyone or to stop the Jonestown defectors from leaving. The intention was to assassinate Congressman Ryan. Cameramen Bob Brown and Greg Robinson were killed just before Ryan because they were filming the assassination. . . .

As absurd a miscarriage of justice as it would appear to be, in the final analysis, a U.S. Congressman was assassinated in full view of at least four dozen people, some of whom . . . have never been identified or even questioned as to what they witnessed. No attempt was made to bring anyone to justice or to even locate the murder weapon. . . . As to who actually killed Leo Ryan, no one seems to care and everyone has a preconceived, precontrived rationale. To a privileged few, Ryan was killed by the CIA. To the rest of the world, Ryan was killed by the crazed Jim Jones. . . .

Obviously, Jones was using the assassination as a mechanism to trigger the experiment [the White Night]. . . .

The first to die in Jonestown were the babes-in-arms. On Jones' order, mothers holding small children were the first to line up in front of the vat of poison where the technicians squirted the potion [grape Kool-Aid and cyanide] into the throats of the children. . . .

The older children were next. One at a time they drank their paper cup of death. The adults followed and so did the trouble as many refused to drink the

UN
IS
SPAWN
OF
THE ILLUMINATI

By MYRON C. FAGAN

Published November 1966 by

CINEMA EDUCATIONAL GUILD, Inc.

P. O. Box 46205, Cole Br., Hollywood 46, Calif.

No. 122

Cover of Myron C. Fagan, *UN Is Spawn of the Illuminati,* published by Cinema Educational Guild in Hollywood, California. Generic cover warning against involvement with the international body.

poison. Force-feeding would have been a waste of precious time. Uncooperative residents were captured by armed guards who had formed two concentric circles around the pavilion. The guards dragged them to the vat of poison where they were injected and somehow labeled involuntary. . . . The last to die were the seniors. . . .

Even with all the preparation and execution, the CIA's task was only half finished with the completion of the experiment. There were many loose ends that, if left untied, might expose the agency's sponsorship of Jonestown. The situation called for a small army of agency propagandists who. . . . are responsible for the mostly false public opinion about Jonestown.

AIDS: The Purposeful Destruction of the Black World?

Haki R. Madhubuti (Don L. Lee)

Since the first reported cases of HIV and AIDS in the United States in the 1980s, some conspiracy theorists have contended that the disease was manufactured by the government as part of a biological weapons program gone awry. Haki R. Madhubuti (Don L. Lee), an author and poet, argued, based on information he obtained from two doctors, that the AIDS virus was created to eradicate the African race throughout the world. In the following excerpt, he contends that the virus was biogenetically engineered in secret research facilities in the United States as a biological weapon and tested as a "vaccine" by the World Health Organization (WHO) in Africa. (From Haki R. Madhubuti [Don Lee], *Black Men: Obsolete, Single, Dangerous? Afrikan American Families in Transition: Essays in Discovery, Solution, and Hope* [Chicago: Third World Press, 1990], 51–58. Reprinted by permission.)

If there was one subject I was sure that I would not write about, it was AIDS. Like most misinformed confirmed heterosexuals, I was convinced that AIDS was a white middle-class homosexual disease that, at worse, would only touch Black homosexuals. I also felt that the AIDS reports coming out of Afrika were exaggerated, and that white people were doing what they normally do with things that had gotten out of hand, *blame the victim*. . . . AIDS, unlike anything else that has invaded the Black World or any world, has the potential of devastating the Afrikan population unlike any weapon we've known since the Afrikan holocaust, the enslavement of Afrikan people by Europeans.

About two years ago, Dr. Frances Welsing sent me some of her research, including the book *A Survey of Chemical and Biological Warfare* (1969). This text details the type of biological and chemical research and warfare being carried on in the Western world. Their work centered on chemical agents for riot control and the rise of biological agents as weapons that could be dispatched unexpectedly on the "enemy." . . . All of this research was/is being supported by the United States, Canada, Britain and West Germany. The crucial thing is that the authors document the early experimentation with viruses that would attack the immune systems of people. . . .

A friend from the West Coast sent me a video tape of the work being done by Dr. [Robert] Strecker. With the tape, he sent piles of other written documentation that convinced me that AIDS is not the next mega-killer, but is *now* ravishing the Black world from Zaire to Haiti, from Zambia to Chicago, from Uganda to Brazil, from Malawi to New York and San Francisco. Here are some of the major misconceptions about AIDS documented in Dr. Strecker's "The Strecker Memorandum" that we need to be immediately aware of:

1) AIDS is a man-made disease
2) AIDS is not a homosexual disease
3) AIDS is not a venereal disease
4) AIDS can be carried by mosquitoes
5) Condoms will not prevent AIDS
6) There are at least six different AIDS viruses loose in the world
7) There will never be a vaccine cure
8) The AIDS virus was introduced into Afrika by the WHO
9) The AIDS virus can live outside the body

Dr. Strecker has unearthed evidence that the AIDS virus was created in a laboratory at Fort Detrick, Maryland from smallpox and hepatitis B vaccines. It is now certain that the World Health Organization introduced the vaccine that contaminated east and central Afrika with the AIDS virus. . . .

We do know that much of this biological/chemical research re-emerged (much of it started during World War II in Germany) after the rebellions of the 1960s, when white men viewed their cities going up in flames set by Black men and could do nothing. Well, part of their answer, as always, was, "How do we *eliminate* (not solve or understand, but eliminate) the problem?" In the United States, according to these people, Black people—more specifically, Black men—are the problem. . . .

Maybe the reader has doubts about this information, and the one question that continues to tug at him or her is, "Why has AIDS been viewed as a homosexual, and now drug-user, disease when in Afrika it was obviously a heterosexual disease?" I think that the answer is not difficult; the two groups that a great many people in the population do not care about and would not be overly-concerned if they disappeared are homosexuals and drug-users. Their logic is that since AIDS is a homosexual and drug-related disease, then—because "I'm not homosexual, don't use drugs, and don't care for either group—I'm safe. Anyway, AIDS is probably the wrath of God against their evil ways." As I said earlier, such racists that blame the world's ills on everybody except themselves. . . .

In the white world when it comes to warfare, there are very few *coincidences*. That is why the United States has war colleges, one of the largest standing armed forces in the world, think tanks, and thousands of secret research projects underway at universities and private companies coast to coast. . . . I do not have an answer to this one, except—*educate* yourselves, be understanding of those that are ill and, as always, be *activists* about this and any other death that threatens our community. As we face life we cannot let the horrors of the world stop us. *Seek preventative health and each day fight for that which is good, just and right, regardless of what others are doing* [emphasis in the original].

The Militia Movement in the United States

John Trochman

In the aftermath of the federal raids at Ruby Ridge in the summer of 1992 and the Branch Davidian compound in Waco, Texas, in spring 1993 that resulted in many deaths, militia movement members in the United States increasingly became more conspiratorial-minded toward the federal government. This paranoia reached a terrible climax when militiamen Timothy McVeigh and Terry Nichols bombed the Alfred P. Murrah Federal Building in Oklahoma City on April 19, 1995—the two-year anniversary of the federal raid on the Branch Davidian compound. In response to the Oklahoma City bombing, the Senate Subcommittee on Terrorism, Technology, and Government Information held hearings in June evaluating the militia movement and the threat of terrorism in the United States. John Trochman, a leading member of the Montana Militiamen, testified on behalf of the militia movement. In the following selection, Trochman denounced terrorism and the Oklahoma City bombing, but at the same time he outlined the purpose and function of the militia movement as the patriotic guardian of the United States. His testimony also revealed his conspiratorial fears of a strong federal government that was plotting a treasonous insurrection to participate in a one-world government. (From Subcommittee on Terrorism, Technology, and Government Information, Committee on the Judiciary, *The Militia Movement in the United States,* 104th Cong., 1st sess., June 15, 1995, 83–85.)

At the present time, we view the militia movement as a giant neighborhood watch. The movement is made up of a cross-section of Americans from all walks of life with a singular mandate which is public and overt—the return to the Constitution of the United States and to your oath to defend that Constitution.

The Declaration of Independence gives excellent insight as to why people feel the need to group together and participate in militia/patriot organizations. This document speaks for itself once again as it did over 200 years ago when flagrant injustice continued out of control by oppressive public servant. . . .

The following are just a few examples as to why Americans are becoming more and more involved in militia/patriot organizations. The high office of the Presidency has been turned into a position of dictatorial oppression through the abusive use of Executive orders and directives, thus leaving Congress stripped of its authority. When the President overrules Congress by Executive order, representative government fails.

When Government defines human begins as a biological resource under the United Nations ecosystem management program, maintaining that State and local laws are barriers to the goals of Federal Government, and when the average citizen must work for half of each year just to pay their taxes while billions of our tax dollars are forcibly sent to bail out the banking elite while our fellow Americans are homeless, starving, and without jobs, Congress wonders why the constituents get upset.

When Government allows our military to be ordered and controlled by foreigners under Presidential order, allowing foreign armies to train on our soil, allowing our military to label caring patriots as the enemy, and then turns their tanks loose on U. S. citizens to murder and destroy [the Branch Davidian compound in Waco] or directs a sniper to shoot a mother in the face while holding her infant in her arms [in Ruby Ridge], you bet your constituents get upset.

When Government refuses to hold hearings on Government-sanctioned abuses and white-washes those hearings that are held and when Government tampers with or destroys evidence needed to solve crime and now considers the very idea of infringing upon the people's right of freedom, speech, assembly, and the right to redress after having destroyed the second and fourth articles, how can Senators and Representatives ever question the loyalty of concerned Americans without first cleaning their own house?. . . .

We the people have about had all we can stand of the twisted, slanted, biased media of America who take their signals from a few private covert special interest groups bent on destroying what is left of the American way. We respectfully request that you rely upon your own investigations, steering clear of the media, and their rumor-gossip mills of misinformation.

Although most everyone in the movement has assembled under the First Amendment. . . . We have not forgotten what our Founding Fathers have stated about the Second. Former President James Madison: "A well-regulated militia, composed of the body of the people, trained to arms, is the best and most natural defense of a free country." Former Vice-President Elbridge Gerry: "I ask what is the purpose of the militia? To offset the need of large standing armies, the bane of liberty."

Why would he call the armed forces the bane of liberty? Why is the Pentagon waging active campaigns to win over the populace, and why does the Military Affairs Manual 41–10 seem to be so applicable in America today—paraphrasing, steps necessary for the overthrow of a nation?

May God be with America as he watches over the shoulders of you who write her laws. A nation can survive its fools and even the ambitious, but it cannot survive treason from within. America has nothing to fear from patriots maintaining vigilance. She should, however, fear those that would outlaw vigilance.

9/11 Conspiracy: A Summary

Michael Pardo

The terrorist attacks on the World Trade Center and the Pentagon on September 11, 2001, have prompted conspiracy theorists to reject the official reports offered by the federal government and to advance numerous alternative theories. Some focus on the government's cover-up of its own failures to prevent the attacks, while others allege that the government used explosives to destroy the Twin Towers and damage the Pentagon. The late Michael Pardo outlines his belief in the following selection: that the U.S. government had prior knowledge of the September 11 attacks and that the attacks were perpetrated not by members of the terrorist organization Al Qaeda, but by the Mossad, Israel's secret intelligence service. (From Michael Pardo, *9/11 Conspiracy: A Summary,* available on http://www.apfn.org/apfn/WTC_summary.htm.)

It can now be reported that there was a dangerous dirty double-dealing and deadly duel of blackmail going on behind the scenes between the United States and Israeli governments right after the 9/11 tragedy, which first resulted in an historic decision by the U.S., for the first time ever, to back a United Nations resolution calling for a free and independent Palestinian state in the Middle East, which subsequently resulted in Israel's bold defiance of weak demands by the United States for Israel to withdraw from the occupied Palestinian territories where brutal massacres are continually perpetrated (accompanied by the failure of Israel to observe numerous United Nations resolutions regarding the current crisis, such similar resolutions which have caused Iraq to be bombed, blockaded, and invaded), and finally resulting in the U.S. government following a long-standing plan drawn up by Israeli double-agents in the Bush administration to prosecute a war on Iraq (The Office of Special Projects), followed by a planned and scheduled regime-change in Iran, Syria, and Saudi Arabia (and an eventual deportation of all Palestinians from the alleged Holy Land), all designed to accomplish the final solution for Eretz Israel: possession/control of all the lands in the Middle East from the Mediterranean Sea to the Tigris and Euphrates rivers.

It can now also be reported that the U.S. government, and many nations of the U.N., are in possession of proof of the duplicity, complicity, and possibly the total responsibility, of the nation of Israel in the 9/11 World Trade Center tragedy. . . .

Initial information springing up right after the 9/11 tragedy . . . indicated that the U.S. government was aware of Israeli prior knowledge of the attack, and considered Israel as a suspect in the masterminding of the conspiracy through an attempt to implicate Arabs, Muslims, and Osama bin Laden in the disaster, for the purpose of turning international opinion, which was mounting against Israel, instead against their Muslim enemies and force the U.S. and the U.N. to brand and consider Palestinian leader Yassir Arafat as a "terrorist" who should be included as an enemy in the subsequent "War on Terrorism. . . ." This was done by the Israeli Mossad master-minding the 9/11 tragedy through remote control of the airplanes by a previously secret radio control system, with subsequent blame being placed on the Islamic Al-Qaeda network and Osama bin Laden through a massive misinformation campaign designed to cover up the real truth in the matter, such misinformation campaign which was perpetrated by the controlled United States media.

Using the 9/11 World Trade Center tragedy as an excuse to promote New World Order policy by implementing Soviet [Union]-like domestic programs in the homeland and attacking the enemies of the New World Order all throughout the world: also build an oil pipeline through Afghanistan and regain control of the Afghanistan heroin trade, by ousting the Taliban government, with whom the Bush administration had been negotiating the year before 9/11 regarding the aforementioned issues; the Bush administration established the "War on Terrorism" which also promoted the goals of the New World Order. . . . This although no proof was ever provided by the U.S. government positively linking Osama bin Laden and Islamic "terrorists" to the 9/11 attack. . . .

At the time of the passage of the U.N. resolution calling for a Palestinian state (shortly after 9/11), the United States was being blackmailed by Israel, with Israel threatening to release sensitive information obtained about U.S. government officials and policies obtained by the multiple levels of Israeli spy rings operating in the United States (some of the sensitive information relating to perverse sexual activities by U.S. officials, obtained through the facilities of the Israeli/Jewish international child pornography/slavery ring), while at the same time, the Bush administration was blackmailing Israel by threatening to curtail Israeli influence in the United States and release information regarding Israel's duplicity, complicity, and total responsibility in the 9/11 tragedy. Subsequently, the Israeli Mossad (with permission from [Israeli prime minister] Ariel Sharon) followed through on their threats and released information in the United States (primarily through the U.S. Patriot and Militia movements, now controlled by Israel, due to the efforts of deep-cover Israeli moles) that implicated the Bush administration in prior knowledge of the 9/11 tragedy. . . .

Previously, and at the same time this was happening, behind the scenes, the Bush administration had launched an investigation into Israeli spying in the U.S., which subsequently resulted in the identification of more than 140 Israeli spies operating in the United States, an investigation which was a natural reaction on the part of a party being blackmailed, in an attempt to remove the source of the blackmailing threat, and which resulted in a new Pentagon policy of excluding foreign nationals (specifically Israelis) from unclassified information. However, this small spy ring was only the tip of the iceberg of Israeli spying, and many other levels of Israeli spies and subversives (*sayanim*) exist all throughout the U.S., including secret agents and offices of the Mossad which have been admitted by former Mossad agents as operating on American soil, despite continual denials by the Israeli leadership.

One of the threats perceived by the United States that would be carried out by such a collection of Israeli agents in the U.S. is the explosion of a nuclear device in an American city, or an attack on a U.S. nuclear power plant, followed by an attempt to implicate Arabs, Muslims, and Osama bin Laden again (and, as needed, Saddam Hussein): warnings about the nuking of an American city then appeared in the Zionist-controlled U.S. press (and in other Israeli/Jewish/Zionist controlled media), with the blame, again, being placed on Arabs, Muslims, Osama bin Laden, and also Saddam Hussein. This particular Israeli threat was connected to the U.S. war plan against Saddam Hussein of Iraq, with President Bush understanding that if he did not do something about Hussein (Israel's biggest enemy and threat in the Middle East), then Israel would have carried through on its threat, which would then have been used to his advantage by Bush and the administration. . . .

However, many people throughout the world were aware of the fact that the Iraqi war ploy was an element of the conspiracy which might eventually catalyze the essential destruction of human civilization. Already heard was the nuclear saber-rattling by U.S. President Bush and Great Britain Prime Minister Blair, who both stated that if weapons of mass-destruction were used by certain Middle-Eastern nations (enemies of Israel), then the U.S. and Great Britain would not hesitate to use nuclear weapons in response. This stated policy, a shift in nuclear policy for both nations, suggests that the U.S. is backing down in fear to Israel's nuclear threat, and follows the pattern of the United States prosecuting the foreign policy of Israel.

The Iraqi war ploy was prosecuted, both by President Bush and the "Team B" cabal (The Office of Special Projects), even though it was largely based on the violation of U.N. resolutions by Iraq: mostly resolutions regarding inspection of certain manufacturing facilities. This while Israel itself is in violation of dozens and dozens of similar U.N. resolutions, has NEVER allowed a U.N. weapons inspector into the country, and has been saved violation of dozens more by U.S. veto. Furthermore, Israel is the only nation in the region which actually possesses nuclear weapons and other weapons of mass destruction: in fact, it is claimed in some intelligence circles that Israel is the third most powerful nuclear force in the world.

But the real truth is that the entire Iraqi war ploy again exemplifies how the Rothschild family still has the upper hand and holds sway over the Illuminist element of the New World Order conspiracy, and can and will have their way whenever they want to; furthermore those who once thought they were not under the thumb of certain people, have found out, and will find out even more in the future, that they really are controlled by the ultimate puppet-masters in the world, and are themselves simply puppets to their real masters. . . .

The pursuit of the Iraqi war ploy was accomplished without the required consent of the United Nations, and the result of the Iraqi war ploy has been the discovery of 0 (zero) weapons of mass destruction by the invaders of Iraq (the alleged reason for the invasion in the first place), which has further turned international concern over the war of aggression into international contempt and fury, and which has aligned many of the nations that were in opposition to the war (and powerful elements of the U.N. Security Council) against the United States and its invading allies. And while it is likely that weapons of mass destruction which existed in Iraq before the war made their way out of the country during the invasion, the discovery of no weapons of mass destruction just fuels the fire of public international opinion against the U.S., Great Britain, and Israel. . . .

At this time, both in Afghanistan and Iraq, U.S./British/Israeli control is limited only to several miles within the capitol and other major cities of the invaded nations, while Islamic war lords and local political parties still control the majority of both nations, resulting not in a complete conquering and destruction of the invaded nations, but a total destabilization of the societies of both nations instead. And while the stated goal of the first two invasions of the alleged "War on Terrorism" has been to get Osama bin Laden and Saddam Hussein, at this time, questions still remain as to whether the captured Saddam is actually Saddam Hussein or just another one of his "doubles," doubts have already been expressed over whether Hussein's sons were really killed (the U.S. government has recently admitted that the photographs taken of Hussein's dead sons were actually wax mockups of them), and it is becoming well-known among the international intelligence community that Osama bin Laden died a few years ago of a kidney/liver disease, and his body was captured and frozen by the Bush administration for presentation to the U.S. public at an appropriate time before the 2004 presidential election. And now, the "War on Terrorism" continues unabated, and reports from throughout the world attest to the continued survival of the ideals which they held while in public power: all while the U.S. and its allies continue to prosecute the war while failing to uncover any true weapons of mass destruction in Iraq. . . .

Since it is the nature of the criminal mind to try to turn their victims into the perpetrators, and paint themselves as the victims, and since blackmailers and their blackmail victims are prone to lie in order to cover up their guilt, it should not be expected that the full truth will ever be admitted by anyone associated with either the U.S., British, or Israeli governments, and it should be expected that subsequent denials and misinformation will be released in a continued attempt to obfuscate the truth in the matter. All in all, the lies that are being told about this matter are some of the biggest lies ever told in the history of human civilization, and the absolute evil manifested in this conspiracy, is some of the greatest evil ever manifested in the history of the world. However, researchers who study the conspiracy as identified herein and keep this article in mind in the near future, will return to discover that what was predicted in this article about future U.S./British/Israeli plans for the Middle East, has all come true, and that fact itself should be enough in itself to convince even the most conservative skeptics about the real truth in the matter.

Hurricane Katrina—Who Benefits?

Sherman H. Skolnick

The mass destruction and the seeming failure of communication between the federal and state government of Louisiana after Hurricane Katrina made landfall on the Gulf Coast in the fall of 2005 has prompted conspiracists to offer alternative theories explaining the origins, the intended purpose, and possible beneficiaries of Hurricane Katrina. The following selection, by the late Sherman H. Skolnick, provides an overview of the many conspiracy theories available about Katrina. Skolnick's long career began in the late 1950s. He founded the Chicago-based Citizen's Committee to Clean Up the Courts in 1963 to prevent corruption in America's courtrooms. He is also the author of *The Secret History of Airplane Sabotage* (1973) that charged that a United Airlines crash in December 1972 was the result of government sabotage, and that twelve of the victims of the crash had been involved in Watergate. (Sherman H. Skolnick, *Hurricane Katrina—Who Benefits?* www.skolnicksreport.com.)

Some meteorologists contend there has been weather-warfare. That is, they say, that there have been two man-made hurricanes, Ivan (The Terrible), 2004, and Katrina, 2005. And, that these storms were created by technology long-known and directed to specific areas.

One weatherman asserted that Russia has long claimed they can send extreme weather and turbulence from Siberia targeting the United States. He proclaimed that Russia did that with Ivan in 2004 and Katrina, 2005.

He appeared on the Coast-To-Coast radio talk show with host George Noory, about a night after Katrina hit the Gulf. In describing how brazenly the hurricane was created and directed, that as an inside signal, it came right over the National Hurricane Center in Florida.

If so, WHO had prior knowledge?

1. As a corruptly installed stooge and scapegoat for the Anglo-American Aristocracy, George W. Bush is a prime suspect having foreknowledge. If it became in time more and more evident of a high-level domestic plot, a new "Pearl Harbor," to carry out a long-planned war-mongering cancel-the Constitution agenda, then putting a Russian-style name in advance on the two later man-made suspected hurricanes, would form the basis for blaming Russia. Or like 9-11, falsely blaming "The Moslems."
2. Did Russian president [Vladimir] Putin, suspecting he might be blamed for Hurricane Katrina, jump the gun? Just prior to Katrina hitting the Gulf, Putin noted that two U.S. Senators were in Russia snooping around off-limits secret facilities. That is U.S. Senator Barack Obama (D-IL) originally from the former British colony of Kenya and a year previous, before Obama was elected, was publicly fingered by me as a British spy; and his accomplice in Russia, U.S. Senator Richard Lugar (R-IN). . . .
3. Some assert that a friendly foreign power, also having high technology, made the man-made Katrina suddenly take a right hook and veer slight-

ly away from New Orleans and directly hit the refineries and facilities of British Petroleum, owned by the British monarchy.

4. In an exclusive bulletin on Cloak and Dagger [conspiracy website], we told how the Bushies' Federal Emergency Management Agency (FEMA), sabotaged the levee which holds back the nearby lake from swamping below-sea-level New Orleans. More than 25 eyewitnesses to this treason are primarily but not exclusively blacks. FEMA operatives vowed to find these finger-pointers and snuff them out. A friendly foreign power is keeping the witnesses safe.
5. Nationwide, the American Red Cross solicited funds for supposed "New Orleans Hurricane Relief. . . ." FEMA in the George W. Bush Administration have been, at great expense, supposedly pre-planning how to deal with an expected New Orleans hurricane disaster. FEMA said that refuge should be sought in the New Orleans Convention Center. And beyond that, FEMA pointed to the nearby Super-Dome sports arena. Eyewitness residents occupied such places. Those that survived bitterly complain that the Red Cross, the National Guard, FEMA helpers, and other supposed rescuers were nowhere to be seen. For almost a week, no food, no bottled water, no medicines for the sick such as diabetics, and no other life essentials were dropped from helicopters or otherwise made available. In two New Orleans hospitals, patients not otherwise in dying condition, died because of lack of essentials.
6. Noting how Hurricane Ivan The Terrible made a mysterious u-turn, Lenny Bloom, co-host of Cloak and Dagger, in 2004, coined the term, HAARPICANE, named after the latest technology to manipulate the weather and the atmosphere, HAARP.
7. When asked by a reporter why Bush was not ordering immediate emergency aid for the suffering residents of New Orleans, a Bush White House official arrogantly barked out, "After all, they did not vote for us."
8. From long experience as a court-reformer, I learned that when we publicly identify a top Judge as a crook, as a bribe-taker, the Establishment, the Ruling Class, "the powers that be," that is THEM—they throw the Judge away like a worn out shoe, and send him to jail for "suddenly" discovered tax evasion and other criminal offenses. I usually cynically comment, "No decent gangster bagman will further bribe such a corrupt identified judge but will look for another crook on the bench." There is reason to believe that now the Anglo-American Aristocracy has extracted all the illicit profit they can out of Bush and may want to throw him away. Hence, the monopoly press is strangely allowing Bush critics to be heard stating that in the Gulf area and elsewhere, Americans are suffering from an "incompetent Bush government." Wow! Why was this truism so long delayed in being heard at the hands of the liars and whores of the press?

9. Oil machinery and other service and equipment faker, Halliburton, has been promised the contract to someday, perhaps not soon, rebuild New Orleans. Vice President Richard Cheney, a top-level criminal, was the CEO of the firm and still receives many millions of dollars per year in delayed "compensation" from them while he stonewalls important White House oil dirty business. The plan for treachery is simple. Residents of New Orleans fled for their life. They obviously did not take along in a plastic bag the deed to their property. So now out-of-town and out-of-work, they do not have the funds to pay their property tax nor do they have their property identification code and number. Sixty six per cent of the population of New Orleans have been blacks, many impoverished, together with a sizeable number of poor whites. So it will be simple for land swindlers like Halliburton and their gang of pirates to grab lots of land from the descendants of slaves or white indentured servants, bull-doze away the hurricane-wrecked houses, and build hotels and other structures to accompany a someday to be newly-enlarged whorehouse district in New Orleans. Some unfeeling critics would like to unfairly point to the whole hurricane mess, as A Red Light District is Bad Karma. Actually, subject to Bad Karma is the highly corrupt, terribly incompetent Bush White House and the Bush Crime Family. And what may happen to the tens of thousands of New Orleans refugees now resident in Texas. . . . The former New Orleans blacks may become property-stripped latter day slaves and the poor whites, likewise plundered of their assets, can expect to become indentured servants, just in time for the new, worthless Bankruptcy Law, same as those many years ago exported from British Debtors' Prisons to Tennessee and elsewhere in the U.S. Cheney and the Halliburton Pirate Flag gang and the Bush Crime Family, together with the Oil Cartel—why do they want the people cleared off the land in New Orleans?

A simple explanation, supplied by savvy sorts, is that New Orleans may be situated on a large pool of oil.

For Further Reading

Section I: Conspiracy in a New Nation

Primary Sources

Backus, Azel. *Absalom's Conspiracy: A Sermon, Preached at the General Election at Hartford, in the State of Connecticut . . .* Suffield, Conn.: H. & O. Farnsworth, 1798.

Bernard, David. *Light on Masonry.* Utica, N.Y.: William Williams, 1829.

Bishop, Abraham. *Proofs of a Conspiracy against Christianity and the Government of the United States.* Hartford, Conn.: John Babcock, 1802.

Clark, Daniel. *Proofs of the Corruption of Gen. James Wilkinson . . .* Philadelphia: Wm. Hall, Jr., & Geo. W. Pierie, 1809.

Morgan, William. *Illustrations of Masonry.* Chicago: Ezra A. Cook, 1827.

Payson, Seth. *Proof of the Real Existence, and Dangerous Tendency, of Illuminism.* Charlestown, Mass.: Samuel Etheridge, 1802.

Pearson, Edward, ed. *Designs Against Charleston: The Trial Record of the Denmark Vesey Conspiracy of 1822.* Chapel Hill: University of North Carolina Press, 1999.

Secondary Sources

Bailyn, Bernard. *The Ideological Origins of the American Revolution.* Cambridge, Mass.: Harvard University Press, 1967.

Davidson, Philip. *Propaganda and the American Revolution, 1763–1783.* New York: Norton, 1973.

Davis, David Brion. "Some Themes of Countersubversion: An Analysis of Anti-Masonic, Anti-Catholic, and Anti-Mormon Literature." *Mississippi Valley Historical Review* 47, no. 2 (September 1960): 205–24.

Gruber, Ira D. "The American Revolution as Conspiracy: The British View." *William and Mary Quarterly* 3d ser., 26 (1969): 360–72.

Kutolowski, Kathleen Smith. "Freemasonry and Community in the Early Republic: The Case for Antimasonic Anxieties." *American Quarterly* 34 (1982): 543–61.

Lepore, Jill. *New York Burning: Liberty, Slavery, and Conspiracy in Eighteenth-Century Manhattan.* New York: Knopf, 2005.

Melton, Buckner F. Jr. *Aaron Burr: Conspiracy to Treason.* New York: John Wiley, 2002.

Wood, Gordon. "Conspiracy and the Paranoid Style: Causality and Deceit in the Eighteenth Century." *William and Mary Quarterly* 3d ser., 39 (1982): 401–41.

Section II: Conspiracy in an Age of Democracy

Primary Sources

Beecher, Edward. *The Papal Conspiracy Exposed, and Protestantism Defended.* New York: M. W. Dodd, 1855.

Beecher, Lyman. *A Plea for the West.* Cincinnati: Truman and Smith, 1835.
Morse, Samuel F. B. *Foreign Conspiracy Against the Liberties of the United States.* New York: Leavitt, Lord, 1835.

Secondary Sources

Anbinder, Tyler. *Nativism and Slavery: The Northern Know Nothings and the Politics of the 1850s.* New York: Oxford University Press, 1992.
Bennett, David. *Party of Fear: From Nativist Movements to the New Right in American History.* Chapel Hill: University of North Carolina Press, 1988.
Billington, Ray Allen. *The Protestant Crusade, 1800–1860: A Study of the Origins of American Nativism.* New York: Macmillan, 1938.
Franchot, Jenny. *Roads to Rome: The Antebellum Protestant Encounter with Catholicism.* Berkeley: University of California Press, 1994.

Section III: Conspiracy in a Divided Nation

Primary Sources

Ayer, I. Winslow. *The Great Northwestern Conspiracy in all its Startling Details . . .* Chicago: Rounds & James, Book and Job Printers, 1865.
Cairnes, John Elliot. *The Slave Power: Its Character, Career, and Probable Designs.* New York: Carleton, 1862.
Goodell, William. *Slavery and Anti-Slavery: A History of the Great Struggle in Both Hemispheres; with a View of the Slavery Question in the United States.* New York: William Harned, 1852.
Miles, Thomas Jefferson. *"To Whom it May Concern": The Conspiracy of Leading Men of the Republican Party to Destroy the American Union . . .* New York: J. Walter, 1864.

Secondary Sources

Davis, David Brion. *The Slave Power Conspiracy and the Paranoid Style.* Baton Rouge: Louisiana State University Press, 1970.
Gara, Larry. "Slavery and Slave Power: A Crucial Distinction." *Civil War History* 15 (March 1969): 5–18.
Hanchett, William. *The Lincoln Murder Conspiracies.* Urbana: University of Illinois Press, 1986.
McGlone, Robert E. "Rescripting a Troubled Past: John Brown's Family and the Harper's Ferry Conspiracy." *Journal of American History* 75 (March 1989): 1179–1200.
Pfau, Michael. *The Political Style of Conspiracy: Chase, Sumner, Lincoln.* East Lansing: Michigan State University Press, 2005.
Rossbach, Jeffrey S. *Ambivalent Conspirators: John Brown, the Secret Six, and a Theory of Slave Violence.* Philadelphia: University of Pennsylvania Press, 1982.
Steers, Edward. *Blood on the Moon: The Assassination of Abraham Lincoln.* Lexington: University Press of Kentucky, 2001.

Section IV: Conspiracy in the Industrial Age through the New Deal

Primary Sources

Baker, E. R. *The Money Monopoly.* Winfield, Kans: H. L. Vincent, 1890.
Cobun, M. W. *The Money Question: A Treatise on U.S. Money.* Great Bend, Kans.: Beacon Book Print, 1892.
Coogan, Gertrude M. *Money Creators.* Chicago: Sound Money Press, 1935.
Dilling, Elizabeth. *Roosevelt's Red Record and Its Background.* Chicago: n.p., 1936.
Elsom, John R. *Lightning Over the Treasury Building.* Boston: Meador Publishing, 1941.
Farmer, E. J. *The Conspiracy Against Silver, or A Plea for Bi-Metalism in the United States.* N.p.: Hiles and Caggshall, 1886.
Means, Gaston B. *The Strange Death of President Harding.* New York: Guild, 1930.

Secondary Sources

Avrich, Paul. *The Haymarket Tragedy.* Princeton: Princeton University Press, 1984.
Kimball, Warren F., and Bruce Bartlett. "Roosevelt and Prewar Commitments to Churchill: The Tyler Kent Affair." *Diplomatic History* 5, no. 4 (1981): 291–311.
Ostler, Jeffrey. "The Rhetoric of Conspiracy and the Formation of Kansas Populism." *Agricultural History* 69, no. 1 (1995): 1–27.
Rauchway, Eric. *Murdering McKinley: The Making of Theodore Roosevelt's America.* New York: Hill and Wang, 2003.
Rives, Timothy. "Grant, Babcock, and the Whiskey Ring." *Prologue: Quarterly of the National Archives and Records Administration* 32, no. 3 (Fall 2000): 142–53.
Summers, Mark Wahlgren. *Rum, Romanism, & Rebellion: The Making of a President, 1884.* Chapel Hill: University of North Carolina Press, 2000.
Weber, Timothy P. "Finding Someone to Blame: Fundamentalism and Anti-Semitic Conspiracy Theories in the 1930s." *Fides et Historia* 24, no. 2 (1992): 40–55.
Young, Bradley J. "Silver, Discontent, and Conspiracy: The Ideology of the Western Republican Revolt of 1890–1901." *Pacific Historical Review* 64 (May 1995): 243–65.

Section V: Conspiracy in the Cold War Era

Primary Sources

Allen, Gary. "The C.F.R. Conspiracy to Rule the World." *American Opinion* 12 (April 1969): 49–68.
Burnham, James. *The Web of Subversion.* John Day Co., 1954.
Carr, William Guy. *The Red Flag over America.* Toronto: National Federation of Christian Laymen, 1957.
Cleaver, Kathleen. "Racism, Fascism, and Political Murder." *Black Panther,* September 14, 1968, 8.
Courtney, Kent, and Phoebe Courtney. *America's Unelected Rulers.* New Orleans: Conservative Society of America, 1962.
Lane, Mark. *Rush to Judgment: A Critique of the Warren Commission's Inquiry . . .* New York: Holt, Rinehart, & Winston, 1966.
Mullins, Eustace. *The Federal Reserve Conspiracy.* Union, N.J.: Common Sense, 1954.

Scully, Frank. *Behind the Flying Saucers.* New York: Henry Holt, 1950.
Smith, Gerald L. K. *The Real Issues in this Fight.* St. Louis: Christian Nationalist Crusade, 1950.
Stormer, John A. *None Dare Call It Treason.* Florissant, Mo.: Liberty Bell, 1964.

Secondary Sources

Dean, Jodi. *Aliens in America: Conspiracy Culture from Outerspace to Cyberspace.* Ithaca, N.Y.: Cornell University Press, 1998.
Fenster, Mark. *Conspiracy Theories: Secrecy and Power in American Culture.* Minneapolis: University of Minnesota Press, 1999.
Goldberg, Robert Alan. *Enemies Within: The Culture of Conspiracy in Modern America.* New Haven: Yale University Press, 2001.
Haynes, John Earl. *Red Scare or Red Menace? American Communism and Anti-Communism in the Cold War Era.* Chicago: Dee, 1996.
Hofstadter, Richard. *The Paranoid Style in American Politics.* Cambridge, Mass.: Harvard University Press, 1996.
Leonard, Kevin Allen. "'I am Sure You Can Read between the Lines': Cold War Anticommunism and the NAACP in Los Angeles." *Journal of the West* 44, no. 2 (2005): 16–23.
Olmsted, Kathyrn S. "'An American Conspiracy': The Post-Watergate Press and the CIA." *Journalism History* 19, no. 2 (Summer 1993): 51–58.
———. *Challenging the Secret Government: The Post-Watergate Investigations of the CIA and the FBI.* Chapel Hill: University of North Carolina Press, 1996.
Posner, Gerald. *Case Closed: Lee Harvey Oswald and the Assassination of JFK.* New York: Anchor Books, 1994.
———. *Killing the Dream: James Earl Ray and the Assassination of Martin Luther King, Jr.* New York: Random House, 1998.
Smith, Toby. *Little Gray Men: Roswell and the Rise of Popular Culture.* Albuquerque: University of New Mexico Press, 2000.

Section VI: Conspiracy in Contemporary America

Primary Sources

Coleman, John. *Conspirators Hierarchy: The Story of the Committee of 300.* Carson City, Nev.: America West Publishers, 1992.
Jasper, William F. "Rubber Stamp Report on OKC." *New American* 15 (February 1, 1999): 21–23.
Keith, Jim. *Black Helicopters over America: Strikeforce for the New World Order.* Lilburn, Ga.: IlumiNet, 1994.
McManus, John E. *The Insiders: Architects of the New World Order.* Appleton, Wisc.: John Birch Society, 1992.
Vidal, Gore. "Yes, Hillary, There is a Corporate Conspiracy Against Bill." *Salt Lake Tribune,* August 16, 1998.

Secondary Sources

Aho, James A. *The Politics of Righteousness: Idaho Christian Patriotism.* Seattle: University of Washington Press, 1990.

Barkun, Michael. "Religion, Militias, and Oklahoma City: The Mind of Conspiratorialists." *Terrorism and Political Violence* 8, no. 1 (1996): 50–64.
Gardell, Mattias. *In the Name of Elijah Muhammad: Louis Farrakhan and the Nation of Islam*. Durham, N.C.: Duke University Press, 1996.
Moore, Rebecca. "Reconstructing Reality: Conspiracy Theories About Jonestown." *Journal of Popular Culture* 36, no. 2 (2002): 200–220.
Simmons, William Paul. "Beliefs in Conspiracy Theories Among African-Americans." *Social Science Quarterly* 86, no. 3 (2005): 582–98.
Stern, Kenneth S. *A Force Upon the Plain: The American Militia Movement and the Politics of Hate*. New York: Simon & Schuster, 1996.
Sturken, Marita. "Reenactment, Fantasy, and the Paranoia of History: Oliver Stone's Docudramas." *History and Theory* 36, no. 4 (December 1997): 64–79.

Index

DONALD T. CRITCHLOW is Professor of History at Saint Louis University and author of, among other books, *The Conservative Ascendancy: How the GOP Right Made Political History; Phyllis Schlafly and Grassroots Conservatism; Intended Consequences: Birth Control, Abortion, and The Federal Government;* and *Studebaker: The Life and Death of an American Corporation* (Indiana University Press, 1997).

JOHN KORASICK is a judicial archivist for the Missouri State Historical Archives.

MATTHEW C. SHERMAN is a doctoral candidate at Saint Louis University, completing his dissertation "Presidential Assassination: The Failure to Protect Lincoln, Garfield, and McKinley."